VISUAL QUICKSTART GUIDE

PALM
ORGANIZERS

SECOND EDITION

Jeff Carlson

 Peachpit Press

Visual QuickStart Guide
Palm Organizers, Second Edition
Jeff Carlson

Peachpit Press
1249 Eighth Street
Berkeley, CA 94710
510/524-2178
800/283-9444
510/524-2221 (fax)
Find us on the World Wide Web at: http://www.peachpit.com
To report errors, send a note to errata@peachpit.com
Peachpit Press is a division of Pearson Education

Copyright © 2002 by Jeff Carlson

Editor: Nancy Davis
Production Coordinator: Connie Jeung-Mills
Copyeditor: Liane Thomas
Compositor: Jeff Carlson
Indexer: Caroline Parks
Cover Design: The Visual Group

ISBN 0-201-74578-X

9 8 7 6 5 4 3 2 1

Printed and bound in the United States of America

Praise for *Palm Organizers Visual QuickStart Guide*

If I had to describe this book in one word, it would be "meaty." ...While each of the Palm-Pilot books to date has unique value, this book is a diamond in the rough and one of my favorites. I highly recommend it.

— Scott Sbihli, *Pen Computing Magazine*

What a great book! If you're a Palm device user, you're going to get a lot out of this book. Jeff Carlson's writing style makes everything easy to understand, yet deep, chock full of valuable information.

— David Gewirtz, Editor-in-Chief, *PalmPower Magazine* (http://www.palmpower.com/)

One strength of the book is in Carlson's out-standing use of the Visual QuickStart Guide format, illustrating each point with plenty of screen shots and examples from the Palm, Windows, and Macintosh operating systems. I can't wait to try some of the new tips and procedures in this terrific book.

— John Nemerovski, Book Bytes Columnist and Reviewer, *My Mac Magazine* (http://www.mymac.com/)

Carlson—clearly an avid Palmist with some accumulated wisdom on the topic—goes beyond merely rehashing the Palm's own documentation.

— David Wall, Amazon.com

Dedication

For Kimberly, who understands me more than I often realize.

Special Thanks to:

Nancy Davis, for getting this book project started in the first place, for remaining flexible and cheerful, and for simply chatting about the New York weather when my brain required a much-needed break.

Liane Thomas, for being a kindred spirit and succinctly nailing the way we both tend to work (despite our best efforts): "think, think, think, plan, plan, think, oh yeah...write!"

Jeff Tolbert for helping to lay out the book, and for listening to me babble about handhelds on frequent trips to the store.

Caroline Parks for shouldering my work schedule in order to get the index done well and on time.

Brian Hall at Mark/Space for answering my questions about the CLIÉ at all hours.

Rosie Pulido for providing me with Palm information and hardware when I needed it.

Kristina Setchfield at Omniserve Wireless for the generous loan of her own Nokia phone for my testing purposes.

Glenn Fleishman, David Blatner, Steve Roth (plus the various long-distance inhabitants) at the Green Lake compound for their advice and experience. More important, for recognizing that look in my eye that says, "I'm totally focused now: go away," and not being offended (or at least not letting me know they were offended).

Nancy Aldrich-Ruenzel, Connie Jeung-Mills, Gary-Paul Prince, and even some non-hyphenated folks like **Kate Reber, Marjorie Baer, Kim Lombardi, Mimi Heft, Paula Baker**, and **Jimbo Norrena** at Peachpit Press. They continue to navigate me through the book process and answer all of my questions.

Kim Carlson, who selflessly fielded bad handwriting and my worries, and gave up far too many evenings because this guy she married remains driven to write books.

TABLE OF CONTENTS

TABLE OF CONTENTS

INTRODUCTION

Palm Organizers

I bought my first handheld, a PalmPilot Personal, in 1997 for a number of reasons. Of course, the gadget factor was pretty high. Plus, the PalmPilot was getting raves for its ability to store volumes of formerly paper-based contact and scheduling information in a device slightly larger than a deck of cards. You could download third-party software directly from the Web, then synchronize those programs and your data with your PC at the single push of a button.

However, I wasn't just looking for a new toy. (What, buy something because it's a cool gadget? Me??) A recent leap into the realm of full-time freelancing convinced me that I needed a greater measure of control over my time and my tasks. Buying a PalmPilot became more of an effort to organize myself and my data than any desire for a geeky electronic device.

This is part of the appeal of a Palm organizer. Yes, it's a cool gadget. Yes, you can accessorize it to your heart's content with styli, cases, and custom flipcovers. Yes, it piques people's curiosity and makes complete strangers walk up and ask, "What's that?" But it's also an efficient, well-thought-out organizational tool that performs its tasks exceptionally well. Instead of being a

Excerpted from an interview with Bill Gates, CEO and Chairman of Microsoft Corporation, on the television show "Charlie Rose," March 4, 1998 (used with permission).

Bill Gates: The future of the PC is to be a tablet-sized device or perhaps larger than a tablet.... But then you also have a lot of other devices, things like—I think I've got one in my pocket.

Charlie Rose: A Pilot is in his pocket.

Bill Gates: No, no, no, no. This is the competitor to the Pilot. Don't say "Pilot." Geez. This is the—

Charlie Rose: Does that look like a Pilot? I rest my case.

self-contained computer in a smaller container, it's an extension of the information that millions of people rely on every day.

Palm Organizers: Visual QuickStart Guide

This book is meant to be a compact, functional extension of a Palm organizer. Not just a how-to approach to using an electronic tool, this Visual QuickStart Guide is a primer on how to effectively get control of your schedule, contacts, and all the data that used to occupy reams of papers and Post-it notes.

My aim for this book is to show you what's possible with Palm devices, from their basic features to tips and tricks for using them smarter and faster. At times I'll personally recommend a product or a technique because it's what I've found useful. As a result, and to keep this book from becoming ten times larger than the device it covers, I don't list every product on the market—I want you to have fun exploring what's available (see Appendix C for some good starting points).

People who swear by their handhelds also tend to integrate them into their lives, moving beyond business meetings to birthdays, home finances, electronic books, and the occasional game of solitaire. It continues to be an invaluable part of my everyday life.

I'd love to know how your handheld helps (or hinders) your life. Feel free to email me with feedback at jeff@necoffee.com.

Part 1
Using Palm Organizers

The Handheld Portal to Your Information

You've probably read articles about them, or seen them in advertisements. More likely, you know someone who has one, and his or her enthusiasm was infectious. That's how I was introduced to Palm organizers, and now it's hard to find me without one.

Chapter 1, **Palm Basics**, introduces you to Palm OS-based organizers, discussing the different models and their hardware controls, battery usage, and available accessories.

Chapter 2, **The Palm OS**, covers the handheld's most undervalued feature: the powerful, yet minimalist, operating system. We'll explore system-wide preferences, memory management, and learn how to write Palm's celebrated—and simple—Graffiti alphabet.

Chapter 3, **HotSync**, examines the feature for synchronizing information from your handheld with the desktop software, including infrared synchronization and using other programs to tie your data into your Personal Information Manager (PIM) software.

Chapters 4–6 (**Date Book**, **Address Book**, and **To Do List & Memo Pad**) deal with the four main built-in programs, showing you why a tiny screen can be so much better than crumpled pages of scribbled appointments and Post-it notes tucked into a bulging "personal organizer."

Chapter 7, **Calculator, Expense, & Clock**, delves into the number-crunching applications provided by Palm, plus the simple but useful Clock application.

Chapter 8, **System Extensions**, opens the door to third-party system extensions that will make you wonder how you ever operated a Palm device without them.

PALM BASICS

The ancestry of today's Palm organizers can be traced to the Pilot, the original creation of inventor Jeff Hawkins. It began as a block of wood that Hawkins carried around the hallways of Palm Computing. It was the essence of the term *hardware*—no buttons, no batteries, no screen (certainly no backlight, though a fluorescent highlighter might have worked), no software.

It was also *simple*. The device in Hawkins's mind didn't take a modern PC and cram its guts into a smaller case, or try to woo consumers with its multimedia capabilities. Instead, the handheld machine focused on performing a handful of essential tasks well, in tandem with the computers and data that people were currently using.

As an evolutionary surprise, today's Palm devices can do much more than their founder's intent: wireless Internet access, color photos, global positioning, and more. And yet, despite the wide array of software and hardware add-ons you can get for them, today's handhelds remain true to Hawkins's original vision: simple to use and simple in scope (though not limited, as you'll discover). It's also become simply essential for millions of owners.

A Rapidly Expanding Field of Palm Devices

Like any product, the PalmPilot evolved over time; there are still thousands of people using even the earliest Pilot models. As more companies have licensed the Palm OS, multiple variations of devices have appeared. **Table 1.1** breaks down the main specifications of the current devices.

Palm m500 series

Palm learned from the phenomenal success of the Palm V that people want a handheld that's thin and light. The m500 series devices share the Palm V's basic shape (**Figure 1.1**), and add a few wrinkles: a built-in vibrating alarm, lighted power button to indicate silent alarms or when the integrated lithium-ion battery is charging, and an expansion port for Secure Digital/MultiMediaCard memory and devices.

The m500 and m505 are also the first organizers from Palm to include a USB-based HotSync cradle. This also means that they have a different style of serial connector, which Palm says is now "universal."

The biggest news is that the m505 achieves what some believe is the current holy grail of Palm devices: a color screen in a thin form factor. The m505's side-lit screen displays 65,000 colors in the same space as the m500's case, an impressive feat of miniaturization. However, what isn't so impressive is the display's brightness: it's surprisingly dark, making it hard to read indoors without the backlight turned on (and there's no brightness setting). Even then, it pales in comparison to color devices from Handspring, Sony, and even Palm's own Palm IIIc. The upside is that the m505 should achieve better battery life, and it's definitely easier to read outside in direct sunlight.

Table 1.1

Current Palm OS Devices and Specifications

Device	Memory[1]	ROM[2]	Screen[3]	OS[4]
Palm m505	8 MB	2 MB Flash	color 65K	4.0+
Palm m500	8 MB	2 MB Flash	mono	4.0+
Palm m105	8 MB	2 MB	mono	3.5
Palm m100	2 MB	2 MB	mono	3.5
Palm Vx	8 MB	2 MB Flash	mono	3.5+
Palm VIIx	8 MB	2 MB Flash	mono	3.5+
Palm IIIc	8 MB	2 MB Flash	color 256	3.5
IBM Workpad c500	8 MB	2 MB Flash	color 65K	4.0+
IBM Workpad c3	8 MB	2 MB Flash	mono	3.5+
HandEra 330	8 MB	2 MB Flash	mono+	3.5+
TRGPro	8 MB	2 MB Flash	mono	3.5+
Sony CLIÉ PEG-N710C	8 MB	4 MB Flash	color 256+	3.5+
Sony CLIÉ PEG-N610C	8 MB	4 MB Flash	color 65K+	4.0+
Sony CLIÉ PEG-S320	8 MB	4 MB Flash	mono+	4.0+
Kyocera Smartphone	8 MB	2 MB	mono	3.5
Handspring Visor Deluxe	8 MB	2 MB	v3	3.1h
Handspring Visor	2 MB	2 MB	v3	3.1h
Handspring Visor Prism	8 MB	2 MB	color 16K	3.5h
Handspring Visor Edge	8 MB	2 MB	mono	3.5h

1 Quantities indicate built-in memory. Items with plus signs (+) are upgradeable by purchasing larger memory chips.

2 Every Palm device contains Read-Only Memory (ROM), which is where the operating system and built-in applications are stored. Some, however, include flash ROM, which means the contents can be rewritten using a special process known as flashing. Recent operating system upgrades require a flash ROM. See Chapter 2.

3 Most models feature monochrome ("mono") screens, which are also capable of grayscale display. Color screens differ by the number of colors they can display; for example, "color 65K" means a color display capable of 65,000 colors. The "+" on the HandEra and Sony CLIÉ devices indicate higher-resolution screens.

4 Numbers indicate the Palm OS version loaded by default. Items with plus signs (+) indicate that the operating system can be upgraded to the most recent version due to the presence of flash ROM. An "h" indicates Handspring's customized version of the Palm OS.

4

Figure 1.1 The Palm m505 brings a color display to the slim and light design made popular by the Palm V.

Figure 1.2 The Palm m100 series has a slightly smaller screen, but is one of the most comfortable devices to hold in your hand.

Palm m100 series

The Palm m100 and m105 represent the entry-level models of Palm's lineup. They're small, like the m500 series, and feature a surprisingly comfortable case design (**Figure 1.2**). Also noteworthy is the m100's weight: at 4.4 ounces, it's the lightest handheld out there.

The only possible drawback is that the screen is a bit smaller than most other devices: it shares the same 160 by 160 pixel resolution, but packed into a 2-inch square. After a few minutes of use, though, you'll barely notice the difference.

The m100 series includes a sensible flip cover that folds flat against the back of the device when open, and sports a window when it's closed: pressing the scroll up button turns the handheld on briefly and displays the date and time.

✔ Tips

- Palm has released a small backlight utility to compensate for the criticism of the m505's screen quality. The Palm m500 Series Backlight Utility (http://www.palm.com/support/m505/backlight_utility.html) remembers the last backlight state, so if you have the light turned on, it will come on the next time you use the device.

- A better alternative is 505LightOn (http://tipandgo.com/), which can keep the backlight on or remember the last state, plus keep the screen lit when the m505 is in the HotSync cradle.

A RAPIDLY EXPANDING FIELD OF PALM DEVICES

Palm VII

The Palm VII is the first—and so far only—handheld device that includes a wireless modem (and isn't a phone/PDA hybrid). Surprisingly, it's embedded in a case not much larger than a Palm III (**Figure 1.3**).

Radio transceiver

The Palm VII's secret weapon is its built-in radio transceiver, which sends and receives data on the Palm.Net network. Raising the antenna activates the radio and makes a connection; you don't have to dial a phone number or tell the handheld where to find a signal. As long as you're in the Palm VII's range of operation, the transceiver does all of the connection work.

Rechargeable battery

The Palm VII operates on two AAA batteries, just like most every other Palm device. However, a separate rechargeable NiCad battery housed above the screen powers the radio transceiver.

The NiCad battery gets its charge from the standard AAA batteries, so expect the first pair of batteries to be used up quickly as the NiCad powers up. The initial charge takes about an hour before you can use it. If you attempt to use the wireless radio before it's charged, the Palm VII will display an alert dialog (**Figure 1.4**). When you're not using the transceiver, the NiCad battery is replenished gradually from the AAA batteries.

✔ Tips

- An extra advantage of the NiCad battery is that it will supply juice to the device if the AAAs go dead, which means your data stays intact until you insert a fresh pair.

- Go to the Diagnostics application, then tap the Details button to view the charging progress.

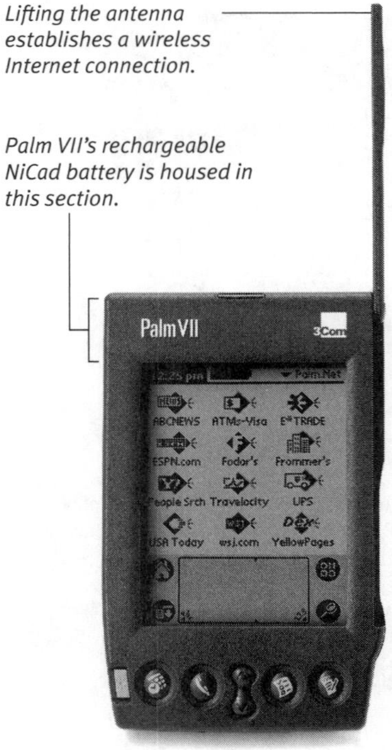

Lifting the antenna establishes a wireless Internet connection.

Palm VII's rechargeable NiCad battery is housed in this section.

Figure 1.3 Getting online is as simple as lifting the antenna, which immediately establishes a connection.

Figure 1.4 While the NiCad batteries are charging for the first time, you won't be able to use the transceiver.

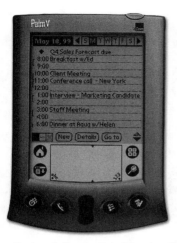

Figure 1.5 Sleek and slim, the Palm V is a handheld that you really can put into a shirt pocket without looking like you're carrying a bulky deck of cards.

Figure 1.6 It's hard to appreciate here, but the Palm IIIc's color screen is quite bright and vibrant. (Feel free to color the image, though we were sadly unable to bundle a set of color pencils with the book.)

Palm V series

Smaller and thinner than Palm devices that preceded them, the Palm Vx and Palm V feature an anodized aluminum case, flared bottom, and smaller overall dimensions (**Figure 1.5**). But more than just looking good, this model introduced significant changes to the Palm hardware: it uses a rechargeable lithium ion battery, and was the first device to adjust screen contrast using software instead of a scroll wheel.

Although the Palm V series is being phased out in favor of the m500 series, it still represents one of the best values for getting a thin and light organizer without paying a high price.

Palm III series

For years, the Palm III was the workhorse of the Palm line of organizers. The golden child of the family is the Palm IIIc (**Figure 1.6**), which features a 256-color active-matrix screen. To accommodate the larger power draw of a color screen, the Palm IIIc includes a rechargeable lithion ion battery, which keeps the unit charged for approximately two weeks of normal use. The good news is that you only have to charge it for a few minutes each day (about the time it takes to perform a HotSync operation) to keep the battery juiced up.

IBM Workpad

The IBM Workpad c3 and c500 devices are essentially the same as the Palm V and Palm m505, licensed by IBM, with black cases (http://www.ibm.com/workpad/).

A RAPIDLY EXPANDING FIELD OF PALM DEVICES

HandEra 330

It's an endless dilemma in the world of computing: enthusiastic users tell a company which features they'd like to see, and the company has to decide which ones are worth implementing. Usually things like expansion ports and more screen space are evolved incrementally, but not in the case of the HandEra 330 (http://www.handera.com/). This is definitely the gadget-lovers gadget.

The first thing you notice is the screen (**Figure 1.7**). Every other Palm device has a large physical screen, but the lower quarter is taken up by the silkscreen area. On the HandEra, the silkscreen area is gone, letting you use the entire vertical space to display your data. If you need to write Graffiti, simply tap the small arrow in the lower-right corner to bring up a virtual silkscreen area. The screen is also notable because it sports a higher 240 by 320 pixel resolution, and because you can optionally rotate the display to view data lengthwise (such as spreadsheets).

The HandEra 330 also features dual expansion ports, accommodating the Secure Digital/MultiMediaCard formats used by the m500 series, but also the more common CompactFlash cards. The engineers have also thrown in a digital voice recorder, a jog dial for browsing data without using the stylus, and a much improved speaker. Oh, and it uses the same serial connector as the Palm III series, which means you can use existing peripherals like keyboards and modems.

All these capabilities require four AAA batteries, versus the standard two in most devices, but it's an acceptable price to pay.

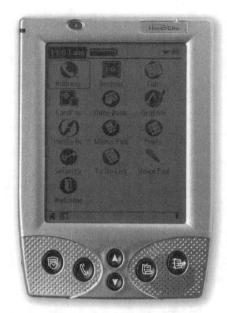

Figure 1.7 The HandEra 330 is an organizer with everything, including a taller screen that puts the silkscreen Graffiti area away when it's not needed.

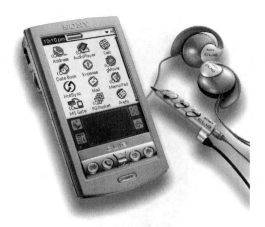

Figure 1.8 Sony's CLIÉ PEG-N710C isn't just an organizer, it's a multimedia playback machine. Play digital music, watch videos, and view photos on its beautiful high-resolution color screen.

Sony CLIÉ

Sony has clearly decided that their Palm OS-based organizers aren't going to be "me-too" devices. The Sony CLIÉ ("clee-ay") series is geared to be the only portable multimedia device you need. The CLIÉ's case is narrower than a Palm m500, but also a bit taller and thicker. And, I have to admit, I love the overall design (which is a huge improvement over the original CLIÉ devices).

In addition to the standard complement of Palm features, the CLIÉ has a jog dial for navigating the interface, and an expansion slot that accepts Sony's Memory Stick modules. The PEG-N710C model (**Figure 1.8**) also supports digital music playback (MP3 and ATRAC3-formatted files), and includes a set of headphones (see Chapter 13). If that weren't enough, the color screen supports a higher resolution of 320 by 320 pixels, which is great for viewing photos or even short movies.

✔ Tip

■ Out of the box, the CLIÉ only works with Windows-based computers. If you own a Macintosh, you definitely want to get The Missing Sync (http://www.markspace.com/missingsync.html) by Mark/Space to synchronize your data and install files onto Memory Sticks (see Chapter 2).

A RAPIDLY EXPANDING FIELD OF PALM DEVICES

Kyocera Smartphone

If you're like me, you may already be suffering from a high-tech malady: gadgetitis. Many people carry a Palm organizer, a cellular phone, a pager, and any number of various devices. The Smartphone (http://www.kyocera-wireless.com/kysmart/) is the result of a novel idea: combine the phone, pager, and Palm handheld in one device!

Flipping down the standard number pad reveals a Palm organizer at the phone's heart (**Figure 1.9**). One upshot to this arrangement is that the Palm OS is actually a part of the phone's inner workings, allowing you to find someone in your Address Book and dial their number with one tap, or easily check your email and other online information.

The Smartphone takes its power from the phone's rechargeable battery. Although it's a bit larger and heavier than the latest crop of cellular phones, this gadget is a clever combination of almost ubiquitous technologies.

✔ Tips

- In addition to being a phone/PDA combination, the Smartphone has a few other helpful features. The Voice Dial application lets you record a spoken word or phrase and associate it with a number, so you can press a button and say a person's name to dial their number. This is a great feature if you have to make a call when driving or are otherwise occupied.

- The Call History application (**Figure 1.10**) offers a detailed breakdown of your calls, without relying on the phone company's records.

- The Smartphone can send and receive data or faxes using the Data/Fax application with the phone in its HotSync cradle.

Figure 1.9 The Kyocera Smartphone integrates a Palm device with a cellular phone, cutting down on the number of gadgets you carry around.

Call History		▼ All
Who	When	Length
📟 Data Call	7/20	03:52
📟 Data Call	7/16	03:49
↗ Carlson, Kim	7/16	00:55
📟 Data Call	7/10	01:42
↗ Tolbert, Jeff	7/10	00:08
↗ Schmitz, Agen	7/10	00:53
📟 Data Call	7/10	07:59
📟 Data Call	7/2	01:46
📟 Data Call	6/21	01:21
📟 Data Call	4/3	01:36
↗ 5088659888	4/3	01:05

Figure 1.10 Don't wait until the phone bill arrives to see your cellular usage.

Figure 1.11 Handspring's Visor family resembles Palm's offerings, but with a few significant twists.

Figure 1.12 Slim and beautiful, the Visor Edge feels more like a futuristic data pad than a big box of cards.

Handspring Visor

In 1998, the creators of the original Palm-Pilot—Jeff Hawkins, Donna Dubinsky, and Ed Colligan—left Palm Computing to form Handspring, Inc. (http://www.handspring.com/). Although some people expected the trio to remake the wheel with their new startup, they focused on revising their original intentions for the PalmPilot: Handspring licensed the Palm OS and developed a low-cost device called the Visor (**Figure 1.11**).

Roughly the same size as a Palm III, the members of the Visor family include the same built-in applications found on the Palm models, but with a few differences: Date Book+ offers more views and options than the built-in Date Book program; City Time gives you a visual display of what time it is around the world; and most significantly, every Visor features the Springboard expansion slot.

Newer devices have built upon the first Visors by adding color (the Visor Prism) and a sleek new form factor (the Visor Edge, **Figure 1.12**).

✔ Tip

- Don't think me rude, but if you own a Handspring Visor, this probably isn't the best book for you. Instead, get my other book, *Handspring Visor: Visual QuickStart Guide*, also published by Peachpit Press (http://www.peachpit.com/vqs/visor/).

Palm Device Overview

No matter which handheld you use, they all share the following characteristics.

Screen

The average handheld's screen accounts for most of the device. The liquid-crystal display (LCD) is normally black and white only, and measures 160 pixels by 160 pixels. (Actually, the screen can display multiple levels of gray, which some developers have taken advantage of; grayscale wasn't officially supported by Palm until Palm OS 3.5.)

Some organizers, like the Palm m505 and Sony CLIÉ PEG-N710C, feature active-matrix color screens that display anywhere from 256 to 65,000 colors. The CLIÉ's screen also has a higher-resolution of 320 by 320 pixels. The HandEra 330 screen is the most unconventional, measuring 240 by 320 pixels and occupying the entire viewing area (part of which is normally occupied by the silkscreen area).

Most important, every screen is touch sensitive, which is why you can interact with it using a stylus.

Power button/backlight

Every device has a power button that turns the organizer on and off (**Figure 1.13**). The handheld will automatically power down after two minutes (you can change the time delay; see Chapter 2).

Holding the power button down for two seconds activates the screen's backlight, which illuminates the screen by lighting the active (black) pixels. In very dark situations, this tends to be more readable, though in moderate lighting it can sometimes be difficult to read the screen.

On most color devices, holding the power button activates the screen brightness control (**Figure 1.14**).

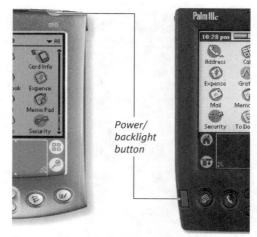

Power/ backlight button

Figure 1.13 The power button doubles as the backlight control on most devices.

Figure 1.14 The Palm IIIc's power button activates the software-based screen brightness setting.

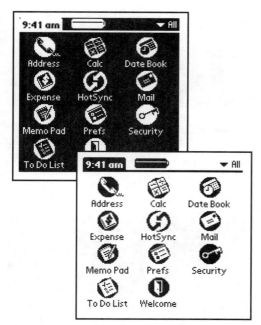

Figure 1.15 Newer Palm OS devices feature inverted backlighting (top, simulated), where only the active pixels are illuminated. Using the "dot-8" shortcut, you can change the backlighting to work like PalmPilots and first-generation Palm IIIs (bottom, again simulated because batteries are not included with this book).

✔ Tips

- The Palm IIIc's default brightness setting is about 25-30 percent of maximum. Although you may be tempted to crank it to the highest level, you'll get more battery life out of a lower setting.

- Every Palm III model includes a plastic flip-top lid that helps protect the screen when you're not using the device. With the Palm IIIc, however, the lid can also provide some shade when it's half open; like most active-matrix computer screens, the Palm IIIc's color display can be difficult to read in direct sunlight.

- The industrial design of the Palm V is impressive, but it seems that Palm skimped when designing the power button. At first glance it looks like you should push the button down to activate the device, but in fact it must be pressed in horizontally (from front to back). Unfortunately, on many units the power button can be flimsy and lose its connection over time. If your power button isn't responding the way it used to, try this: push down diagonally at a 45-degree angle. If that doesn't work, contact Palm to see if you can get a replacement device.

- If you don't like the new method of backlighting, you can specify that the inactive pixels, not the active pixels, are illuminated when you turn backlighting on. Go to the Memo Pad, create a new record, then write "ℒ · 8": the shortcut stroke (like a cursive L), a period (two taps), then the number 8. You should see the words "[Inverting Backlight]" which reverses the backlighting effect (**Figure 1.15**). Repeat the steps to return to the default backlighting style.

Stylus

The stylus is your main method of interacting with the handheld, though just about anything that isn't sharper than a No. 2 pencil can work (that includes fingers and toes too!). In most cases, the stylus is made of a metal barrel that comes with a plastic tip and end pieces that screw at each end.

✔ Tip

■ Unscrew the top or bottom sections of the stylus to find a surprise: a pin that pushes the handheld's reset button.

Silkscreen Graffiti area

This is where you input text using Graffiti, the Palm's method of handwriting (see Chapter 2). It's usually referred to as the "silkscreened" area, because the Graffiti input area and the buttons on either side of it are printed on a layer of glass by a silkscreening process. The Applications (also known as Home) and Calculator buttons are located here, as well as the triggers for accessing menus and using the Palm OS's Find feature (**Figure 1.16**).

Application buttons

The plastic buttons on the case immediately activate the Date Book, Address Book, To Do List, and Memo Pad or Note Pad (**Figure 1.17**). I rarely launch these programs any other way.

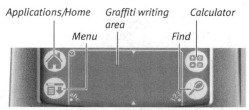

Applications/Home   Graffiti writing area   Calculator
Menu   Find

Figure 1.16 Use the silkscreened area to input text using Graffiti, plus launch certain functions.

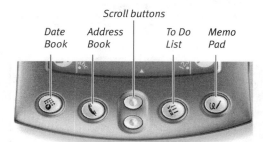

Scroll buttons
Date Book   Address Book   To Do List   Memo Pad

Figure 1.17 The plastic application buttons take you directly to the built-in programs. The scroll buttons are often a better substitute for tapping the scroll arrows found in many applications.

Infrared port

Figure 1.18 The infrared port can be used to beam information between Palm organizers, and for synchronizing with an IR-equipped PC.

Contrast button

Figure 1.19 Some devices (like the Palm m105 shown here) put the contrast control button in the silkscreen area.

Scroll buttons

These up and down buttons are a handy way to scroll through text and other information.

Infrared port

Every handheld includes an infrared port that enables you to "beam" information from one device to another (**Figure 1.18**). See Chapter 2 for more information about beaming applications, and program-specific chapters (such as Chapter 4) for more on beaming individual records and categories.

Contrast control

Adjust the screen's contrast using the button in the silkscreened area (**Figure 1.19**).

✔ Tips

- Pressing one of the application buttons when your handheld is powered down will turn it on and launch that program.

- You can launch any program—not just the built-in ones—by pressing one of the application buttons. To remap their functions, go to the Buttons section of the Preferences application (see Chapter 2).

- To put the contrast button to better use, install Contrast Button App Hack (http://www.synsolutions.com/). You can program the button to launch any program. See Chapter 8 for more information on Palm OS extensions, or "hacks."

Reset button

There will probably come a time when something has happened that renders your handheld unusable (it will stop responding to your input). To get back to business, locate the tiny reset hole in the back of the unit (**Figure 1.20**). Use the reset pin located in the stylus, or straighten part of a paperclip, and insert it into the hole to reset the Palm OS (known as a *soft reset*—it won't erase your data).

HotSync cradle

The ability to synchronize information between the handheld and a desktop computer is one of the reasons for Palm's success. Every Palm device comes with an angled HotSync cradle (**Figure 1.21**) and synchronization software for your PC. Place the device into the cradle so that the connector at its base slides into the cradle's serial port. To begin synchronizing, press the HotSync button on the front of the cradle.

Newer cradles are USB-based. If you use a Macintosh that doesn't have USB, you'll need to purchase the Macintosh Serial Adapter. Older cradles with serial cables can be made to work with USB-equipped computers using the PalmConnect USB Kit. See Palm's online store (http://store.palm.com/) for more information.

✔ Tip

■ The cradle is also where devices with internal lithium ion batteries are recharged.

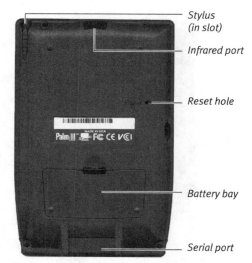

Stylus
(in slot)

Infrared port

Reset hole

Battery bay

Serial port

Figure 1.20 The back of a Palm looks bland, but it's riddled with features.

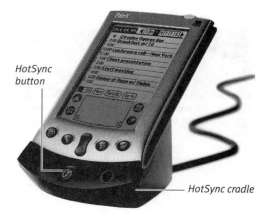

HotSync button

HotSync cradle

Figure 1.21 To transfer data between the handheld and your PC, use the accompanying HotSync cradle: slide the organizer into place and press the HotSync button in front to synchronize the information.

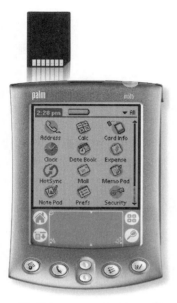

Figure 1.22 The Palm m500 series accepts Secure Digital/MultiMediaCard expansion cards.

Expansion Cards

The latest Palm organizers have begun offering slots for expansion ports, enabling you to add removable memory or peripherals without occupying a device's serial port. Handspring has offered their Springboard slot since the first Visor; the following formats are also available. For information on transferring data to and from cards, see Chapter 2.

Secure Digital/MultiMediaCard

The Palm m500 and m505 feature a slot for either Secure Digital or MultiMediaCard expansion cards (http://www.palm.com/products/accessories/expansioncards/). Both formats use the same physical specification, which is only about the size of a postage stamp (**Figure 1.22**). Current cards add more memory or include reference materials like electronic books or other data; look for devices such as digital cameras, GPS receivers, and wireless modems in the future.

CompactFlash

The HandEra 330 includes two expansion card slots: a Secure Digital/MultiMediaCard bay, and a CompactFlash bay. CompactFlash is a card standard used in several types of devices, and therefore offers a wide variety of uses. The HandEra can accommodate up to 1 gigabyte of memory, GPS receivers, modems, Ethernet networking cards, and other accessories.

Sony Memory Stick

Sony's expansion card offering is the Memory Stick, a card that's literally about the size of a stick of gum. Memory Sticks offer more memory, and can be swapped between multiple devices (from Sony Vaio computers to the AIBO electronic pet). Sony has several types of Memory Sticks: the MagicGate variety supports encrypted data.

Battery Use

Most Palm organizers run either on two AAA batteries or on a built-in rechargeable lithium ion battery, and last anywhere between four and six weeks (except for color models, which average 2 weeks). Feel free to read that sentence again, especially if you're a laptop computer (or Windows CE device) owner who's used to measuring battery life in *hours*. The battery use is minimal (the CPU is asleep most of the time, even when powered on), so even if you use it often, you can still expect about three weeks of life from one set.

AAA batteries

A new set of two store-bought AAA batteries will give you 3 volts of power. When they approach 2 volts, the device will begin to warn you that it's time to install a fresh pair. Although some people go ahead and swap out the old batteries after the first warning, you can probably get several more days of moderate use before switching. Since I hate being nagged about such things, I usually go ahead and replace the batteries after the first or second warning.

Rechargeable lithium ion battery

More devices, especially smaller ones like the m500 series or any model with a color screen, include built-in lithium ion batteries that recharge whenever they're in their HotSync cradles; a light on the cradle or the handheld indicates that the battery is charging.

Battery level indicator

Figure 1.23 The battery level is shown at the top of the Applications screen.

✔ Tips

- It only takes a few minutes each day to refill a rechargeable battery. Under normal use, the charge applied during a HotSync should be sufficient to top off the gauge (**Figure 1.23**). The fact that the batteries won't fall out or get knocked loose accidentally makes these devices the most solid handhelds I've used.

- If you've just opened your brand new device with a rechargeable battery, stop! Be sure you charge the unit for three or four hours before first use to ensure that the battery is fully charged. Not following this simple step can cause the battery to hold less of a charge over the long run.

- The Palm VII has a secret weapon: the radio transmitter located at the top of the device. Since it requires its own power supply, the first AAA batteries you put in fill the rechargeable radio battery. (When you're not using the wireless access features, the battery charges back to full strength from the AAAs.) This means that if your regular batteries are way past dead, it's likely that your data isn't in the grave as well: the Palm VII will trickle enough power from the radio's battery to keep the contents of its memory intact.

- It's almost inevitable that at some point you'll find yourself without power. If you have a rechargeable device such as the Palm V, consider buying a TCL Emergency Charger (http://members.aol.com/gmayhak/tcl/e-charge.htm), a small attachment that connects to a 9-volt battery and offers extra juice until you can fully recharge the device.

BATTERY USE

Recommended battery types

Palm recommends using Alkaline batteries, which have a steady rate of discharge (as opposed to nickel-cadmium, or NiCad, batteries, which drop off suddenly when they're spent; you may not have enough juice to HotSync your data before installing new batteries). Many users also report longer battery life using the newer Duracell Ultras and Energizer Advanced Formula batteries.

If you want to use rechargeable batteries, go with rechargeable alkalines like Rayovac Renewal. Just be sure to recharge them at around 50 percent capacity—don't wait until they're dead—to get the best use out of them.

To change batteries:

1. HotSync your data. There are provisions built into Palm devices to prevent data loss during a battery swap, but the best is to have a backup of your data. For more on synchronizing data, see Chapter 3.

2. Shut off your handheld, turn it over, and remove the battery door (**Figure 1.24**).

3. Pull out the old batteries and replace with the new ones. Palm recommends swapping them one at a time (i.e., bad battery out, good battery in, repeat). You have about 60 seconds from the point when you remove the batteries to when you install fresh ones to avoid data loss.

4. Replace the battery door, and turn the device back on.

✔ Tip

■ If you're using different battery types (Alkaline/NiCad/Rechargeable Alkaline/ NiMH), write the following in a text field (such as the Memo Pad) to toggle between more accurate battery gauges: "ᘔ · ⅂" (shortcut, period, 7).

Remove the battery door, then replace the batteries, first one, then the other.

Figure 1.24 Batteries are included with your new Palm device. When it's time to replace the AAA batteries, you have about 60 seconds to swap them out before your data is lost.

Screen Care

Your screen is the gateway to your data, so take care of it. You shouldn't have to do much besides wipe it with a clean cloth every once in a while, but there are several solutions for keeping the glass clear of scratches and giving the silkscreened Graffiti area a better "writing" feel beneath the stylus.

Screen protectors

Several companies offer clear plastic or vinyl strips that fit over your handheld's screen. I've used WriteRights, by Concept Kitchen (http://www.conceptkitchen.com/), which keep the screen clear of scratches and provide for a better writing texture. Applying them successfully is an art in itself, but the end result works well for me.

✔ Tips

- Perhaps the most popular low-tech solution is to put strips of tape (Scotch 811, in the blue box, is the preferred variety) over the Graffiti area, which gets the most stylus use. Other people have used Post-it notes, tape flags, and transparency film.

- If a damp cloth is outmatched by the grime on your screen, Concept Kitchen also offers PDA Screen Clean, a set of cloths and wet/dry formulas.

SCREEN CARE

Accessorizing

A characteristic of a successful product is how well you can accessorize it, so it's not surprising to find a cottage industry that caters to handheld accessories. These range from stylish styli to screen protectors to clothing specially designed with PDA-ready pockets.

Styli

As you might expect, you can buy replacement styli, ranging from brass styli that fit into the stylus slots to hybrid pens such as the Cross Digital Writer (http://www.cross.com/). The LandWare Floating•Point stylus, for example, has a special nib that replicates the feel of writing on paper (http://www.landware.com/) (**Figure 1.25**). See PDA Panache (http://www.pdapanache.com/) for more variations.

Cases

There are numerous case variations on the market, ranging from Palm's Slim Leather Case (**Figure 1.26**) to RhinoSkin's Cockpit (http://www.handheld-cases.com/), a titanium hard case with a melting point of 1,666 degrees Celsius! There are also varieties of belt-loop cases, zippered pouches, carriers with shoulder-straps. For a few good resources on cases, check out Fredlet's Pilot Page (http://www.fredlet.com/palm/) or the Gadgeteer (http://www.the-gadgeteer.com/).

Other accessories

Depending on your needs, a variety of other helpful goodies can be ordered. Examples include extra HotSync cradles, travel kits and chargers, and extra HotSync cables.

Figure 1.25 Replacement styli range from simple substitutes to pen/stylus combinations to traditional pens with PDA nibs. The LandWare Floating•Point stylus is shown here.

Figure 1.26 Handheld case manufacturers have taken advantage of this new niche market—you can buy a style of case customized for your needs.

Figure 1.27 The Palm Portable Keyboard is a full-size keyboard that folds up to a size slightly larger than a Palm device, and weighs only about 8 ounces.

Figure 1.28 LandWare's GoType! Pro keyboard includes a power socket for charging a Palm V while in use, and a serial connector and cable to perform a HotSync directly from the keyboard.

Keyboards

The Palm's pen has proved mightier than the chiclet keyboards on many other PDAs, but there are times when a real physical keyboard can come in handy. Anyone who's tried to work on a regular-sized laptop computer in an airplane's coach seat knows that space is at a premium.

Over the past couple of years, a handful of external keyboards have appeared. Although perhaps overkill for everyday handheld usage, they're great for typing long memos, emails, and especially taking notes during a meeting. Of the keyboards available, two models stand out.

Palm Portable Keyboard

Of all the handheld peripherals I've carried around lately, this is the one that knocks people out. Designed by Think Outside (http://www.thinkoutside.com/) and sold by Palm (http://store.palm.com/), the Palm Portable is a full-size keyboard that folds into a compact rectangle not much larger than a Palm device (**Figure 1.27**). In addition to being small and light, it has special keys that launch applications and access Palm OS features like command shortcuts.

GoType! Pro

LandWare (http://www.landware.com/) struck gold with the GoType! Pro keyboard, an all-in-one clamshell design with a slot to plug in a handheld (**Figure 1.28**). It features special Palm OS-specific keys to access applications, commands, and shortcuts. The GoType! Pro for Palm V also has a built-in serial port for performing a HotSync operation with your PC, plus a power slot to recharge the device's internal battery.

KEYBOARDS

Palm Desktop

Most of this book concerns the Palm OS and the handhelds that use it, but there's also another very important component to the organizer: the desktop software. A Palm OS handheld is primarily intended to be an extension of your personal data, so the desktop software acts as the core.

You also have the option of using other PIM programs like Microsoft Outlook or Lotus Notes. But Palm Desktop is the one that most closely resembles what you find on the palmtop.

Palm Desktop makes it easy to access your data when you're working on your computer, printing information, installing software on the handheld, or just need to enter a lot of data without cramping your fingers writing Graffiti. At the very least, Palm Desktop provides the framework for keeping backup copies of the data on your handheld.

Throughout the book, I'll cover specific features of each module in their respective chapters (such as Chapter 4, *Date Book*).

Palm Desktop for Windows

Most of the functionality found on the Palm translates directly to the Windows version of Palm Desktop (**Figure 1.29**). On the desktop, however, you get the advantage of a computer's larger screen size, so you can see more information at a glance than on a handheld.

Palm Desktop is also the place to access archived data (which you've deleted from the handheld but want to store on the PC).

Figure 1.29 Palm Desktop for Windows replicates most of the Palm OS's functionality, but puts most of the information on the same screen.

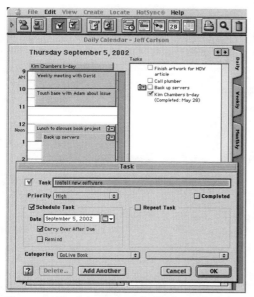

Figure 1.30 The Palm Desktop for Macintosh includes the features of Claris Organizer, upon which it was based.

Figure 1.31 You can store more data, although not all of it will transfer to the handheld.

Palm Desktop for Macintosh

The first incarnation of the Macintosh Palm Desktop only synchronized the built-in applications, with no way for developers to write additional conduits (software bridges between the Palm OS and the desktop). For a few years, Pilot Desktop 1.0 remained the only choice for Palm-owning Macintosh users. Eager to reestablish contact with its Mac user base, Palm made an interesting choice when updating the desktop software: it bought Claris Organizer from Apple. Rather than build something new from scratch, they built upon Organizer.

The result is a vastly different desktop PIM from both Pilot Desktop 1.0 and the Windows counterpart (**Figure 1.30**). Although it shares basic functionality with Palm Desktop for Windows, there are notable differences: some features, such as support for a second address field (so you can store home and work addresses, for example), exist only on the desktop, not in the Palm OS (**Figure 1.31**); you can assign sub-categories to records; and, of course, the interface is quite a bit different.

The new software isn't free of shortcomings. For example, private records on the desktop cannot be hidden, though they will retain their Private setting under the Palm OS.

However, as of this writing Palm is working on a version of Mac Palm Desktop that handles private records, runs natively under Mac OS X, and other goodies the developers aren't ready to divulge.

✔ Tip

■ If you don't have at least version 2.6.3 of Mac Palm Desktop, get it. It solves a host of crashing problems dealing with the Instant Palm Desktop extension.

THE PALM OS

Much is said and written about the portability of Palm organizers and the ease of synchronizing data with a desktop PC. When the attention is turned to the software running inside it, though, the focus usually shifts to how many events can be stored, or how quickly one can look up an address.

I would argue that the Palm Operating System (Palm OS) is actually the strongest, and most overlooked, of the Palm device features. Like a well-scored movie soundtrack, which adds to the atmosphere of a film without drawing attention to itself, the Palm OS provides a lot of power while remaining essentially invisible to most owners. If you're used to the shaded buttons and colors of Windows, the Palm OS probably looks sparse and boring (and if you're a Macintosh user, you may think you've returned to the early days of System 6!). As a result, using a Palm device for the first time is surprisingly easy.

Yet it isn't just ease of use that makes the Palm OS notable. Beneath the uncluttered interface lies an operating system that's been designed with an emphasis on efficiency and usability. After using the Palm OS for only a few hours, you'll realize that your stylus is only tapping its surface.

Navigating the Palm OS

There are three basic methods of interacting within the Palm OS, all of which depend on the stylus (or a similar writing instrument). Since the screen is touch-sensitive, there's no need for a "proxy" device such as a mouse.

Tap

Most of the elements you encounter require a tap with the end of the stylus. Tapping a record selects it by either opening up a new window or placing a cursor within the text. You also use taps to manipulate the following interface elements (**Figure 2.1**):

- **Icons.** In the Applications screen, tapping a program's icon or name launches it. Smaller custom icons, such as the alarm clock and note, are also used.

- **Buttons.** Similar to the buttons found under Windows and the Mac OS, these rounded-corner boxes are used to activate commands or confirm actions.

- **Menus.** When you tap a title bar or the silkscreened Menu icon, drop-down menus become visible at the top of the screen. Tap to select menu items.

- **Scroll arrows.** When data spills beyond the size of the screen, tap the up/down scroll arrows to move the active information up and down. You'll also encounter left/right scroll arrows, like the Date Book arrows that move between weeks (see Chapter 4).

- **Popup menus.** Whenever you see a small triangle pointing down next to a word, it indicates that more options are available via a popup menu.

- **Checkboxes.** Tap on a checkbox to mark or unmark it, toggling the action that is assigned to it (such as the Private indicator in most records' detail screens).

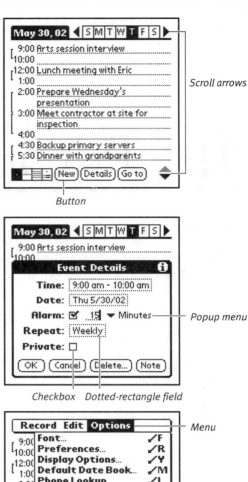

Scroll arrows

Button

Popup menu

Checkbox   Dotted-rectangle field

Menu

Icon

Figure 2.1 Tapping just about any interface element in the Palm OS evokes a response.

Tap and hold original item...

...to drag it to a new location.

Figure 2.2 The Memo Pad provides one example of dragging a list item to a new location.

Figure 2.3 Tap to set your cursor, then drag through letters to highlight them.

◆ **Dotted-rectangle fields.** These fields display the information that has been selected for them, but also indicate that tapping the field allows you to change it.

Drag

In a few cases, you will want to drag an item using the stylus. The most common examples include (but are not limited to):

◆ **Scroll bars.** If you have more than 11 memos displayed in the Memo Pad, a vertical scroll bar appears at the right side of the screen. You could tap the arrows at the top or bottom of a scroll bar, but a quicker way to view the full list is to tap and hold on the dark solid portion of the scroll bar, then drag it vertically.

◆ **Custom ordered memos.** In the Memo Pad and some applications, you can "grab" an item and drag it to a new position within a list (**Figure 2.2**). A thick dotted line indicates where the item will be placed when it is "dropped" (i.e., when you lift the stylus from the screen).

◆ **Highlighting text.** To select a series of letters or words, tap to place your cursor, then drag to select the text (**Figure 2.3**).

◆ **Weekly Date Book entries.** In the Date Book's week view, you can select events and reschedule them by dragging to a new date and time. (See Chapter 4.)

Write

Using the silkscreened Graffiti area, you can use the stylus as a pen and write letters that appear within text fields. See "Graffiti," later in this chapter.

✔ Tip

■ Under Palm OS 3.5 and later, double-tap to select a word; triple-tap to select a line.

Accessing Menus

Although hidden to conserve valuable screen space, drop-down menus similar to those found in Windows and the Mac OS are available for most applications. Access menus to take advantage of commands not displayed on the current screen, and to edit text using Cut, Copy, Paste, and Undo commands.

To access menus in applications:

1. Tap the Menu icon located in the lower-left corner of the silkscreened area of the screen. You'll see a row of words appear at the top of the screen such as Record, Edit, or Options.

2. Tap a word to see a drop-down menu of related commands (**Figure 2.4**). You don't have to maintain contact with the stylus; these menus are "sticky" and will stay visible until you tap the stylus on a command or elsewhere on the screen.

3. Tap the desired menu item to perform its action.

✔ Tips

■ Palm OS 3.5 finally added the ability to tap a program's title bar (the solid black area in the upper-left corner) to access its menus. You may never tap the Menu icon again!

■ If you're not running Palm OS 3.5, you can get the same functionality by installing the HackMaster extension MenuHack (http://www.daggerware.com/mischack.htm). (For more about similar system enhancements, see Chapter 8.)

To make menus visible...

...tap this icon first.

Figure 2.4 It may not make much sense to jump from bottom to top to access menus, but it's nice that menus are normally hidden to save space.

Figure 2.5 Tap the "circle-i" icon in the upper-right corner of dialog boxes to access help and other information.

Figure 2.6 It's worth checking out a new program's Tips screens—often you'll find real tips, not just online help.

Onscreen Help and Tips

Nestled within the tight memory confines of the Palm OS exists a handy location for accessing onscreen help and application tips. Most dialog boxes (windows that are identified by a thick outside line and a black title bar at the top) include a "circle-i" information icon in the upper-right corner (**Figure 2.5**). Tapping this small icon displays a screen titled Tips, which often provides instruction or pointers for using an application's features (**Figure 2.6**). It's often worth poking around the dialog boxes of a new program to see if there are any "hidden" features that may be revealed on the Tips screen.

Using the Onscreen Keyboard

The Palm OS includes two methods for entering information: Graffiti, the style of lettering you use to write individual letters (see the next section), and a virtual keyboard for tapping letters on the screen. The keyboard can be accessed only when your cursor is in a text field. Activating it brings up a new window containing the text field (or as much as can be displayed in the smaller space), with the keyboard located below (**Figure 2.7**).

Three separate keyboards are available: the abc keyboard, which is laid out in Qwerty format (like most computer and typewriter keyboards); the 123 keyboard, which gives you access to numbers and common symbol characters; and the Int'l ("international") keyboard, which creates common letters with diacritical marks (such as é) as well as characters like ß, ¿, and æ. Switch between layouts by tapping the corresponding button beneath the keyboard.

To activate the keyboard:

There are three ways of accessing the keyboard: tap either the abc or 123 dots in the lower corners of the Graffiti area; select Keyboard from the Edit menu (when available); or write ╱-K in the Graffiti area. Tap Done when finished.

✔ Tips

- If you like the onscreen keyboard but find the Qwerty layout difficult, install Fitaly (http://www.twsolutions.com/), which arranges letters based on frequent usage.

- If you don't mind Qwerty, but don't like tapping the small letter squares, install DotNote (or ".Note") (http://www. utilware.com/) to display larger keys.

Figure 2.7 If you'd prefer to tap on letters instead of write them, bring up one of the onscreen Keyboard layouts. This is often the best way to access symbol and international characters.

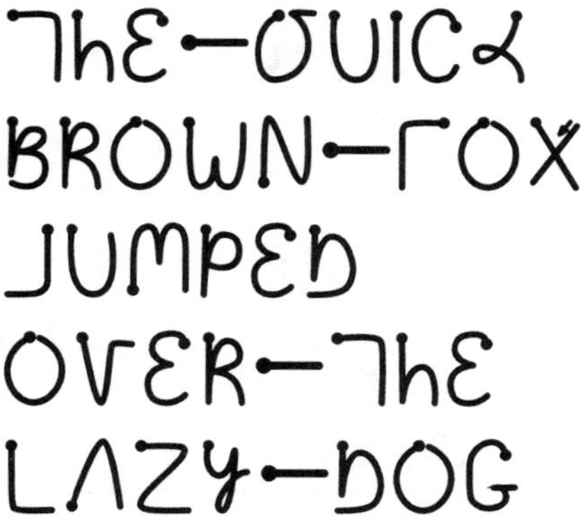

THE QUICK BROWN FOX JUMPED OVER THE LAZY DOG

Figure 2.8 At first glance, Graffiti looks like an alien scrawl, but pretty soon you'll find yourself writing like this on everything—not just your handheld.

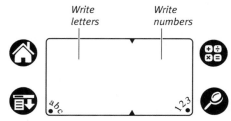

Write letters   *Write numbers*

Figure 2.9 Create Graffiti letters on the left side of the Graffiti area; write numbers on the right.

Graffiti

One of the only things that makes potential Palm organizer buyers hesitate before purchasing is the prospect of hand-writing letters on the screen. Some are concerned that they'll have to learn a new "language." Others are gun-shy after hearing about the difficulties with handwriting recognition that plagued other handhelds (notably Apple's discontinued Newton MessagePad). In the Palm OS, you use the stylus to write the Graffiti alphabet, which translates those written gestures into proper text characters (**Figure 2.8**).

Call me a Graffiti evangelist, but I'm here to reassure you that: (a) Graffiti is simpler than you think (you'll pick up the basics in the first few hours, I promise); and (b) because it doesn't technically do any handwriting recognition, your chances of writing something like "The quack bruin fax junked over the hazy fog" are fairly minimal (unless that's what you meant in the first place).

The Graffiti area

One of the key differences between traditional handwriting recognition and Graffiti is that you don't write directly on the active portion of the screen using Graffiti. Instead, you form letters in the silkscreened Graffiti area, where they are interpreted and displayed wherever your cursor happens to be.

The Graffiti area is split into two sections: write letters on the left side, numbers on the right (**Figure 2.9**). This is an important distinction, because some characters, such as B and 3, can be written using identical strokes.

Writing Graffiti

Here's the big secret about Graffiti: nearly every character can be written with only one stroke of the stylus. (The exception is X, which requires two strokes—but you can also use an alternate version of X that's still just one stroke.) The identity of the character is determined both by the shape of the stroke, and by the combination of the stroke's origin point and direction. As an example, let's write the word "Tack" (**Figure 2.10**).

To write basic Graffiti characters:

1. First, you need to be in an application where you can write text. Press the Memo Pad button on the front of the handheld, then tap New to create a new memo. Place the tip of the stylus at the left side of the Graffiti area.

2. Write the Graffiti stroke for T (⌐), starting at the dot. Make sure you write the complete stroke without lifting the stylus until the end (**Table 2.1**). You should see a capital T in the memo above.

3. Using the same side of the Graffiti area, write the stroke for A (∧), again starting at the dot. Repeat the process for C (C), and—my favorite letter to write—K (⋖).

4. Admire your (sharp) handiwork.

Writing numbers is exactly the same, only you write strokes in the right side of the Graffiti area (**Table 2.2**).

✔ Tip

■ You probably noticed that the first letter was automatically capitalized, and subsequent letters were in lowercase. When you begin a new field, or write an end-of-sentence punctuation such as a period or exclamation point, the Palm OS assumes that you want a capital letter.

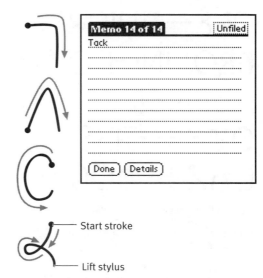

Figure 2.10 Each character can be written using one stroke of the stylus in the Graffiti area. Start at the dot (but don't try to draw the dot), and lift the stylus at the end of the stroke.

Table 2.1

The Graffiti Alphabet

Letter	Graffiti	Letter	Graffiti
A	∧	N	N
B	β	O	O
C	C	P	P
D	∂	Q	Ơ
E	Ɛ	R	R
F	Γ	S	S
G	G	T	⌐
H	h	U	U
I	I	V	V
J	J	W	W
K	⋖	X	X
L	L	Y	y
M	m	Z	Z

Table 2.2

Graffiti Numbers and Special Strokes

Symbol	Graffiti	Symbol	Graffiti
1	I	8	8 8
2	2	9	9
3	3	0	O O
4	L	backspace	→
5	5 b	return	/
6	6	shift	I
7	7	space	—

Table 2.3

Graffiti Punctuation (with Alternates)

Symbol	Graffiti	Symbol	Graffiti
.	• •	+	• ∝
,	• /	=	• Z
'	• I	|	• ∫
?	• ? ⌐	<	• <
!	• I	>	• ⌐
-	• —	\	• \
(	• C	{	• ε
)	• ⊃	}	• 3
/	• /	[	• ε
$	• S	]	• 3
@	• O	~	• N ~
#	• Ⴈ h	`	• \
%	• ૪	;	• /
^	• ∧	:	• l
&	• ४	"	• N
*	• ✕	tab	• ⌐
—	• • —		

In Graffiti, there are no separate strokes for upper- and lowercase letters. Instead, as when typing on a computer keyboard, you need to specify when to enable Caps Shift.

To write uppercase letters:

1. Write the Caps Shift stroke (I) in either side of the Graffiti area (Table 2.1). An up arrow symbol (↑) will appear in the lower-right corner of the screen to indicate that Caps Shift is enabled.

2. Write a normal Graffiti letter. You'll see the uppercase version appear in the text field. The up arrow will disappear.

3. If you're going to write a series of uppercase letters, you can enable Caps Lock by writing two Caps Shift strokes. The up arrow is replaced by an underlined up arrow (↥).

To write punctuation:

1. Tap once on either side of the Graffiti area to enable Punctuation Shift. You'll see a large dot in the lower-right corner.

2. Write the stroke for the punctuation mark you want (**Table 2.3**).

✔ Tip

■ If you change your mind and want to switch back to normal writing before committing to a capital letter or punctuation character, write a Back Space stroke (→), which effectively "deletes" the Shift or Punctuation Shift stroke you just made.

To write symbols and extended characters:

1. Enable the Symbol Shift mode by drawing a diagonal line in either side of the Graffiti area, starting at the top-left corner and finishing at the lower right. You'll see a similar line (╲) in the lower-right corner of the screen.

2. Write the stroke for the symbol you want (**Table 2.4**).

To write accented characters:

1. It takes two strokes to create accented characters. First, draw the letter you want to apply the accent to, such as E (Ɛ).

2. Write the corresponding accent stroke. The character changes to the new accented letter (**Table 2.5**).

Navigating using Graffiti

You can move your cursor within a field or to an adjacent field without erasing the letters you've already written using Graffiti navigation strokes (**Table 2.6**).

Command strokes

There's a better way than menu items to access commands. Rather than use three taps to access a menu item (tap the Menu icon, tap the menu name, tap the menu item), it's much easier and faster to write a command stroke. Draw a diagonal line from the bottom-left to the upper-right of either side of the Graffiti area (Table 2.6). You'll see the word Command:, or the Command Bar (see next section), appear at the bottom of the screen. Write the stroke that activates the menu item you want (such as ╱-C for Copy).

Table 2.4

Graffiti Symbols/Extended Characters

SYMBOL	GRAFFITI	SYMBOL	GRAFFITI
●	╲ ·	X	╲ ╱
TM	╲ ꟽ	÷	╲ 𝔛
®	╲ Ꝛ	=	╲ Z
©	╲ C	¢	╲ C
'	╲ Γ	¥	╲ 𝖸
,	╲ 7	£	╲ L
"	╲ N	¿	╲ L
"	╲ Ɯ	i	╲ I
§	╲ S	ß	╲ B
.	╲ O	µ	╲ ꟽ
+	╲ ∝	f	╲ S
—	╲ —	ø	╲ O

Table 2.5

Graffiti Accent Characters

SYMBOL	GRAFFITI	SYMBOL	GRAFFITI
à	∧ ╲	è	Ɛ ╲
á	∧ ╱	é	Ɛ ╱
â	∧ ∧	ê	Ɛ ∧
ä	∧ 𝔛	ü	U 𝔛
å	∧ O	ç	C
ñ	N N	æ	Ɛ

Table 2.6

Graffiti Navigation Strokes

COMMAND	GRAFFITI	COMMAND	GRAFFITI
cursor right	⟶	next field	╏
cursor left	⟵	shortcut	ℛ
previous field	╏	command	╱

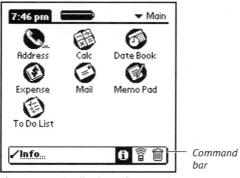

Figure 2.11 In Applications, the command bar provides access to common features, like the Info or Delete screens.

Figure 2.12 With nothing selected, the command bar offers few choices.

Figure 2.13 With a record selected, the command bar displays icons for commands which work in that context.

The Command Bar

Palm OS 3.5 and higher takes the concept of command strokes one step further with the command bar (**Figure 2.11**). When you write a command stroke, the command bar displays icons for actions that are usable depending on the current context.

For example, with no records selected in the To Do List, the only icon to appear is the Security icon (**Figure 2.12**). However, with a task selected, the Beam Item, Paste, and Delete Item options appear (**Figure 2.13**).

If you don't act within three seconds, the command bar disappears until invoked again.

To access the command bar:

1. Draw a diagonal line from the bottom-left to the top-right corner of either Graffiti area (✓).

2. Tap an icon on the command bar to perform an action. You can tap and hold on the icons to see their description; when you lift the stylus, the action is executed.

✔ Tips

- The command bar is an addition to the Palm OS's command-stroke function; if a command isn't represented by an icon, you can still invoke it by writing the command shortcut letters found in the application's menus.

- If you've tapped an icon but decide not to invoke its action, drag the stylus away from the icon before lifting it from the screen's surface.

Graffiti Improvement Tips

Simple tips for improving Graffiti recognition

- **Write large.** Feel free to use the full Graffiti area to write your letters—that way, more touch-sensitive sensors are registering your strokes.

- **Write at a natural speed.** If you write too slowly, you can confuse the sensors and generate errors.

- **Don't write on a slant.** Try to keep vertical strokes vertical, and horizontal strokes horizontal.

Alternate characters

If you're finding that the downstroke on the B is creating a D and vice-versa, or if you just want to write faster, there are a number of built-in alternate strokes that work just as well (or sometimes better) than the standard Graffiti set (**Table 2.7**).

TealEcho

Install TealEcho (http://www.tealpoint.com/) to see Graffiti characters as you write them. Having that visual feedback helps improve Graffiti skills by showing you exactly why your scribbles may be incomprehensible. See Chapter 8 for more about TealEcho.

TealScript

If you'd rather go in and tinker with each individual Graffiti character, install Teal-Script (http://www.tealpoint.com/). By marking the Enable Globally checkbox on the main screen, you can replace Palm's Graffiti alphabet (though you're not deleting the original) with the infinitely configurable TealScript. You're still using Graffiti, but you can set up a TealScript profile that reacts better to the way you write (**Figure 2.14**).

Table 2.7

Normal and Alternate Characters				
LETTER	GRAFFITI		LETTER	GRAFFITI
A	∧		T	⊐
B	ß ß 3		U	U
C	C <		V	∨ ∨
D	Ð Ω ℓ		W	ω
E	Ɛ ⋛ ℓ		X	X ℓ
F	Γ Γ		Y	ɣ ɣ ſ
G	G 6		Z	Z
H	h		1	I
I	I		2	2 ς
J	J J		3	3
K	⋉		4	∟ C <
L	L ∠		5	5 5 S
M	m m		6	6
N	N ∧ ∼		7	7 ⊃
O	O O		8	8 8 ℓ ɣ
P	P P ſ		9	9
Q	Ʊ Ʊ		0	O O
R	ß ß ℝ		æ	Ɛ
S	S ⟨ ら			

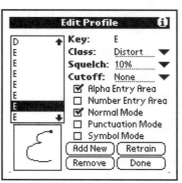

Figure 2.14 TealScript builds profiles based on your Graffiti usage.

Palm's Welcoming Committee

Your handheld includes a program called Welcome that automatically runs when starting the device for the first time, or after the memory has been completely wiped (such as from a hard reset or battery failure) (**Figure 2.15**).

It initially sets up the date, time, and localization options, then calibrates the digitizer, which maps pen taps with the correct pixels on screen (**Figure 2.16**). You then have the option to follow a short tutorial on writing Graffiti characters (**Figure 2.17**).

Once you've run Welcome, however, there's little reason to go back to it unless you want to refresh yourself using its brief tutorials; all of the settings (and more) can be accessed from the Prefs application.

✔ Tips

- If you want to easily change your basic settings (such as when you travel to a different time zone), the Welcome application can be a quicker method than accessing the Prefs program.

- The Graffiti tutorial in Welcome replaces Giraffe, a favorite game of early Palm owners that taught Graffiti by forcing you to write letters falling from the top of the screen before they hit the bottom.

  If you miss the old animal, don't worry: you'll find the file "Giraffe.prc" in the Add-on folder that was created during the Palm Desktop installation.

Figure 2.15 You probably found Welcome when first powering on.

Figure 2.16 Welcome establishes the date and time settings from the start.

Figure 2.17 Welcome offers a formal area to practice writing Graffiti.

Setting General Preferences

The Prefs application looks mundane at first, but closer inspection reveals that the rest of the OS hinges upon the settings you choose here. To access the preferences, tap the popup menu in the upper-right corner (**Figure 2.18**).

To set General preferences:

1. Choose General from the Preferences popup menu (**Figure 2.19**).

2. As a battery-saving feature, a device will shut itself off after a period of inactivity. Tap the Auto-off After popup menu to choose a delay of 30-seconds, one minute, two minutes, or three minutes.

3. If you own a device with a rechargeable battery, check the Stay on in Cradle box to prevent the device from powering off when it's docked in the HotSync cradle. This is a good way to use your organizer as an expensive desk clock.

4. Specify the volume settings for the System, Alarm, and Game default sound levels as High, Medium, Low, or None.

5. If you own a Palm m500 or m505, use the Alarm Vibrate and Alarm LED controls to enable or disable those features.

6. Specify whether people can beam to you using the Beam Receive popup menu.

✔ Tip

- Leaving the Beam Receive option on can drain your battery at a higher rate. However, returning to Prefs each time you wish to receive something can be a pain. Instead, write the ShortCut ℛ .I (shortcut stroke, period, I) in any text field, which turns on Beam Receive for a single instance.

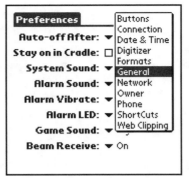

Figure 2.18 All of the Preferences settings can be accessed via the popup menu in the upper-right corner.

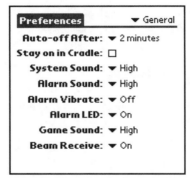

Figure 2.19 Set several volume levels, as well as choose if you want to receive beamed materials. Devices that use rechargeable batteries can be left on while in their recharging cradles.

Do Your Prefs Look Different?

Palm has modified the Preferences screens several times during the progression of the Palm OS. The screens I'm using are for Palm OS 4.0. If you don't see something where I'm describing it, check another screen. The best example is setting the date and time: in Palm OS 4.0, the controls have been moved to their own screen, but in previous versions the settings lived in the General screen.

Figure 2.20 Time keeps on slippin', slippin', slippin'...sorry, having a Steve Miller Band moment.

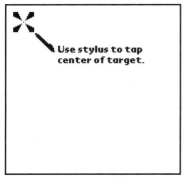

Figure 2.21 Set your time zone here. If you travel frequently, this screen makes it easy to change the handheld's clock when you reach your destination.

Figure 2.22 Tapping the targets ensures that your touch-sensitive screen is accurately registering the tap locations.

Setting the Date and Time

Palm OS 4.0 breaks out these controls into their own Preferences screen (**Figure 2.20**).

To set the Date and Time:

1. Tap the Set Date field to select today's date from a calendar.

2. Tap the Set Time field to configure the hour and minute values.

3. Tap Set Time Zone to select your location from the list provided (**Figure 2.21**).

4. If Daylight Saving time is in effect, select On from the popup menu.

✔ Tip

■ Be careful about changing the time to reflect new time zones on your handheld and laptop when traveling. Since the time and date stamps are referred to when you perform a HotSync, having your organizer and your PC living in separate zones can cause data to be overwritten incorrectly.

Setting the Digitizer

Due to temperature variations, repeated use, and the general passing of time, the digitizer can gradually slide off track. If your pen taps don't seem to be working the way they used to, run the Digitizer.

To calibrate the Digitizer:

1. Choose Digitizer from the Preferences popup menu.

2. Tap the center points of the X shapes that appear (**Figure 2.22**). This process ensures that the pixels you tap on the screen correspond with the pixels that the Palm OS thinks you're tapping.

SETTING DATE, TIME, AND DIGITIZER

Customizing Buttons

Although the plastic application buttons on the case and the silkscreened icons near the Graffiti area are handy for directly launching the built-in applications, there are times when you might want to specify different programs, such as Super Names (http://www.standalone.com) instead of the Address Book application (**Figure 2.23**).

To customize buttons:

1. Choose Buttons from the Preferences popup menu.

2. Select the button you wish to replace, and tap the popup menu to the right of its icon.

3. Choose an application from the popup list. To return to the Palm OS factory settings, tap the Default button.

✔ Tips

- You can configure not only the plastic buttons and the silkscreened icons, but also the one-stroke pen drag. In the Buttons screen, tap Pen, then tap the popup menu in the center (**Figure 2.24**). You can choose to turn on the backlight, activate the onscreen keyboard (this is the default), display Graffiti help, turn off and lock the device, or (using Palm devices with infrared capability) beam data. Setting this feature to turn on the backlight is better than pressing the power button for two seconds.

- Install Swipe (http://www.doublebang.com/) to get six more one-stroke commands, using different areas of the screen (**Figure 2.25**).

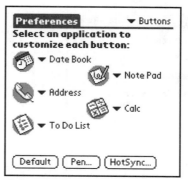

Figure 2.23 Launch other programs from the physical application buttons.

Figure 2.24 Specify an action for the bottom-to-top screen stroke shortcut.

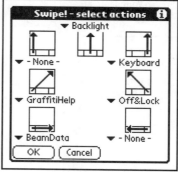

Figure 2.25 Swipe gives you six more options for customizing strokes.

CUSTOMIZING BUTTONS

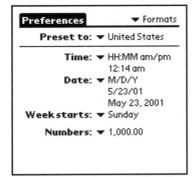

Figure 2.26 The Formats screen offers preconfigured settings for 24 countries.

Figure 2.27 The Owner screen can be filled with whatever text you like, though most people enter contact information.

Changing Formats

If you dream of traveling abroad, select Formats from the Preferences popup menu and tap the Preset to popup menu to select the country in which you'd like to reside. Otherwise, it's probably a better idea to choose your current location.

To change time, date, week, and number formats:

1. The formats have already been configured for each country, but you can adjust them individually by tapping each setting's popup menu (**Figure 2.26**).

2. Switch to another application or Preferences menu item to apply the settings.

Editing the Owner Screen

Since you'll likely become attached to your handheld, you should go ahead and put your name in it (thereby resolving any potential playground ownership disputes by asserting that yes, your name *is* on it!).

To set up the Owner screen:

1. Select Owner from the Preferences popup menu.

2. Write your contact information (or other text) on the lines provided. If you should misplace your Palm device someday, the honorable person finding it can learn where to ship it back (**Figure 2.27**).

✔ Tip

■ After configuring your preferences, return to the Owner screen before switching to another program. This should speed up access the next time you open the Preferences application, as some sections— especially ShortCuts—take longer to load.

Using ShortCuts

Graffiti is an efficient way to input data, but you'll soon get tired of entering commonly used words and phrases letter by letter. Instead, set up ShortCuts that substitute full texts when you enter an abbreviation.

To create and edit ShortCuts:

1. Select ShortCuts from the Preferences popup menu (**Figure 2.28**).

2. Tap New to create a ShortCut, or Edit to change an existing one. The Palm OS includes seven built-in ShortCuts.

3. In the ShortCut Entry window, write the abbreviation under ShortCut Name. The shorter the abbreviation, the fewer the letters you'll have to write to activate it, but you're not limited to just two or three (**Figure 2.29**).

4. Write the full text that will replace the abbreviation when you activate the ShortCut. Tap OK when you're done.

To use a ShortCut:

1. In any text field, write the ShortCut Graffiti character (𝒳); you will see it appear in your text.

2. Write the abbreviation for the word or phrase you're going to use. The abbreviation and ShortCut character will be erased and replaced by the full text.

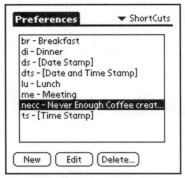

Figure 2.28 All but one of the predefined ShortCuts are named with two-letter abbreviations, but you're not bound to that limit.

Figure 2.29 ShortCuts make entering frequently used texts much easier.

Figure 2.30 Preconfigure a variety of methods of moving data to and from your handheld.

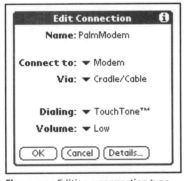

Figure 2.31 Editing a connection type controls how the OS interacts with devices such as modems.

Figure 2.32 Changing the speed or editing the initialization screen can sometimes improve a poor connection.

Setting Connection Preferences

If Palm OS devices are truly "connected organizers," as Palm says, then they need to connect with a variety of devices. Under Palm OS 3.3 and later, the Connection preferences handle peripherals like modems as well as serial and infrared connections.

To create or edit a configuration:

1. Select Connection from the Preferences popup menu (**Figure 2.30**).

2. Tap the New button, or tap a configuration to highlight it, then tap Edit.

3. From the Connect to popup menu, choose the type of connection that fits your purpose: PC, Modem, or Local Network (**Figure 2.31**).

4. Next, use the Via menu to choose the route the connection will take: Cradle/Cable or Infrared.

5. If connecting to a modem, choose Touch-Tone™ or Rotary from the Dialing popup menu, and specify the loudness from the Volume popup menu. These aren't available if connecting to a PC or network.

6. Tap the Details button (**Figure 2.32**).

7. Select a data speed from the Speed popup menu. If you're running into HotSync problems under a serial connection, reducing the data speed may help.

8. If you're using a modem, the Country and Init String options will be available. Choose your country and enter a modem initialization string if you need one.

9. Set the flow control on the Flow Ctl popup menu. Flow control regulates the rate of incoming information. Leaving this set to Automatic should be fine in most cases.

Setting Network Preferences

Attaching a modem to your handheld enables you to connect directly to an Internet Service Provider (ISP) (**Figure 2.33**).

To set up Network preferences:

1. Select Network from the Preferences popup menu.

2. Choose the name of your ISP under the Service popup menu. If yours is not listed, select New from the Service menu, or write ✁-N.

3. Write the name you use to connect in the User Name field.

4. Tap the dotted box next to Password to write your login password. If you leave this blank, you will be prompted for your password each time you connect.

5. Choose a connection mode from the Connection popup menu (this setting comes from the Connection screen; see the previous page).

✔ Tip

■ The Palm OS keeps a log of network connections; select View Log from the Options menu (**Figure 2.34**).

Figure 2.33 The Network preferences screen allows you to connect directly to an Internet service provider.

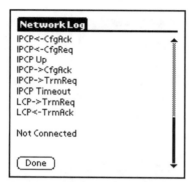

Figure 2.34 Secret code? Not if you know how to read modem commands. Use the Network Log to troubleshoot your connections.

Figure 2.35 Tapping the Phone field in the Network preferences screen displays several dialing options.

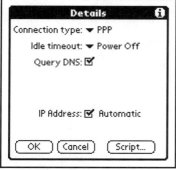

Figure 2.36 Choose the type of Internet connection, along with the action to take if the connection is idle.

To configure Network phone settings:

1. Tap the dotted box next to Phone to configure dialing options (**Figure 2.35**). In addition to the phone number required to dial, you can specify that a calling card be used, that a prefix be dialed (for example, dialing 9 to reach an outside line), or that call-waiting be disabled (if your phone package includes this; the signal tone generated by call-waiting services often breaks existing Net connections). Tap OK.

2. Tap the Details button to continue with the setup (**Figure 2.36**). Depending on the service you use to connect to the Internet, choose PPP, SLIP, or CSLIP from the Connection type popup menu.

3. Use Idle timeout to specify when the network connection should be disconnected if there is no activity. The default Power Off setting ensures that an active connection continues until the unit shuts off—even if you switch between applications.

4. Use Query DNS (Domain Name System), to instruct your Internet application (such as an email client or Web browser) to ask your ISP's server to resolve domain names (addresses) on the Internet. If you uncheck this box, you will need to enter your primary and secondary DNS server addresses.

5. Check IP Address: Automatic to grab a random IP (Internet Protocol) address from your ISP, which identifies your machine on the Internet. If you have a fixed IP address, uncheck the box and enter it into the blanks that will appear below.

6. Finally, tap the Script button to create a customized login script to facilitate connecting to your ISP's server. If you don't require one, leave the first line so that it reads "End."

SETTING NETWORK PREFERENCES

Setting Phone Preferences

Palm OS 4.0 includes built-in support for using a mobile phone to connect to the Internet. You need to have installed Palm's Mobile Internet Kit, which comes with some devices (like the Palm m505), or is also sold separately.

To set Phone preferences:

1. Choose Phone from the Preferences popup menu.

2. Select a connection from the Connection popup menu (**Figure 2.37**). If your phone doesn't appear in the list, you can choose Edit Connections to set up a profile.

3. Tap the Test button to make sure the handheld and phone are communicating (**Figure 2.38**).

Setting Web Clipping Preferences

Palm's Mobile Internet Kit gives any Palm device the capability to use the Web Clipping technology introduced with the Palm VII (see Chapter 10).

To set Web Clipping preferences:

1. Choose Web Clipping from the Preferences popup menu (**Figure 2.39**).

2. If you have a MyPalm account set up (see http://my.palm.com/) and you've used the MyPalm application to get online with a Palm VII or VIIx, your user name appears in the User ID field.

3. Tap the Server field to manually change the proxy server information.

4. A Palm VII's communication with nearby radio towers can identify its location. If you're uncomfortable with this, mark the checkbox for Warn when sending personal information.

Figure 2.37 You can connect to a cellular phone by selecting a profile on the Phone screen.

Figure 2.38 Use the Test feature to make sure your handheld and phone are communicating clearly.

Figure 2.39 Web Clipping allows you to access Web information quickly and easily.

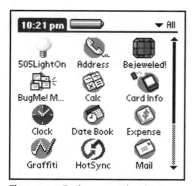

Figure 2.40 Each program has its own icon, listed alphabetically on the Applications screen.

Figure 2.41 You can also view applications in a list format, and group them into categories.

Launching Applications

Now that you have all of your preferences set up, you can finally start using applications. (You've probably been using applications from the beginning, but I felt it was important to cover the preferences early.)

Unlike nearly all personal computers, a Palm device has no hard drive or floppy disk to store its data—everything is held in RAM (random access memory), including third-party applications and their data (the built-in applications and the core Palm OS files are stored in separate read-only memory, or ROM). As a result, you technically never have to open or quit programs. All the applications are running concurrently, paused at the state where you last left them. Although I may refer to "launching" or "opening" applications throughout this book, Palm OS is actually only switching between them. (But "launching" sounds more exciting.)

To open an application:

1. Bring up the Applications screen by tapping the silkscreened Applications icon.

2. Tap a program's name or icon to launch it (**Figures 2.40** and **2.41**).

✔ Tips

- If you have more programs than will fit onto a single screen, write the first letter of the program you want in the Graffiti area to make it visible.

- Repeatedly tapping Applications switches between application categories (see "Categorizing Applications" later in this chapter).

Installing Applications

Many handheld owners get by just fine using the built-in applications. However, one of the platform's strengths is that there are thousands of third-party programs and utilities available to install. In most cases, you can download the software from the Web on your desktop computer, then install it onto your Palm organizer.

To install applications using the Palm Install Tool (Windows):

1. Launch the Palm Install Tool either from the Windows Start menu, or by clicking the Install button from within Palm Desktop.

2. Click Add to select the programs to install. Palm OS applications end with the extension .prc (no matter whether you use a PC or a Mac). You can also drag the program files from the Windows desktop to the Palm Install Tool window to add them to the list (**Figure 2.42**).

3. When you've added the programs you want to install, click Done.

4. Perform a HotSync to transfer the programs into the handheld's memory.

To install applications using the HotSync Manager (Macintosh):

1. Launch the HotSync Manager.

2. From the HotSync menu, choose Install, or press Command-I.

3. Click the Add to list button to locate the .prc file you want to add. You can also drag the files to the installation window from the Finder to add them to the list (**Figure 2.43**), or even just drag them to the Finder's HotSync Manager icon.

4. Perform a HotSync operation.

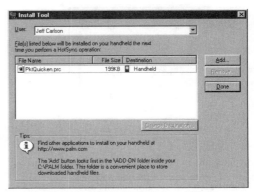

Figure 2.42 Under Windows, click the Add button to prepare programs to be installed. Alternately, you can drag the files to the Palm Install Tool window.

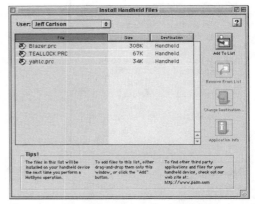

Figure 2.43 The Macintosh installer looks different than its Windows cousin, but works much the same. Clicking the Application info button displays attributes of the selected file, such as creation date and version number.

Figure 2.44 My Little Buddy creates a floating toolbar that gives you access to application files, Palm Web sites, the Palm Desktop, and more.

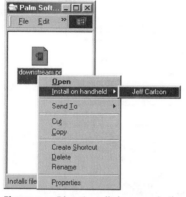

Figure 2.45 DirectInstall shows up in the Windows Explorer contextual menu, flagging a file to be installed at the next HotSync.

Dropping a file onto Palm Buddy's desktop window installs it immediately.

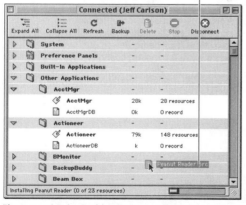

Figure 2.46 Palm Buddy eliminates the need to install applications via HotSync on the Macintosh. Just drag and drop your .prc file onto Palm Buddy's window to immediately install it.

Other Installation Options

Although the Palm Install Tool is the main method of adding files to your handheld, other third-party programs feature streamlined methods of doing the job.

My Little Buddy (Windows)

On the Windows side, I've found My Little Buddy (http://www.precise-solutions. cix.co.uk/pilot.htm) to be an important fixture on my desktop. My Little Buddy is a floating toolbar that lets you quickly open Palm Desktop and the HotSync Manager, install batches of files, store Web URLs for easy access, and more (**Figure 2.44**).

DirectInstall (Windows)

Another nifty Windows installation helper is the near-invisible DirectInstall (http://www. rob.cybercomm.nl). Simply right-click a Palm data file or application, then select a Palm user from the Install on handheld popup menu (**Figure 2.45**). The file will be transferred at the next HotSync operation.

Palm Buddy (Macintosh)

One of my favorite Mac programs is Palm Buddy (http://perso.wanadoo.fr/fpillet/), which doesn't synchronize files but rather makes installing and backing them up a breeze (**Figure 2.46**). Palm Buddy maintains a live connection to the handheld, so you don't have to HotSync to install files: simply drag and drop any .prc file onto Palm Buddy's window. Be aware, though, that leaving Palm Buddy and the handheld actively connected will drain your batteries much quicker.

However, as of this writing, the program doesn't support USB. But it's worth mentioning, since hopefully by the time you read this Palm Buddy will be updated.

Categorizing Applications

Grouping all of your applications onto the same screen isn't always helpful. That's why the Palm OS lets you set up categories to help organize your programs.

To switch between views:

1. In Applications, choose Preferences from the Options menu, or write /-R.

2. Choose either Icon or List from the View By popup menu.

To categorize applications:

1. In Applications, choose Category from the App menu, or write /-Y.

2. You'll see a list of all installed applications. Tap a category name from the popup menu to the right of a program.

3. If you don't see the category you want, select Edit Categories from the popup list to create a new category or edit an existing one (**Figure 2.47**).

To remember the last category:

1. All categories are shown if you switch to the Applications screen from another program. To keep the same category visible, choose Preferences from the Options menu, or write /-R (**Figure 2.48**).

2. Mark the Remember Last Category box.

✔ Tip

■ Tapping the Applications button repeatedly scrolls through the categories, but you won't see everything: Unfiled programs don't appear. So, to take advantage of this switching view, be sure to file your unfiled programs.

Figure 2.47 Tap the popup menus at right to specify a program's category. New applications are set to Unfiled.

Figure 2.48 Viewing applications by category lets you organize them according to your preference. Tapping Remember Last Category prevents all applications from being viewed the next time you tap the Applications icon.

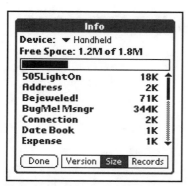

Figure 2.49 View your memory usage from within Applications by choosing Info from the App menu.

Figure 2.50 The Info dialog box is also where you can see the version numbers of the Palm OS and installed software.

Memory Management

Palm data is teeny compared to data on a typical PC, but you can still get carried away and load your memory to maximum capacity.

To view the amount of free memory:

1. From the Applications screen, choose Info from the App menu, or write ╱-I. Under Palm OS 3.5 and later, you can tap the Info icon (❶) on the command bar.

2. The Size button displays memory usage in kilobytes (**Figure 2.49**); tap the Records button to view how many records are stored in each application; tap the Version button to see each program's version number (**Figure 2.50**).

3. Tap Done when finished.

Deleting Applications

At some point you'll install a program that doesn't hold your attention, or maybe you'll just need to free up some memory to add more applications. Deleting the ones you don't want is a painless process.

To delete applications:

1. From within Applications, choose Delete from the App menu, or write ✓-D. Under Palm OS 3.5 and later, you can also tap the Delete icon (🗑) on the command bar.

2. Choose the application you wish to remove, then tap the Delete button and confirm your choice.

✔ Tips

■ You cannot delete the Palm OS's built-in applications; they are stored in ROM.

■ When you delete an application, any data files associated with it are deleted as well.

■ To quickly jump down to the program you want to delete, write the first letter of its name in the Graffiti area.

Installing Apps into Flash ROM

If you purchased any Palm OS handheld except for the Palm m100 series, Palm IIIe, the original Palm VII, or the Handspring Visors, you may have noticed that it included not only standard memory, but also flash memory, or flash ROM.

The Palm OS, as well as the built-in applications like Date Book and Address Book, are all stored in the device's read-only memory. This enables everything to start up immediately when you first turn the Palm device on, and ensures that the OS and the main applications don't get erased if your batteries die or you suffer a hard reset. Current models include 2 MB or 4 MB of flash memory.

The Palm designers opted to store the basic software in flash ROM, memory that can be written to using a technique known as "flashing." This way, future system updates could be distributed as software and flashed onto existing hardware. However, the Palm OS and built-in applications take up only about 1.3 MB of room, leaving approximately 700K of unused flash memory in most devices!

The clever folks at the HandEra (http://www.handera.com/) wrote a nifty application called FlashPro to take advantage of that wasted space. This means you can store some of your frequently used programs in that 700K memory space, freeing up more room for other programs in RAM. Plus, if you should have to perform a hard reset and lose all of your data, those flashed programs will be there when you restart.

Not all programs work well in flash memory; be sure to check HandEra's Web site for a list of compatible applications.

Replacing the Applications Application

The Applications screen does its job moderately well, but people with more than a handful of programs soon grew weary of scrolling. It wasn't long before an enterprising programmer built a way out of the old Applications box.

The result was Eric Kenslow's LaunchPad, one of those programs that make you want to say, "Why didn't they think of that sooner?" Currently, there are multiple variations of LaunchPad including Synergy Solutions' Launch 'Em (http://www.synsolutions.com/), and Bozidar Benc's Launcher III (http://www.benc.hr/).

Instead of one long scrolling field, these launchers provide a configurable tabbed interface, visual and numeric battery level display, and time and date display (**Figure 2.51**). They also hook into many features of the Palm OS such as Show/Hide Records, backlighting, Lock & Turn Off, and dragging programs to a trash icon to delete them.

Perhaps the best improvement is the ability to categorize applications by simply dragging their icons to a tab. Forget the endless popup menus in Applications' Category screen.

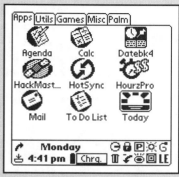

Figure 2.51 A familiar tabbed interface greets users of Launch 'Em, a replacement application launcher based on Eric Kenslow's LaunchPad utility.

✔ Tips

■ Select the Always use option in the Preferences screen to make the launcher your default application screen. However, be sure to uncheck this option if you need to delete or update the launcher, or risk hitting an error requiring a soft reset.

■ You still need to use the Applications program to view free memory and, depending on which launcher you use, delete files. You can either tap the Applications program icon (not the silkscreened icon) to go there, or you can select Apps/Memory (or equivalent) from the Pilot or Apps menu (again, depending on your choice of launching programs), which will take you to Applications.

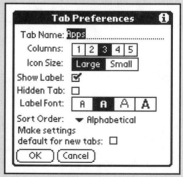

Figure 2.52 Launch 'Em provides many more options for working with, and viewing, your applications.

■ Launch 'Em includes an extra feature that allows you to hide individual tabs, so you can keep some programs and their data under at least one level of security (**Figure 2.52**).

The Security Application

You're probably carrying around your most important information in a device no bigger than your hand. Although you're no doubt careful with your organizer, there's a half-decent chance that it may get swiped, or even left on top of your car as you're rushing off to work. The Palm OS's built-in security features provide a first line of defense in case your Palm is picked up by the wrong person.

The Security application controls whether or not records marked private—no matter which program they reside in—are either shown or hidden (**Figure 2.53**). Palm OS 3.5 enhanced Security by adding a third option that masks private records. It also provides a means for changing the global security setting within individual programs, saving a trip to the Security application itself (**Figure 2.54**).

To set up a password:

1. Tap the dotted Password box, which should read Unassigned if this is your first time using Security.

2. Enter a password and a hint, then tap OK.

3. Reenter your password to verify it.

To change or delete a password:

1. Tap the dotted Password box, which should read Assigned.

2. Enter your current password.

3. Write a new password to change it; tap the Delete button if you want to not have an assigned password at all.

4. If you changed your password, reenter it to verify it.

Figure 2.53 Security controls whether records marked as Private throughout the Palm OS are shown or hidden.

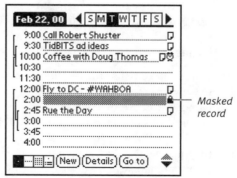

Masked record

Figure 2.54 Palm OS 3.5 added the capability to mask private records instead of just hiding them.

Figure 2.55 If you want to see your data again, write your password in the blank provided.

Figure 2.56 If you've forgotten your password, your private records will be deleted until the next HotSync.

Figure 2.57 To be diligent about securing your data, enable the Auto Lock Handheld feature.

To use the Lock & Turn Off feature:

1. In the Security application, tap the Lock & Turn Off button. You will be prompted to verify your choice.

2. The next time you turn on your handheld, enter your password to access your data (**Figure 2.55**).

To access a forgotten password:

1. If you've forgotten your password, you can remove it, but at a price. Tap the Password field, then tap the Lost Password button in the Password screen.

2. If you wish to proceed, tap Yes (**Figure 2.56**). The state of the Password field will revert to Unassigned.

To automatically lock your handheld:

1. Tap the Auto Lock Handheld field.

2. Select a time period to have Security automatically lock your device. The default is Never, but you can choose to engage the feature whenever the handheld is turned off, at a specific time of the day, or after a delay of several minutes or hours (**Figure 2.57**). Tap OK.

✔ Tips

- You don't have to set up a password if you don't want to. Setting Security to hide or mask records without specifying a password still makes private records unreadable. You won't be asked to provide a password if you switch to Show Records.

- Don't use easy passwords: birthdates, addresses, family members' names, and especially pet names. The best passwords are a combination of letters, numbers, and symbols.

- Unlike earlier releases, Palm OS 4.0 recognizes upper- and lowercase letters.

Beaming Applications

Recent Palm devices possess the ability to send data between similar devices equipped with infrared hardware. In addition to sending records (such as addresses), you can transfer full applications.

To beam applications:

1. From the Applications screen, choose Beam from the App menu, or write ╱-B. Under Palm OS 3.5 and later, you can also tap the Beam icon (🕿) from the command bar.

2. Select an application from the list that appears (**Figure 2.58**). Programs marked with a padlock symbol beside them cannot be beamed.

3. Aim your infrared port at the recipient's handheld and tap the Beam button.

To receive beamed applications:

1. Go to the Preferences application and make sure that Beam Receive is set to On in the General preferences screen.

2. Aim your infrared port at the sender's handheld and wait for them to initiate the transfer.

3. When the application has been beamed, choose to accept or deny the program.

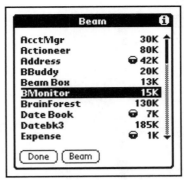

Figure 2.58 Rather than transfer programs to a friend via your PC, beam them from the Applications screen.

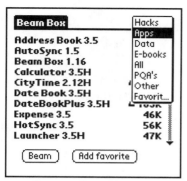

Figure 2.59 Beam Box can beam just about anything, provided the recipient also has Beam Box installed (which you can beam to them if they don't!).

✔ Tips

■ Palm asserts that infrared transfers can be achieved from a maximum distance of one meter (39.37 inches).

■ Write the ShortCut ℓ .I (shortcut stroke, period, I) in any text field, which activates Beam Receive in the General preferences for a single instance.

■ Beaming records and applications is helpful, but out of the box you can't beam data (such as a BrainForest outline) or system extensions (see Chapter 8). Beam Box (http://www.inkverse.com/) allows you to beam nearly anything on your handheld, as long as the recipient also has Beam Box installed (**Figure 2.59**).

■ If you don't have much free memory on your organizer, you may run into trouble trying to beam applications or records to another handheld. When you beam something, the Palm OS needs enough free memory to store a temporary copy of what you're beaming. So if you're trying to beam a large application and getting an out of memory error, you'll need to delete some files before you can send it. The good news is that if the recipient's handheld has plenty of free space on it, you can temporarily beam smaller files to her, delete them from your device, then get them back after you've transferred the larger file.

BEAMING APPLICATIONS

Using Expansion Cards

Expansion cards provide extra memory to store more data: but how do you access the data and copy it to and from the cards? Palm OS 4.0 supports data transfers from the Applications screen; the Sony CLIÉ and HandEra 330 models use different (but similar in functionality) programs for transfers.

To access files under Palm OS 4.0:

Insert an expansion card into the slot on the Palm device. The Applications screen will display a new category containing the programs stored on the card. The category name includes an icon indicating that you're looking at the card's contents (**Figure 2.60**).

To transfer files under Palm OS 4.0:

1. On the Palm m500 or m505, go to the Applications screen.

2. Choose Copy from the App menu, or write /-C. The Copy dialog box appears.

3. Set the Copy To popup menu to the file's destination (**Figure 2.61**). The From popup menu changes automatically.

4. Highlight a file and tap the Copy button.

5. Tap Done.

To transfer files on the Sony CLIÉ:

1. Launch the MS Gate program.

2. From the popup menu in the upper-right corner, select either MS (Memory Stick) or Internal to choose files to copy.

3. Locate and tap the file you want to transfer. Data on Memory Sticks are stored hierarchically with a Windows-like interface. Tapping folders opens them; tapping the up arrow exits a folder (**Figure 2.62**).

4. Tap the Copy or Move buttons to transfer the file, or Delete to get rid of it.

Figure 2.60 Expansion card files show up in the Applications screen as if they belong to another catgory.

Figure 2.61 You don't need a special application to transfer data files under Palm OS 4.0.

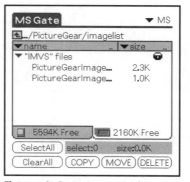

Figure 2.62 Sony Memory Sticks are formatted hierarchically like Windows disks.

HotSync

The underlying approach to functionality in the Palm OS is almost more philosophical than practical: the handheld is not a computer in itself, but an extension of one's computing environment. It recognizes that people aren't going to abandon PCs in favor of PDAs, but rather use both tools to accomplish the greater task of organizing and managing one's information. For it is this goal, grasshopper, that leads to greater productivity, plus the justification to purchase yet another cool electronic gadget.

The key that unlocks this data convergence is the HotSync feature, the ability to synchronize data between the handheld and the PC—not just copy it from one box to the other. This is an important distinction, because it means both platforms will always have the most current information at your disposal.

HotSync Overview

Performing a HotSync operation is essentially a one-step procedure: push a button and it happens. You can do this when connected directly to your PC, or over a modem or network. However, knowing about what's going on in the background will help you deal with potential problems in the future.

How HotSync works

In normal copy operations, such as when you copy a file from a floppy disk to your hard drive, the PC's operating system checks to see if a similarly named file exists in the location you're copying to. If a match is found, it checks the modification dates of each file to determine which is newer, then throws up a dialog box requesting confirmation to continue (under some operating systems, this feature can be disabled). If the user clicks OK, the old file is overwritten. The problem here exists when both files have been separately modified; if so, the older data is wiped out (**Figure 3.1**).

In contrast, the Palm OS (by way of the Hot-Sync Manager on the PC) compares every record within a file like the Address Book database. If you make a change to different records on the handheld and the desktop, the changes appear on both platforms following a HotSync. If you make separate changes to the same record on each platform, both versions are retained, and you are notified of the duplication (**Figure 3.2**).

Standard file date comparison

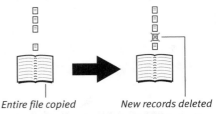

Entire file copied   *New records deleted*

Figure 3.1 Most files on your PC are "synchronized" by comparing their modification dates and overwriting the older file—big trouble if both files have changed.

HotSync synchronization

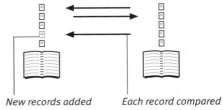

New records added   *Each record compared*

Figure 3.2 HotSync synchronization compares each record within Palm database files, ensuring that you have up-to-date information on your handheld and on your PC.

Figure 3.3 Your data is stored on your PC's hard drive, in the user folder matching your Palm user name.

Table 3.1

User Folder Contents (Windows)

FOLDER	CONTENTS
address	Address Book data
Backup	Nearly everything except data for the built-in applications. This includes program files, related database files, Doc text files, some preferences files, etc.
datebook	Date Book data
expense	Expense application data
Install	Program files to be installed at the next HotSync. See the Tip on this page for important information about this folder.
Mail	Email data
memopad	Memo Pad data
todo	To Do List data

Table 3.2

User Folder Contents (Macintosh)

FOLDER	CONTENTS
user name	No funky truncation of the user name on the Mac—in my case, the folder is titled "Jeff Carlson." The file within, which is also the full user name, contains all of the built-in databases' data, plus the following:
Conduit Settings	Preferences for each conduit
Archived Files	Records deleted from the device, but stored on the desktop computer
Files to Install	Files to be transferred at the next HotSync
Backups	Everything else

Where HotSync stores your data

A HotSync operation copies data from the handheld to the PC and vice-versa, which means that information has to live on your hard drive—but where?

When you install the Palm Desktop software, enter your name (or whatever name you wish to use) at the Create User Account screen. This name becomes the name of the device.

You'll find a new folder on your hard drive named "Palm" (unless you specified a different location and folder name during setup). Within that folder is a folder that closely matches your User Name; on my PC, for example, the files are located in the folder "CarlsoJ" (**Figure 3.3**), though on my Mac it comes up as "Jeff Carlson." The information in **Table 3.1** and **Table 3.2** detail the folder structure on each platform.

✔ Tips

- When you run the Palm Install Tool, the programs you choose are stored in the Install folder within your user folder. However, under Windows you can't just toss .prc files there and expect them to be transferred at the next HotSync. The HotSync Manager needs to be told that the Install folder is "active" before it will copy the files located within. Running the Install program once toggles this setting—so, after you install one program using the Palm Install Tool, switch to the Windows desktop to copy new program files to the folder in bulk.

- The Backup(s) folder stores all programs you've installed on your handheld—even ones you've deleted from the handheld. So, if the folder size seems impossibly large, don't be alarmed.

- It's a good—no, great—idea to regularly make backups of your user folder.

HOTSYNC OVERVIEW

63

Configuring HotSync Manager

The HotSync Manager isn't often seen, but it does quite a bit of work behind the scenes to ensure that your data is transferring properly. Its primary task is to monitor the port reserved for the HotSync cradle so it can act when the handheld signals a sync operation.

To access the HotSync Manager under Windows:

From within Palm Desktop, choose Setup from the HotSync menu. You can also click the HotSync icon on the Taskbar, then select Setup from the popup menu (**Figure 3.4**).

To access the HotSync Manager under Mac OS:

Launch HotSync Manager from the Palm folder on your hard disk, or choose Setup from the HotSync® (*active user name*) sub-menu of the Instant Palm Desktop menu (next to the Applications menu in the upper-right corner of your screen; **Figure 3.5**).

To enable HotSync port monitoring:

Make sure the cable attached to your HotSync cradle is connected to one of your PC's USB or serial ports.

Access the HotSync Manager as described above and go to the Setup screen. Under Windows, you have three options for enabling port monitoring (**Figure 3.6**):

◆ **Always available.** Activates HotSync Manager when you start your computer.

◆ **Available only when Palm Desktop is running.** Automatically enables and disables port monitoring when you use Palm Desktop.

Figure 3.4 The HotSync icon on the Windows Taskbar offers a quick way to configure HotSync settings.

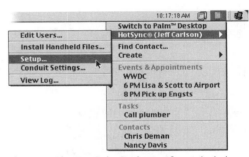

Figure 3.5 The Mac Palm Desktop software includes the Instant Palm Desktop menu, where you can access HotSync Manager commands.

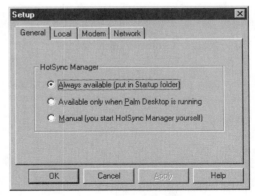

Figure 3.6 Choose when HotSync Manager will be active to avoid port conflicts with other devices.

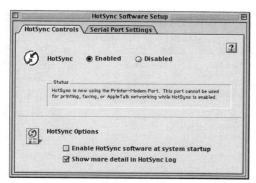

Figure 3.7 Enable HotSync port monitoring from the HotSync Controls tab on the Macintosh.

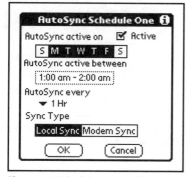

Figure 3.8 Schedule your HotSync operations at a more convenient hour with AutoSync.

◆ **Manual.** Starts port monitoring at your discretion, freeing up the port for other uses when you're not using HotSync.

Under the Mac OS, you can leave HotSync running all the time by selecting Enable HotSync software at system startup under HotSync Options, or you can choose the Enabled or Disabled radio buttons at the top of the screen (**Figure 3.7**).

✔ Tips

■ Do you find yourself forgetting to Hot-Sync during the course of your busy day? Let the Visor do the work for you: Auto-Sync (http://www.rgps.com/AutoSync.html) can automatically HotSync your handheld according to one or two schedules. Be sure to have your computer running and the handheld in its cradle, then let it go to work (**Figure 3.8**).

■ There never seem to be enough ports on a computer. Older PowerBooks, for example, have only one port that shares duties with printers, external modems, and LocalTalk network connections. If you don't want to switch cables each time you need to print or perform a HotSync, consider buying an inexpensive hub that connects multiple devices.

■ If you use a Macintosh with a serial port (as opposed to newer machines with USB), make sure that AppleTalk is disabled before attempting to perform a HotSync: in the Chooser, select the AppleTalk Inactive radio button. Apple-Talk can hog the serial port and not allow other applications, like HotSync Manager, to use it. The same is often true of fax software.

CONFIGURING HotSync MANAGER

Setting Up Conduits

Each of the built-in applications, as well as the Palm OS and the program installer, has its own conduit, a software translator that specifies how records should be compared and copied between platforms. In addition, many third-party applications, such as AvantGo and HourzPro, include their own conduits for manipulating their specific data.

To configure conduits:

1. Choose Custom from the HotSync menu in Windows. In the Mac OS, launch the HotSync Manager and choose Conduit Settings from the HotSync menu, or press Command-H.

2. Highlight the conduit you wish to edit, then click the Change (Windows) or Conduit Settings (Mac) button. Double-clicking a conduit also lets you modify its settings (**Figure 3.9**).

3. Choose an action for that conduit (**Figure 3.10** and **Table 3.3**). Click the Set as default checkbox (Windows) or the Make Default button (Mac) to make the new setting permanent each time you do a HotSync. Click OK.

Under Windows, clicking the Default button in the Custom dialog box restores the conduit settings to the last default state.

✔ Tip

■ Many people use PIMs such as Microsoft Outlook and Symantec's ACT! instead of Palm Desktop. In addition to the Outlook conduits included with the Palm software, a variety of third-party applications, like Desktop to Go (http://www.dataviz.com/) and PocketMirror (http://www.chapura.com/), replace the built-in conduits with ones that synchronize data with your favorite desktop PIM.

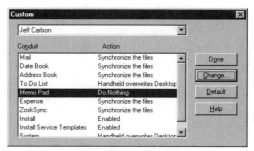

Figure 3.9 Conduits control the way each program's data is handled during a HotSync.

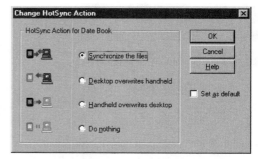

Figure 3.10 Multiple HotSync actions let you override the default synchronization settings.

Table 3.3

HotSync Conduit Actions

SETTING	ACTION
Synchronize the files	All records are compared individually; newer records overwrite older records.
Desktop overwrites handheld	Individual records are not compared; entire desktop file replaces handheld file.
Handheld overwrites desktop	Individual records are not compared; entire handheld file replaces desktop file.
Do nothing	Records are skipped; no action is taken.

The Two Faces of HotSync

Palm OS 3.1 and earlier assumed two approaches to HotSyncing data: Local Sync, which used the device's serial port to interface with a HotSync cradle or cable, and Modem Sync, for synchronizing over a modem connection (**Figure 3.11**). Tapping one of the two buttons would initiate that type of HotSync. (Pressing the physical button on the HotSync cradle would automatically trigger the correct connection.)

Palm OS 3.3 acknowledged that there are more ways to HotSync data, so Palm added Connections, an option in the Preferences application that lets you create different configurations based on the connection type (see Chapter 2 for more on the Connections screen). Now, Palm devices running Palm OS 3.3 or later still have the option to select between Local and Modem synchronization, but a connection popup menu beneath the single HotSync button lets you specify which type of local or modem connection to use (**Figure 3.12**). This also affords the flexibility of specifying your own devices, like wireless modems. To edit connection configurations from within HotSync, choose Connection Setup from the Options menu, or write ∕-S.

Given the inevitable march of progress, why is this important? Some handheld models, like the Palm m100 and Handspring Visors, store the operating system in standard read-only memory (ROM); since Palm OS 3.3 and Palm OS 3.5 are flash upgrades (meaning they replace a writeable version of the ROM), these devices can't be upgraded from earlier versions—you need to purchase a more recent model to get the new HotSync version. This doesn't mean they're crippled in any way, just that there are two slightly different approaches to accomplishing the same task.

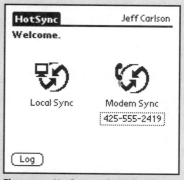

Figure 3.11 HotSync under Palm OS 3.1 assumes there are only two ways to synchronize your data.

Connection popup menu

Figure 3.12 Palm OS 3.3 and later includes a popup menu to specify different connection types.

Local HotSync

Most of your HotSync actions fall into the category of Local HotSync, in which the handheld and PC are connected directly by either a serial cable or cradle, or via infrared.

To set up a Local HotSync:

1. Launch Palm Desktop or the HotSync Manager and choose Setup from the HotSync menu.

2. Click the Local tab (Windows, **Figure 3.13**) or the Serial Port Settings tab (Mac).

3. From the Serial Port popup menu, specify the COM port to which your HotSync cable or cradle is connected.

4. Specify the speed of the connection from the Speed popup menu. Click OK, or close the window.

5. From the Windows Taskbar popup menu, specify that Local HotSync monitoring should be activated by clicking the name; a checkmark appears. On the Macintosh, this information is available in the Serial Port Settings window.

✔ Tip

- If you're having trouble maintaining a connection, reduce the speed setting in the Setup dialog box.

To perform a Local HotSync:

1. Place your device in the cradle.

2. Push the HotSync button on the front, or press the button in the HotSync application on the handheld. A short series of tones indicates a successful connection.

3. A window appears on the desktop indicating the HotSync progression. A similar screen also appears on the handheld (**Figure 3.14**). Another set of tones indicates when the synchronization is done.

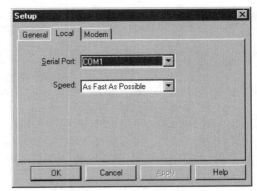

Figure 3.13 Use the Local tab to specify which port your HotSync cradle is connected to.

Figure 3.14 Pressing the HotSync button on the cradle activates the HotSync; the progression is visible on both the handheld and the PC.

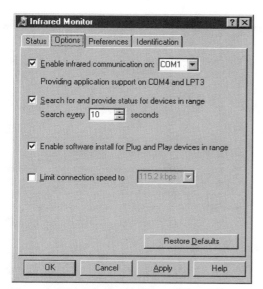

Figure 3.15 If your laptop or desktop PC is equipped with an infrared port, you can set your preferences to recognize the handheld and perform a HotSync.

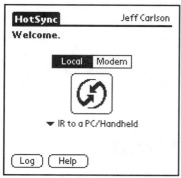

Figure 3.16 Use the HotSync application on the Palm to initiate an infrared HotSync operation.

Infrared HotSync

Knowing a good opportunity when it zaps them in the head, the engineers at Palm incorporated infrared HotSync capabilities into the Palm OS. The system's IR communication is built upon the IrCOMM protocol. If you're using a Macintosh PowerBook G3 Series or later, or a PC laptop running Windows 98 or later, IrCOMM support should be built in.

To set up infrared HotSync (Mac):

1. Open the HotSync Manager, and switch to the Serial Port Settings tab.

2. Choose Infrared from the Port popup menu under Local Setup.

To set up infrared HotSync (Win):

1. Open the Infrared Monitor from the Settings folder and click the Options tab.

2. Check the box labeled Enable infrared communication on, and choose the COM port (usually COM4 or COM5) used by the infrared port (**Figure 3.15**).

3. In the HotSync Manager, choose the COM port as the Local source.

To perform an infrared HotSync:

1. Launch the HotSync application on the Palm device, and make sure that IR to a PC/ Handheld is selected from the Connection popup menu.

2. Tap the large HotSync button to begin (**Figure 3.16**).

✔ Tip

■ Visors running Palm OS versions earlier than 3.5 need the SerIrCommLib.prc file from Palm (http://www.palm.com/support/downloads/irenhanc.html), or the third-party program IRLink (http://www.iscomplete.com/).

INFRARED HOTSYNC

Modem HotSync

Make sure you have disabled any programs on your PC (such as fax software) that may cause HotSync headaches.

To set up a Modem HotSync on your computer:

1. Choose Setup from the HotSync menu to bring up the Setup dialog box.

2. Click the Modem tab (Windows, **Figure 3.17**) or the Serial Port Settings tab (Mac).

3. From the Serial Port popup menu, specify the COM or serial port to which your modem is connected.

4. Specify the speed of the connection from the Speed popup menu. Click OK, or close the window.

5. From the Taskbar popup menu, specify that Modem HotSync monitoring should be activated by clicking the name; a checkmark appears. On the Macintosh, this information is available in the Serial Port Settings tab—click the Modem Setup or Both Setups radio button (**Figure 3.18**).

To set up a Modem HotSync on your Palm device:

1. Launch the HotSync application.

2. Choose Conduit Setup from the Options menu, or write /-D.

3. Choose which conduits should be run by marking the checkboxes to the left of each program's name (**Figure 3.19**). Tap OK.

4. If you haven't set up your Modem preferences, go to the Prefs application and select Connection (or Modem) from the popup menu in the upper-right corner (see Chapter 2).

Figure 3.17 As with a Local HotSync, specify your modem's COM port and speed, as well as the model.

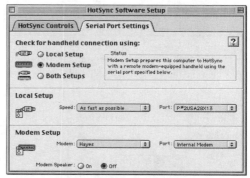

Figure 3.18 The Modem Setup information on the Macintosh shares the same screen as the Local Setup.

Figure 3.19 To save some connection time, mark only the conduits you want to have synchronized.

Figure 3.20 With everything configured, simply tap the HotSync button.

Figure 3.21 Modem Sync looks slightly different in Palm OS versions prior to 3.3, but accomplishes the same task. Tap the Modem Sync button.

To perform a Modem HotSync:

1. Go to the main HotSync screen. If you're running Palm OS 3.3 or later, tap the Modem button.

2. Tap the dotted Enter Phone # box (under the Modem Sync icon; or, under the Connection popup menu in Palm OS 3.3 or later) to specify a phone number.

3. Attach a modem (connected to a phone line, of course) to your handheld (see Chapter 9).

4. If you're using a modem with a HotSync button on the case, push it to initiate the HotSync (and skip the next step). If not, launch the HotSync application on the handheld.

5. Tap the main HotSync button (**Figure 3.20**), or the Modem Sync icon in devices running Palm OS 3.1 (**Figure 3.21**). You should hear the startup tones.

6. When the HotSync is complete, you'll hear the tones signaling the end, and the connection will terminate.

MODEM HOTSYNC

LANSync/Network HotSync

Network HotSync extends your range and flexibility by providing a method to synchronize your data from any computer on your PC network—whether it's using someone else's HotSync cradle down the hall or several states away. (Network HotSync isn't available for Macintosh computers.) If your network has dial-in remote access, you can also connect using a compatible modem.

To set up a Network HotSync:

1. Launch the HotSync application.

2. Depending on which mode you're in, pressing the HotSync icon (or the Local Sync or Modem Sync icon for devices running Palm OS 3.1) will attempt to connect directly to the PC attached to the current HotSync cradle, or to your PC out on the network. If you're dialing in to a modem that acts as the gateway for a network, choose Modem Sync Prefs from the Options menu, or write ∕-O. Tap either the Network or Direct to modem button to specify the Modem Sync action (**Figure 3.22**).

   If you're connected directly to the network, choose LANSync Prefs from the Options menu, or write ∕-L. Choose between LANSync and Local HotSync (**Figure 3.23**).

3. Choose Primary PC Setup from the Options menu, or write ∕-P. In most cases, you shouldn't have to change this information, since it's downloaded from your PC when you perform a HotSync.

4. On your PC, bring up the HotSync settings by choosing Setup from either the HotSync menu within Palm Desktop or from the popup menu on the Taskbar.

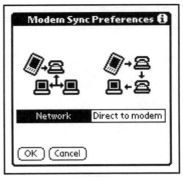

Figure 3.22 The Modem Sync Preferences dialog box lets you choose between a direct dial-up connection or a dial-up network connection.

Figure 3.23 By choosing LANSync or Local HotSync, you dictate the action of the main screen's Local Sync icon.

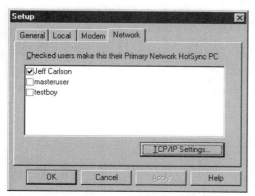

Figure 3.24 The Network tab in the HotSync Setup screen sets up your PC for LAN synchronization.

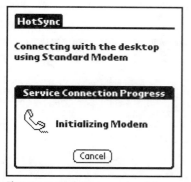

Figure 3.25 Dial up your network by tapping the Modem button, then the HotSync button.

5. Tap the Network tab, then place a checkmark next to the users who will have access to your machine (**Figure 3.24**).

6. If you need to adjust the TCP/IP configuration, click the TCP/IP Settings button. Otherwise, click OK.

To perform a Network HotSync:

◆ If the computer you're connecting from is on the same local area network (LAN) or wide area network (WAN), and you've set the LANSync preferences to LANSync, tap the Local button, then tap the HotSync icon to connect. Under Palm OS 3.1, tap the Local Sync button.

◆ If you need to dial in via modem to connect to your network, and you've set the Modem Sync preferences to Network, tap the Modem button, then tap the single HotSync button. Under Palm OS 3.1, tap the Modem Sync icon to dial the number and establish a connection (**Figure 3.25**). Once connected, the HotSync operation should proceed normally.

✔ Tip

■ If you have a Palm m500 or m505 and a wireless network based on the 802.11b protocol (sometimes called Wi-Fi) check out the Xircom Wireless LAN Module for Palm Handhelds (http://www.xircom.com/). It's a device that attaches to the back of the handheld and offers wireless network access.

Viewing the HotSync Log

The details of each of the last ten HotSyncs are stored in a text file on your computer. Although the information usually isn't important, the HotSync Log is the first place to turn to if you're having HotSync problems (fortunately, most error messages are written in understandable English; **Figure 3.26**).

To view the HotSync Log:

◆ **Windows:** Choose View Log from the HotSync menu within Palm Desktop, or from the HotSync popup menu located on the Taskbar (**Figure 3.27**).

◆ **Mac OS:** Choose Log from the HotSync menu within the HotSync Manager.

◆ **Palm OS:** Tap the Log button on the main HotSync screen. However, don't get angry with me for suggesting it, since the Palm HotSync Log gives only the most basic of information (like the scintillating "OK Date Book").

◆ Alternately, open the log file itself with a word processor or text editor. You'll find the log in your user folder.

✔ Tip

■ To record a detailed log on the Macintosh (instead of the minimal log that's stored on the handheld), mark the Show more detail in HotSync log checkbox at the bottom of the HotSync Controls screen.

```
HotSync started 09/03/01 02:12:12
    - Installed file:
C:\Palm\CarlsoJ\Install\giraffe.prc
OK Install
OK Mail
OK Date Book
OK Address Book
OK To Do List
OK Memo Pad
OK Expense
ZoskSync Conduit 2.3.3 Begin:
    ZoskSync: No reports were transferred
from the handheld.
OK ZoskSync Conduit End
OK System
```

Figure 3.26 A typical HotSync Log looks like this, with plain-English comments to indicate the steps taken.

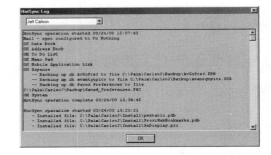

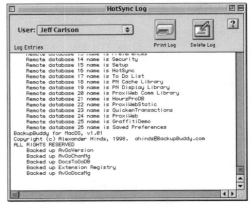

Figure 3.27 The HotSync Log can be viewed from within Palm Desktop (Windows and Mac versions shown here), or you can use a word processor or text editor to read the file from your hard drive.

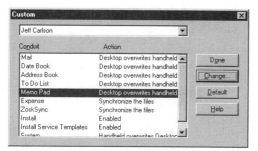

Figure 3.28 In the event of a hard reset, your first HotSync should be set so that the desktop information overwrites the handheld's data.

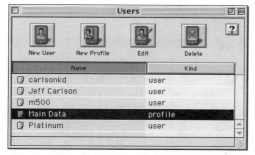

Figure 3.29 Sharing one computer with multiple Palm devices entails creating a new user account for each person. The Macintosh screen is shown here.

Multiple HotSync Options

The majority of owners use their handhelds on an individual basis: one organizer, one PC. However, there are some cases where you may want to synchronize one device with multiple machines, or several organizers on the same machine.

Since HotSync *synchronizes* your data, not overwrites it, the information on each machine should remain updated without any special work on your part. Simply HotSync as you normally would; the desktop software keeps track of multiple users.

However, if you should happen to lose your handheld's data (for example, due to a hard reset), customize your first HotSync as described here.

To set up a first HotSync on an empty Palm device:

1. On your PC, choose Custom from the HotSync popup menu on the Taskbar, or from the HotSync menu in the Palm Desktop application.

2. Specify Desktop overwrites handheld for all of the conduits (**Figure 3.28**). Press OK.

3. Perform a HotSync. Your data on the handheld should be in the state it was before it was lost.

4. Before you HotSync again, change the conduit settings back to Synchronize.

To set up a new user:

1. In Palm Desktop, select Edit Users from the User submenu of the HotSync menu (Mac), or select Users from the Tools menu (Windows).

2. Click the New (Windows) or New User (Mac) button (**Figure 3.29**) and type a name. Click OK.

File Link

Frequently updating memos or addresses is made simple for Windows users. Using the File Link feature, you can create a Windows file that is in plain text (.txt), comma separated (.csv), or Palm archive format that gets transferred to the handheld according to scheduled intervals (**Figure 3.30**).

To create a File Link:

1. Prepare the file you wish to link. For example, let's say everyone who accesses my PC needs each week's movie box office listing. Save it as either straight text, comma-separated, or as a Memo Pad archive (see later in this chapter for details). If you're saving a list of addresses (say, the month's new clients), save the file as either comma-separated or as an Address Book archive.

2. Choose File Link from the HotSync menu in Palm Desktop, or the HotSync popup menu on the Taskbar.

3. Select a user name, make sure the Create a new link radio button is activated, and click the Next button.

4. Choose either Memo Pad or Address Book from the Application name popup menu.

5. If you know the path to your file, type it into the File path field. Otherwise, click the Browse button to locate it.

6. Linked file data is stored in its own category to avoid conflicts with your other data. Enter a name in the Category name field (**Figure 3.31**), and click Next.

7. A dialog box confirming your link settings appears. By default, the file will be queued for HotSync whenever it changes. If this is okay, click the Done button.

Figure 3.30 Set up a File Link that points to a file filled with important information that changes often.

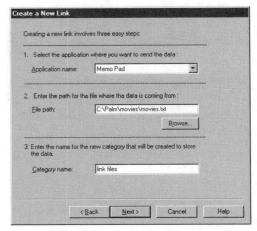

Figure 3.31 Choose the application, file path, and specify a category name to set up a File Link.

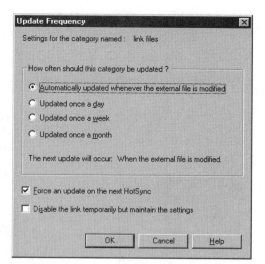

Figure 3.32 You can set the frequency at which the linked file is transferred to the handheld.

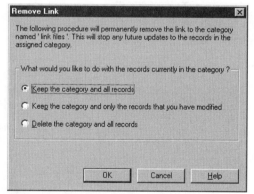

Figure 3.33 If you want to put your File Link into hibernation for a while, choose to keep the category and records, or just the category, for later.

To schedule a File Link update:

1. If you want to specify other options (such as daily, weekly, or monthly updates), click the Update Frequency button on the Confirm your Link Settings dialog.

2. Specify the interval for how often the category should be updated (**Figure 3.32**).

   If you know the file isn't going to change for a while, mark the checkbox next to Disable the link temporarily but maintain the settings.

3. Click OK to exit the Update Frequency dialog box, then click the Done button.

To remove a File Link:

1. Choose File Link from the HotSync menu in Palm Desktop, or the HotSync popup menu on the Taskbar.

2. Choose a user name, and select the option marked Modify or remove an existing link. Click the Next button.

3. Highlight the link you wish to delete and click the Remove button. The Remove Link dialog box appears.

4. Choose how you'd like to handle your existing linked data (**Figure 3.33**).

5. Click OK.

✔ Tips

- Although it may look like something's gone wrong, don't be surprised if, after you've set up a link, the category you set up appears to be empty. The linked data won't get copied to Palm Desktop until you perform a HotSync.

- Unfortunately, File Link is not available on the Macintosh.

Working with Archived Records

When you delete a record from the handheld or the Palm Desktop, you're given the option to save it on your PC by marking the Archive deleted program item(s) at next HotSync checkbox (**Figure 3.34**). This is a great feature if you've accidentally deleted something, or if you need to free up some memory on your handheld, but don't want to lose the information permanently. But where does it go? And how do you get it back?

Each of the built-in applications creates an archive file (such as an Address Book archive (.aba) or Date Book archive (.dba)) for each category that contains deleted records. Those files are stored in each application's folder, although recent deleted items won't show up until you perform a HotSync (**Figure 3.35**).

To restore archived records:

1. In Palm Desktop, go to the Palm application module you want to restore records from (such as the Memo Pad). Choose Open Archive from the File menu.

2. In the Open Archive dialog box, highlight the archive file named after the category you're looking for (such as "Personal.mpa"), and click the Open button.

   Your deleted records are now visible in the main window. You'll see the name of the file, followed by "(Archive)" in the window's title bar (**Figure 3.36**).

3. Highlight the records you want to restore, and choose Copy from the Edit menu (or press Control/Command-C).

4. Switch back to your active Palm records by choosing Open Current from the File menu.

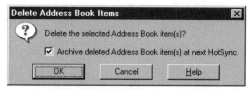

Figure 3.34 You may have seen this dialog dozens of times...but do you know where the data actually goes? If you mark the checkbox, you can retrieve deleted records from your PC's hard drive at any time.

Figure 3.35 Archives are named according to the deleted records' categories.

Archive icon

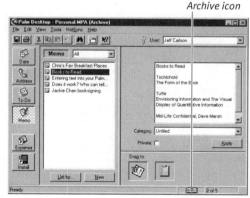

Figure 3.36 Opening an archive file is straightforward, but the records are displayed in the main window, which can be confusing if you're not paying attention. Look to the title bar or an icon in the lower-right (Palm Desktop 3.1 and earlier) to signal that an archive is currently active.

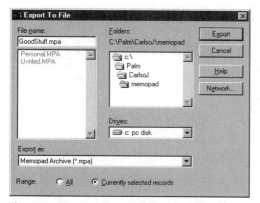

Figure 3.37 You don't have to limit yourself to using archives for resurrecting deleted data. Export selected records, or your entire set of addresses, to-do items, and memos into archive format.

Figure 3.38 Records can be imported from tab-delimited files, in addition to Palm's archive formats.

5. Choose Paste from the Edit menu, or press Control/Command-V to paste the restored records.

6. Perform a HotSync to restore the data to your handheld.

You can also use the archive format to create customized archives, rather than just files containing deleted records. This can be useful if you need to email a batch of addresses to another Palm device owner, for example.

To export archive files in Palm Desktop:

1. Go to the Palm application module you wish to export. If you want to export only certain records, highlight them.

2. Choose Export from the File menu. In the Export To File dialog box, choose Currently selected records if you're not exporting the entire contents of the application. Give the file a unique file name, then click the Export button (**Figure 3.37**).

Note that if you have private records hidden, you will need to choose Show private records from the View menu before exporting them.

To import archive files in Palm Desktop:

1. Go to the Palm application module you wish to import.

2. Choose Import from the File menu. In the Import dialog box, highlight a file and click Open.

✔ Tips

■ You can also import records in text-only and comma-delimited file formats (**Figure 3.38**).

■ Change the category for many records at once: export them, switch to the new category, then import them back in.

Creating HotSync Profiles

Profiles allow you to set up a group of master records that can be transferred to new Palm devices. For example, you can set up a profile containing your company's important meetings to be copied to each person's handheld. However, the profile erases any existing data, so you can only copy a profile to a brand new or empty device.

To create a HotSync profile:

1. Windows: In Palm Desktop, select Users from the Tools menu.

   Macintosh: In Palm Desktop, go to the HotSync menu and select Edit Users from the User submenu.

2. Windows: In the Users dialog box that appears, click the Profiles button to view a list of profiles. Click the New button (**Figure 3.39**).

   Macintosh: Profiles are marked in the Users window with a different icon (**Figure 3.40**). Click New Profile.

3. Windows: Highlight the name of your new profile and click OK.

   Macintosh: After your profile is created, click the close box in the upper left corner, or press Command-W.

4. Stock your profile with the information that you want to appear on every Palm device you copy it to. Enter the data by hand, or switch between the profile and a user account to copy and paste records.

✔ Tip

■ To preserve your existing categories when copying records to the profile, first set up the category names in your new profile. Then, in your user account, view by category and copy the records you want. Switch to the profile, view the similarly named category, and paste the records.

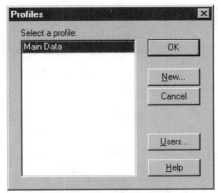

Figure 3.39 In the Profiles screen, you can toggle between the Users and the Profiles lists.

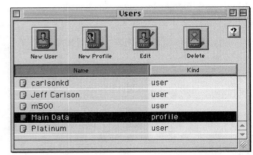

Figure 3.40 On the Mac, profiles are displayed using a separate icon. Click the Edit button to rename them.

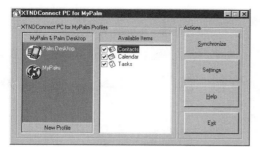

Figure 3.41 The MyPalm sync software synchronizes your handheld data with both Palm Desktop (or the PIM of your choice) and the MyPalm Web-based calendar.

The Really Expensive Calculator

It may seem odd to use the Web to track your schedule, since that's what your handheld is for (which doesn't need Internet access). Isn't this a step backward?

Rather, it's more like having the option to step to the side when needed. Once when I was traveling in Britain, the only electronic gadget I took with me was my PalmPilot. Like any good geek, I'd stored trip notes, emergency phone numbers, and a host of other important information on my convenient organizer. Unfortunately, while sitting at the train station in Chepstowe, I replaced the batteries, fumbled the job, and lost my data! Normally, this would be no big deal, but my laptop was thousands of miles away.

If I had put my data online, I could have connected the handheld to a PC at an Internet café later in Windermere (I was smart enough to carry a HotSync cable, apparently), then transferred my data back to the handheld. Instead, I carried around a very swanky calculator for two weeks.

Synchronizing with Web-Based Organizers

A handheld organizer is intended to be an extension of your personal data, but just how extended do you want to be? Several Web services have appeared in recent years that let you store your calendar and contacts online. The idea is that you can check your schedule from any place with a Web connection: a client's office, Kinko's, an Internet café, or even some other far-flung destination.

Most of the services available now are free, and can store your addresses, to do items, and memos as well as calendar items. I'm using the MyPalm service (http://www.palm.net/) as an example; others include Yahoo! (http://calendar.yahoo.com/) and Intelli-Sync (http://www.intellisync.com/).

To set up a MyPalm account:

1. Go to http://www.palm.net/ to set up an online account. You can use any login name and password you like; it doesn't have to be the same as on your handheld.

2. Make sure you have a backup of your Palm data for safekeeping, then download and install the MyPalm Sync software (currently only for Windows).

3. Choose Synchronize Palm Desktop from the XTNDConnect PC icon that appears in the Taskbar (**Figure 3.41**).

4. Click the Settings button, then the Data Sources tab.

5. Click Palm Desktop Address Book in the list at left, then choose a Palm device name in the dialog box that appears. Or, click the Change button and select a name if the dialog box doesn't appear.

6. Click OK.

7. Click the Synchronize button.

To update the Web information:

1. Use the forms provided on the Web page to create or edit appointments, addresses, and other information (**Figure 3.42**).

2. From the XTNDConnect PC icon in the Taskbar, choose Synchronize Palm Desktop. The data on your PC and on the Web are now the same.

3. HotSync your Palm device to update the handheld's data. The information is now the same as the online data when the synchronization is finished (**Figure 3.43**).

✔ Tips

■ The MyPalm synchronization software currently doesn't recognize user names with spaces, so it may report that your data is not available to sync. One option is to wipe your handheld, give it a new name, and start over; however, I have several programs that use registration codes based on my user name. Palm has posted something of a workaround while their engineers are working on the problem. Go to http://www.palm.net/Corporate/support.jsp and do a search for incident number 010328-0125.

■ Be sure to read the terms of agreement when you sign up with a service to ensure that the company will safeguard the integrity of your data.

■ As Web calendars have become more sophisticated, more features are now available, such as making a version available to friends or the general public, online chat forums, and the like.

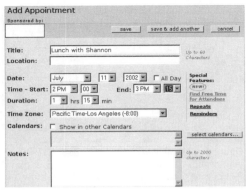

Figure 3.42 The advantage of a Web-based calendar is that you can add appointments from any computer connected to the Web.

Figure 3.43 After a HotSync, the handheld and Web versions contain the same appointments.

DATE BOOK

My mother called me at college one night to see how things were going. After updating her on my classes, friends, and the usual local intrigue, I inquired what was new with her. "Not much," she replied. "We just finished my birthday cake."

Oops. So, my brain isn't hardwired for dates and holidays—that doesn't mean I have to forever miss important events and appointments. Although Mom was good-humored about my chronological ineptitude, it made me realize that I needed more than just the rusting calendar in my head.

Now several years later, I use Date Book to store meetings, social occasions, and holidays, confident that they're quickly available at hand.

Plus, unlike the calendar that hangs in my kitchen, Date Book can remind me of events before they happen, not after. My mom should be proud.

Setting Preferences and Display Options

The 160 by 160 pixel screen on most Palm devices can display 25,600 pixels, which sounds like a lot until you consider that the minimum PC screen resolution today is 640 by 480 pixels (or a total of 307,200 pixels). It's easy to see why every effort has been made to keep the Palm's small screen uncluttered yet understandable. Date Book displays time in daily, weekly, and monthly views. The Agenda view, introduced in Palm OS 3.5, displays a day's events with tasks from the To Do List (**Figure 4.1**).

Changing some of the display options allows you to specify how dense or sparse your calendar will appear.

To set Date Book preferences:

1. Choose Preferences from the Options menu.

2. If you've ever wished you could set your own hours, here's your chance. Select the Start Time and End Time by tapping the arrows to the right of the time boxes (**Figure 4.2**).

3. The Preferences dialog box also contains settings for Date Book's alarm. Checking Alarm Preset specifies that each new event includes an alarm, which will go off according to the number of minutes you specify.

4. You can also specify which sound the alarm will use, how often it plays when the alarm goes off, and at what interval it will play until you dismiss it.

5. Tap OK to return to the Date Book views.

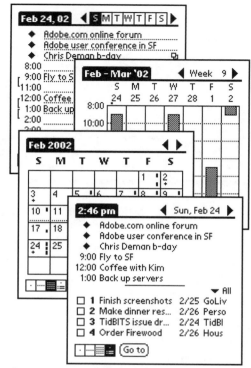

Figure 4.1 The Date Book displays your time in (from top) daily, weekly, and monthly views. The Agenda view (bottom), introduced in Palm OS 3.5, shows tasks as well.

Figure 4.2 Most people choose regular business hours, but for some of us that means all day long, as shown here. Checking the Alarm Preset box adds an alarm to each new event you create.

Figure 4.3 Date Book's Day view makes the best of its limited screen real estate, displaying elements such as time bars and icons while hiding unused time lines.

Figure 4.4 You can control the degree of clutter in the day and month views. I prefer to see everything.

Figure 4.5 Choose from three fonts to display the Day view records (this example uses the largest font).

Day View

Whenever you access the Date Book, either by tapping its icon from the Applications screen or by pressing the physical Date Book button at the lower-left of your device, you are presented with the Day view. From the other Date Book views, you can also tap the first box (containing one dot) in the lower-left corner of the screen. This is where you enter and edit events, and generally manage your schedule (**Figure 4.3**).

Day view features

◆ Events of the day appear on the dotted lines beside their allotted times, which adjust to conform to your schedule (a meeting ending at 9:45, for example, is marked as such, instead of displaying somewhere before 10:00). If there isn't enough space on the screen to view all your events, the Date Book removes any unused lines. To disable this feature, deselect Compress Day View in the Display Options dialog box (**Figure 4.4**).

◆ If you select Show Time Bars in the Display Options dialog box, the black brackets at left will indicate an event's time span—a handy way to see if you've scheduled overlapping events.

◆ Tap the days of the week buttons at the top of the screen to switch days. Tapping the arrows on either side of the buttons moves you forward or backward in weekly increments.

◆ The icons at right signify that an event contains a note (⬚), an alarm (⏰), or that it is a repeating event (⬚).

◆ You can also specify which font is used to display event text (**Figure 4.5**). Select Font from the Options menu (or write ╱-F) and choose from three styles.

DAY VIEW

✔ Tips

■ The Day view provides a fine overview of the day, but doesn't tell you what time it is now. Tap the date tab in the upper-left corner to briefly display the current time (**Figure 4.6**). This works in each Date Book view except for the Agenda view, which shows the time by default.

However, tapping the title bar under Palm OS 3.5 and later brings up the program's menus, so although the time appears, it's quickly obscured by the menu. Instead, tap and hold to view the time, then move your stylus off the tab (without lifting the stylus) to return to normal without engaging the menu.

■ For those times when manipulating the stylus is inconvenient, or just to save time, press the Date Book button on the case to switch between views.

■ In school, I knew a kid who (for whatever irrational reason) always hated those blue horizontal lines on the notebook paper we had to use. If he has a Palm device now, I'm sure he'll be happy to learn that he can get rid of the Day view's dotted lines. Set the Start Time and End Time to the same hour, and only the existing events will be displayed (**Figure 4.7**).

■ On color devices, red time bars indicate time conflicts between appointments (**Figure 4.8**).

Figure 4.6 What time is it? Tap the tab in the upper-left corner to view the current time.

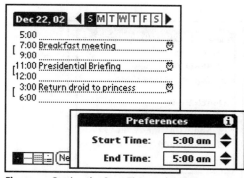

Figure 4.7 Setting the Start Time and End Time to the same hour displays only the lines that contain events.

Conflict in red

Figure 4.8 A subtle but helpful touch on color devices is the red time bar indicating conflicting appointments.

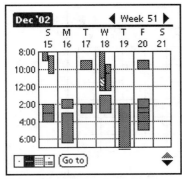

Figure 4.9 The Week view isn't necessarily a weak view: time blocks show how busy your week is, with overlapping events shown as thin bars.

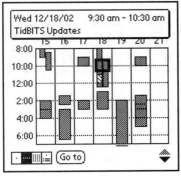

Figure 4.10 Deciphering the identity of a time block is easy—tapping one brings up its description at the top.

Week View

Viewing an entire day's schedule is helpful, but I often want to know what's coming up during the week without having to switch between multiple day views. To get an idea of my schedule's density, I display the Week view by tapping the second box (containing a line of four dots) in the lower-left corner.

Week view features

◆ Events in the Week view are represented by gray bars that span vertically across the displayed hours. If the appointments overlap, the bars become narrower and sit side-by-side on the week's grid. If you have several items happening at once, subsequent events are displayed with a diagonal pattern (**Figure 4.9**).

◆ To see what a particular bar indicates, tap it once to bring up a floating window at the top of the screen containing the description you entered in the Day view, and its specific time span (**Figure 4.10**).

◆ Tapping the arrows in the upper-right corner of the screen move you forward or backward one week, indicating the week's number in the year. Pressing the up or down button on the device case also shifts between weeks.

◆ Tapping the weekday abbreviation at the top of the screen switches to the Day view for that day. The current day is in bold.

◆ Unlike the Day view, the week grid does not compress to fit all events onto one screen. Items appearing before or after the visible 11-hour period are indicated by a solid horizontal line appearing above or below the day's column. A dot at the top indicates an untimed event. You can scroll to these events by tapping the arrows in the lower-right corner.

Month View

So, you're the type of person who likes to see the big picture? The Month view is your viewfinder, although at first glance you may think you've stumbled upon Morse code: who added all those dots? Tap the third box in the lower-left corner (containing a grid of 16 dots) to switch to the Month view.

Month view features

◆ This screen displays the entire month in a typical calendar format, with the days of the week running along the top of each column. Today's date, if you're viewing the current month, shows up as white text within a black square (**Figure 4.11**).

◆ To move forward and backward among months, tap the arrows at the top-right corner of the screen, or press the up and down buttons on the handheld case.

◆ Event blocks are indicated by black bars on the day in which they occur. Due to a lack of space, events are noted by the period of the day they occur: morning, midday, and evening. Similar to the Week view, this gives you an idea of the density of your schedule (**Figure 4.12**). Note that the day's month view will only display one bar for that part of the day, even if you have multiple appointments.

◆ If you have selected the Show Daily Repeating Evts box in the Display Options window, repeating events show up as a line of dots running along the bottom of the days they occupy. This option, the equivalent to "banners" in most desktop calendar programs, is off by default.

◆ If you have selected Show Untimed Events in the Display Options dialog box, these items are shown as little plus-signs at the bottom left of the day's square.

Figure 4.11 Your entire schedule is displayed using a minimum of space.

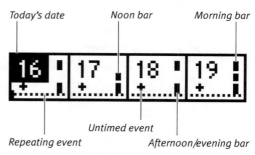

Today's date *Noon bar* *Morning bar*

Repeating event *Untimed event* *Afternoon/evening bar*

Figure 4.12 Realizing the limitations of their screen, Palm's designers opted for a "less is more" approach to the Date Book's Month view.

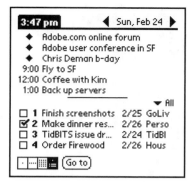

Figure 4.13 View the day's events and to do items in the Agenda view.

Agenda View

Recognizing that what you do is often tied to when you do it, Palm's programmers added a fourth view to Date Book in Palm OS 3.5. The Agenda view is similar to the Day view, but also contains the day's tasks from the To Do List in the lower half of the screen (**Figure 4.13**). Tap the fourth box in the lower-left corner to bring up the Agenda view.

Agenda view features

◆ Tap an appointment to switch to the Day view, where it will be actively selected. Similarly, tapping a task switches to that record in the To Do List.

◆ Tap the horizontal scroll arrows at the top of the screen to move forward or backward one day.

◆ The to do items are displayed just as they appear in the To Do List. To see data such as the due date or category name, enable those options in the To Do List.

◆ View different To Do List categories by selecting them from the category popup menu above the to do items.

✔ Tip

■ If you have the Agenda view displayed, then switch to another application, the Agenda will appear when you come back to the Date Book. Normally, the Date Book returns to the Day view when you switch back to it. To keep the Agenda view, make sure it's active before you exit Date Book.

Date Book Navigation: Jumping Through Time

I've become so dependent upon my hand-held for scheduling that if an event isn't in Date Book, then it isn't happening. (This approach has prevented several event conflicts!) As a result, I find myself frequently looking ahead to specific dates, a process the Palm designers have streamlined pretty well.

To jump to specific dates:

1. From any Date Book view, tap the Go to button. The Go to Date dialog box is context sensitive based on your previous view. So, the Day view gives you the option to jump to a specific day, the Week view jumps to weeks, and the Month view jumps to months (**Figure 4.14**).

2. Select a year using the arrows at the top of the page.

3. Select a month and a date or week. (If you came from the month view, selecting the month will take you there immediately.)

   If you've been time-traveling and want to get back to the present, tap the Today, This Week, or This Month button.

✔ Tip

- A faster method of jumping to today's date is to press the Date Book button on the handheld's case—the first press will return you to today's Day view from anywhere in the Date Book (except the Agenda view under Palm OS 3.5 or later).

Figure 4.14 Tapping the Go to button brings up the day (top), week (middle), and month (bottom) navigation screens, depending on your previous view.

Figure 4.15 Splitting the time into two vertical bars may appear odd at first, but this approach puts the controls in a smooth path for your stylus.

Figure 4.16 After exiting the Set Time window, go ahead and name your event.

Entering and Deleting Date Book Events

I'm sure Mrs. Wilson, my second-grade teacher, would pale at the sight of my handwriting. All that cursive training, wasted! Date Book allows me to enter legible events quickly, using a variety of methods—and delete them just as easily without the mess of strikethroughs and scribbles.

To enter an event using the New button:

1. In the Day view, tap the New button to bring up the Set Time dialog box. You can also choose New Event from the Record menu, or write /-N in Graffiti.

2. Specify a starting time. If you tap the Start Time box, the day's beginning time (from Date Book's Preferences) is entered by default. The time in the End Time box automatically sets to one hour after the Start Time. Tap on an hour and minute (the first and second vertical columns) to change the Start Time (**Figure 4.15**). The All Day button (Palm OS 3.5 and higher) enters the time span you set up in the preferences.

   You can also elect to create an untimed event by tapping OK before specifying Start and End Times, or by tapping the No Time button if those fields are already filled. Birthdays, anniversaries, and other holidays work best as untimed events.

3. Change the End Time, if desired, and tap OK.

4. Write a descriptive title (**Figure 4.16**).

✔ Tip

- A slightly faster way to enter an event is to tap directly on one of the times running down the left side of the display.

To enter an event by naming it on the appropriate line:

1. The quickest method for creating a new record is to tap the line belonging to the time you wish to use. Date Book creates a one-hour event and positions the text cursor on the line for you to name the record; no dialog boxes or OK buttons are involved (**Figure 4.17**).

2. Tap on a null area of the screen to enter your new event. To modify the event's time, tap either the time itself or the Details button.

To enter events in the Week view:

1. In the Week view, tap on a day and time for your new event—a black rectangle appears (**Figure 4.18**).

2. When you remove the stylus from the screen, Date Book changes to the Day view and automatically enters an untitled record at the time you specified.

✔ Tips

- If you're feeling like a hunter-gatherer while poking at all of these buttons and locations, consider using a more expressive method to enter Date Book events. In the Day view, begin writing your event's Start Time using Graffiti's number-entry area (the right portion). A new record will be created at that time.

- A similar approach is to just start writing the title of a new appointment in Graffiti. An untimed event appears; use the Details button or tap the time to schedule it.

- Also, if you're tired of pecking at the vertical hour and minute columns in the Set Time dialog box, you can write Graffiti numerals that will show up in the Start Time box (and also in the End Time box after selecting it).

Figure 4.17 Tap directly on the time you wish to create an event for, and bypass the Set Time dialog box.

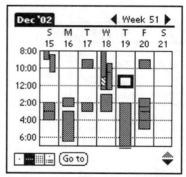

Figure 4.18 In the Week view, tap the time for a new event (indicated by the box with a dark border).

Figure 4.19a Set up your "pencil-in" notation by creating a ShortCut in the Palm OS Preferences application.

Figure 4.19b Write the Graffiti characters you set up as a ShortCut, then enter the event's title.

Figure 4.19c Your event is now easily recognizable as a temporary date/time. After confirming the specifics, remove the "pencil-in" notation.

"Pencil-in" Events

One capability I miss from paper-based organizers is being able to "pencil-in" an event, which you can then confirm later. In the Date Book, temporary and confirmed appointments show up the same. What I'd really like to see is the ability to write an event in gray, but until that day comes, here's a simple workaround using the Palm OS's ShortCut feature (**Figures 4.19a**, **4.19b**, and **4.19c**).

To add a "pencil-in" event:

1. From the Applications screen, launch the Prefs utility and select ShortCuts from the popup menu in the upper-right corner.

2. Tap New and name your ShortCut something like "pn".

3. Figure out how you'd like penciled items to display—I've always liked the curly brackets, so I enter both characters under ShortCut Text.

4. Tap OK and return to Date Book.

5. When you want to create a penciled-in event, preface its title with the shortcut you just created. In my case, the brackets appear and I either tap to put my cursor between them, or use the Graffiti cursor-left stroke (➔).

6. When the event is confirmed, remember to remove the "pencil-in" notation.

✔ Tip

■ I hoped that Palm OS 3.5's color support would let me create events in gray, but that's still not yet the case, even under Palm OS 4.0. However, DateBk4 (http://www.pimlicosoftware.com/) can: create an event, tap the Details button, then tap the Font field to set the color. You can also set up a template to create new penciled-in events. (See later in this chapter for more on DateBk4.)

"PENCIL-IN" EVENTS

Editing and Deleting Existing Events

Once created, events aren't set in stone. The ways to change their attributes are as varied as creating new appointments.

To change an event's time and/or date (the long way):

1. In the Day view, tap a record to select it, then tap the Details button.

2. In the Event Details window, tap the Time field or the Date field (**Figure 4.20**).

3. Adjust the time in the Set Time window, and the date in the Set Date window.

To change an event's time (the short way):

1. In the Day view, tap on the time to the left of the event you wish to edit.

2. Adjust the time in the Set Time window.

To change an event's time and/or date (the shortest way):

1. In the Week view, tap and hold the event you wish to edit (**Figure 4.21**).

2. Drag the event to its new time and/or date (within the same week).

To delete an event:

1. In the Day view, tap the event to select it and then tap the Details button.

2. In the Event Details window, tap Delete, choose Delete Event from the Record menu, or write ╱-D .

3. If you want the record to be saved on your PC the next time you perform a HotSync, be sure to mark the Save archive copy on PC option; uncheck the box to banish it forever (**Figure 4.22**).

Figure 4.20 You can easily change the date and time of any event by accessing the Event Details window.

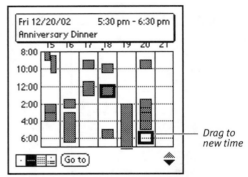

Drag to new time

Figure 4.21 The quickest way to change an event's time and date is to tap and drag it in the Week view.

Figure 4.22 If you don't want an event taking up valuable memory in your handheld, you can keep a copy of it on your PC's hard drive.

EDITING AND DELETING EXISTING EVENTS

Figure 4.23 Traffic likely to be bad? Specify a longer time period for the alarm to go off before an event.

Figure 4.24 The alarm's Reminder screen appears before an event, accompanied by a cheerful chime (Palm OS 4.0 shown here).

Figure 4.25 Date Book gives you several options for alarms, including repeating reminders and seven different sounds.

Setting Alarms

Remember the days of carrying a travel alarm clock? They're long gone, my friend.

To set an alarm:

1. After you've created an event, tap Details and mark the Alarm checkbox.

2. Choose the amount of time before the event that the alarm should go off. Minutes is the default, but you can also select Hours or Days (**Figure 4.23**).

To respond to an alarm:

◆ Tap OK to dismiss the Reminder screen when the alarm activates (**Figure 4.24**).

◆ Under Palm OS 3.5 or later, tap the Snooze button to give yourself a few extra minutes before the alarm goes off again. Palm OS 4.0 displays a small indicator at the upper-left corner of the screen to indicate the impending alarm.

◆ Under Palm OS 4.0, tap the Go To button to display the event in Date Book.

To change alarm options:

1. Go to the Date Book Preferences dialog box (choose Preferences from the Options menu, or write ∕-R).

2. Choose your favorite Alarm Sound.

3. Choose the "snooze" options: Remind Me specifies how often the alarm will go off before you dismiss it. Play Every sets the time between reminders (**Figure 4.25**).

✔ Tip

■ If you've missed multiple alarms, Palm OS 4.0 displays a screen summarizing them, which you can clear individually or all at once. Previous versions forced you to tap OK on several screens before you could use the handheld again.

Creating Repeating Events

Scheduling meetings, appointments, and reminders is a great use for Date Book, but one of the primary reasons I wanted an electronic organizer was to keep track of those recurring events that I never seem to remember: birthdays, holidays, weekly meetings, and the like. Date Book's repeating events feature allows me to do just that.

To create a repeating event:

1. Select an event and tap the Details button.

2. Next to the word Repeat, tap None. This brings up the Change Repeat dialog box (**Figure 4.26**).

3. Specify if the event is a daily, weekly, monthly, or yearly event by tapping one of the boxes at the top of the screen.

4. Write the numerical frequency of the event in the Every field.

5. If the event stops repeating on a certain date, select Choose Date from the End on popup menu; otherwise, leave it set to No End Date.

6. Depending on your selection in step 3, you can specify additional event criteria.

   Weekly events can be set to repeat on certain days by tapping in the appropriate Repeat on boxes.

   Monthly events can be repeated by day ("The 1st Wednesday of every month"), or by date ("The 5th of every month") (**Figure 4.27**).

   Yearly events, by default, are set to repeat according to the date of the first event.

7. Tap OK to exit the dialog; you'll see the repeating event icon appear to the right of your record in the Day view, and a dotted line in the Month view if Show Untimed Events is selected in Display Options (**Figure 4.28**).

Figure 4.26 Why manually add the same events over and over? Repeating events allow you to specify multiple days of the week, among other options.

Figure 4.27 Date Book is smart enough to base the repeated event depending on the date that's selected.

Day view

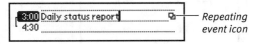

Repeating event icon

Month view

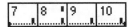

Figure 4.28 Repeated events are shown with an icon in the Day view, and a dotted line in the Month view.

Figure 4.29 If you change an existing repeating event, you're asked how you prefer to implement the changes.

Figure 4.30 Yearly occasions that fall on a particular day of the week can be set up as monthly, not yearly, repeating events, such as Thanksgiving.

To change a repeating event:

1. Tap any occurrence (you don't have to edit the first record you create) to select it, then tap the Details button.

2. Make any changes you like, including time, date, or attached notes, then tap OK.

3. Choose whether you wish to apply the change to the Current record, All instances of the event, or if you'd rather Cancel (**Figure 4.29**).

Palm OS 3.5 added another option: Future leaves past occurrences intact and deletes only the current and future repetitions.

If you only change the title of the event, the change is automatically applied to all occurrences without displaying the Repeating Event dialog box.

✔ Tips

■ What about those events, like Thanksgiving, that occur yearly but are based on a particular day of the week? Since the yearly repeat option only specifies the event's date, you have to out-think Date Book. Set up a monthly repeat that occurs every 12 months, and choose Repeat by Day (**Figure 4.30**).

■ One of my biggest scheduling problems is not being aware of an event, such as a birthday, until the day is upon me. One workaround is to set alarms to go off several days before the event. Another solution is to install Birthdate (http://www.birthdate.com/), a shareware utility that collects birthdates from other areas of the Palm OS (such as the Address Book) and optionally notifies you when they are coming up.

CREATING REPEATING EVENTS

Attaching and Deleting Notes

Initially, I thought the ability to attach notes was a superfluous add-on, best used when you wanted to record snide (er, I mean "constructive") comments during a meeting.

Since then, I've seen the light. Not only are they good for jotting random thoughts in context, but they have become indispensable for storing information that I know I will need at a particular time.

To attach a note to an event:

1. Tap an event to select it.

2. Tap the Details button, then tap Note. Alternately, choose Attach Note from the Record menu, or write /-A.

3. Compose your note using Graffiti or the onscreen keyboard (**Figure 4.31a** and **4.31b**).

4. When you are finished, tap Done.

✔ Tip

- To edit the attached note later, follow the steps above to access the note. If you want a quicker method, however, go to the Day view and tap the note icon (▯) to the right of the event's name.

Navigating a note

- If your note occupies more than one screen, use the scroll bar on the right side of the screen to move within the text.

- Choose Go to Top of Page from the Options menu to jump quickly to the beginning (this and the next command apply only to Palm OS 3.1).

- Choose Go to Bottom of Page from the Options menu to jump quickly to the end (**Figure 4.32**).

Figure 4.31a Tap the Note button in the Event Details window to attach more text to an event.

Figure 4.31b A new note presents you with a slightly limited version of the Memo Pad application.

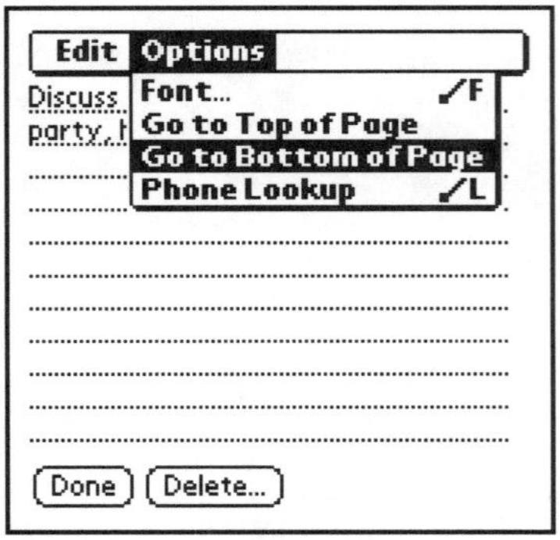

Figure 4.32 For longer texts (up to 4,025 characters), use the quick-navigation commands located under the Options menu (Palm OS 3.1).

Figure 4.33 Move through a long note quickly by "select-scrolling" the stylus through the text.

Figure 4.34 When you no longer need a note, delete it—keep in mind that you don't have the option to archive it to your PC, as you do with memos.

✔ Tip

■ A quicker option, though harder to navigate, is to "select-scroll" through long notes (**Figure 4.33**). Position your cursor somewhere in the middle of the text, and, without lifting the stylus from the screen, drag down the screen. The text will be highlighted, and soon you'll find yourself at the bottom of the note (or whichever point you chose to lift the stylus).

To delete a note:

1. In the Day view, choose Delete Note from the Record menu, or write ╱-O.

   Or, if you're on the note editing screen, tap the Delete button. The Delete Note dialog box appears.

2. Click Yes or No to confirm if you really want to delete the note (**Figure 4.34**).

Performing a Phone Lookup

Luckily for those of us who value good data, the built-in applications don't live independently of each other. One of the handier features employed in the Palm OS is the ability to perform phone number lookups from the Address Book.

To perform a phone lookup:

1. If you know the name of the person you're scheduling an event with (such as "Coffee with Pedro Finn"), write his or her name into a field in the Day view.

   If you don't know the person's name, just leave that part blank (i.e., "Coffee with ").

2. Choose Phone Lookup from the Options menu, or write ╱-L.

3. If a name in your Address Book matches the name you wrote, the phone number will be added to your event's description. If not, or if you didn't specify a name, scroll through the list of names and highlight the one you want (**Figure 4.35**).

4. Tap Add to include the phone number in the Date Book record (**Figure 4.36**).

✔ Tip

■ The Palm OS searches for last names when performing a lookup, so you can write a person's last name and, if theirs is the only instance of that name, the phone number will appear without making a trip to the Address Book screen.

Figure 4.35 Finally, contact information that's convenient to contact. Performing a phone lookup lists the names in your Address Book with phone numbers.

Figure 4.36 The looked-up number automatically gets added to the time line you created.

Figure 4.37a Tap the Private checkbox to keep an event safe from curious onlookers.

Figure 4.37b If the Current Privacy setting in the Security application is set to Show Records, you are reminded that the event is not yet hidden.

Figure 4.38 Under Palm OS 3.5 and later, changing the security setting alters it in every application.

Marking Events Private

I have a tendency to show my handheld to anyone who asks, but I don't always want them to see everything in my schedule. (Okay, so maybe I don't have very much information that needs to be kept secret, but it's good to know I can when I need to.)

When you mark Date Book events as Private, their appearance depends on the state of the Show/Hide Private Records option in the Palm OS's Security application (Palm OS 3.5 and later lists this as the Current Privacy setting). If you've specified an alarm for a hidden private record, a Reminder screen will still appear when scheduled.

To mark events Private:

1. Select an event and tap the Details button.

2. In the Event Details dialog box, mark the Private checkbox (**Figure 4.37a**). If the Show/Hide Private Records setting is switched to Show, you will receive a warning dialog about how to hide private records after you tap OK (**Figure 4.37b**).

To change the security setting:

1. Choose Security from the Options menu, write ∕-H, or tap the lock icon from the command bar. The Change Security dialog box appears.

2. From the Current Privacy popup menu, choose Show Records, Mask Records, or Hide Records (**Figure 4.38**). This changes the security setting in all applications on your handheld.

✔ Tip

- To easily read a masked record under Palm OS 4.0, tap it and enter your password. When finished it becomes masked again.

Beaming Events

In the movies, conspirators are always synchronizing their watches to make sure everyone's on the same schedule. In the real world, I use the Palm OS to beam appointments to colleagues and family members, and thereby avoid having anyone say, "Why didn't you tell me there's a meeting today?"

To beam an event:

1. Tap an event to select it.

2. Choose Beam from the Record menu, write ╱-B, or tap the Beam Event icon (☏) from the command bar (**Figure 4.39**). If the recipient's Beam Receive preference is set to On and the IR ports are aimed at each other, the record will be transferred (**Figure 4.40**).

To receive a beamed event:

1. Make sure your Beam Receive preference is set to On. Aim your IR port at the other person's Palm device.

2. After you've received the beamed record, you will be asked if you wish to add it to the Date Book. Tap Yes or No.

Figure 4.39 Palm devices equipped with infrared capabilities can beam records to one another easily.

Figure 4.40 Be sure your Palm device is pointed at the recipient, and within seconds the record is transferred.

Figure 4.41 Some people choose to leave their past behind them—select Purge to wipe away old events.

Figure 4.42 I know people who have saved every event for as long as they've been able. Others wipe the old information and store it on their PCs.

Purging Old Events

Although the Palm OS has been written to accommodate very small file sizes, there comes a point at which the volume of past events begins to eat into your available memory. Will you have to shoulder the weight of the past forever? Luckily, you don't have to.

Date Book gives you the option to permanently delete older records from your device, while still maintaining an archive of the past on your PC.

To purge old events:

1. From the Day view, choose Purge from the Record menu, or write ╱-E in the Graffiti area (**Figure 4.41**). The Purge dialog box appears.

2. Choose the time frame of records that will be purged by selecting an item on the Delete events older than: popup menu. You can select 1 Week, 2 Weeks, 3 Weeks, or 1 Month (**Figure 4.42**).

3. If you want to maintain a copy of the purged records on your PC, be sure the checkbox next to Save archive copy on PC is marked; otherwise, uncheck the box. Tap OK.

Palm Desktop Special Features

For the most part, you'll find that working within Palm Desktop's Date Book is similar to using the Palm OS Date Book: click New Event to create new events, Edit Event to change them, and view them using either the Day, Week, Month, or Year views. However, the desktop software also includes several features that make it easier to create and modify appointment times, and add events based on phone lookups. And because it operates on your PC, you can also print your calendar.

To edit events in the Day view:

1. Select the day you need in the calendar to the right.

2. Click on the time that you'd like to schedule your event. You can click either the time numerals in the left column, or click an empty area in the right column.

3. Type your event's description, then press Enter.

4. To add an alarm or a note, right-click on the event to bring up a contextual menu. You can also delete the record here, as well as access the main Edit dialog box.

5. If you need to quickly move the event to another date, drag it to the calendar in the pane at right. It retains the same time.

To edit events in the Week view:

◆ Click on an empty time slot, or click the time numerals, to create a new event.

◆ As in the Day view, drag events to new times and dates using the event handle, or reschedule lengths using the duration handle (**Figures 4.43, 4.44,** and **4.45**).

◆ Right-click on any event to bring up the editing contextual menu.

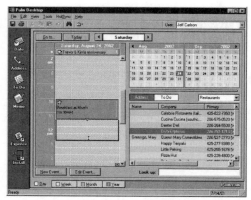

Figure 4.43 Click and drag an appointment's bottom handle to change its time span; click and drag the right-side event handle to reschedule its time or date.

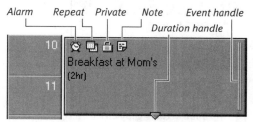

Figure 4.44 Events are more configurable in the desktop Day view than in the Palm OS Day view.

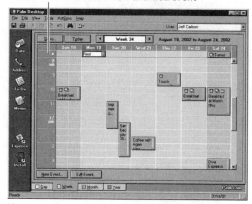

Figure 4.45 Untimed events appear in the upper field marked by a diamond. The field expands to accommodate the number of untimed events.

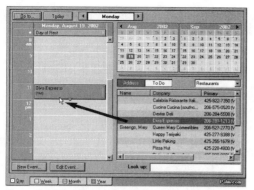

Figure 4.46 Quickly create an appointment with a phone lookup by dragging a name from the Address pane at lower right to the time of the event.

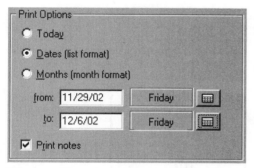

Figure 4.47 Choose how you want your schedule printed. Clicking on the tiny calendar icons gives you a popup calendar to specify the date ranges.

To perform a phone lookup in Palm Desktop:

1. Switch to the Day view, and select the date on which you wish to create an event.

2. Click Address in the lower-right pane to display your Address Book entries.

3. Locate the contact either by scrolling through the names, or typing in the Look up field.

4. Drag the contact's name to the time of the appointment (**Figure 4.46**).

✔ Tips

■ For whatever reason, Palm Desktop 4.0 doesn't include the phone number in the title of an event that's been created by dragging a contact.

■ You can also drag a To Do item from the lower-right pane onto your day to schedule a task. Although the records aren't linked (changing the date on one won't affect the other), this capability is good for setting aside blocks of time to complete your tasks.

To print your appointments:

1. In any Date Book view, select Print from the File menu, or press Control-P. The Print Options dialog box appears.

2. Choose a print option: Today's appointments, a list of Dates, or a time span in Months format (**Figure 4.47**).

3. If printing in month format, you can use the small calendar icons to specify which days you want to print.

Macintosh Palm Desktop Special Features

Most cross-platform applications share the same interface and features, but that's not the case with the Macintosh Palm Desktop software. Because it's built on top of Claris Organizer (see Chapter 1), you'll find many features that don't exist in the Windows version of Palm Desktop.

Navigating Palm Desktop for Macintosh

One of the first things you'll notice is the presence of a toolbar at the upper-left corner of the screen (**Figure 4.48**). Clicking on the buttons offers a quick alternative to common actions, such as:

- **Create Appointment** (or press Command-Option-A). This opens the Appointment dialog box, allowing you to enter the schedule information without finding the time and date on the calendar first (useful when you're entering several events at different times). Click Add Another to stay in the dialog box and enter multiple events instead of switching back to the calendar view (**Figure 4.49**).

- **Create Event Banner** (or press Command-Option-B). Event banners are equivalent to untimed events in the Palm OS. See the next page for details.

- **Go To Date** (or press Command-R). This jumps to a specific date (**Figure 4.50**).

- **Go To Today** (or press Command-T). Jump to the current date. Carpe diem, etc.

- **View Calendar** (or press Command-Option-C). If you're viewing to do items or contacts, clicking this button takes you to the last calendar view you were using.

Create Appointment   Go To Date   View Calendar

Create Event Banner   Go to Today

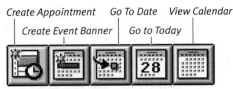

Figure 4.48 Palm Desktop for Macintosh features a floating toolbar with buttons to work within the Date Book module.

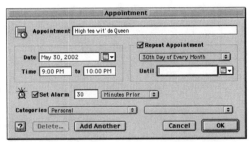

Figure 4.49 Click the Add Another button to create a new event without exiting the dialog box.

Figure 4.50 Go To Date switches your current calendar view to the date you specify. This small window is also handy when you're viewing the Day or Week views, giving you a monthly calendar without switching to the Month view.

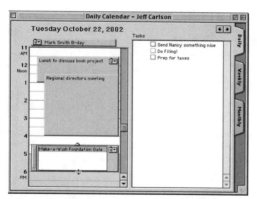

Figure 4.51 Click and drag within the Day or Week views to create a new event.

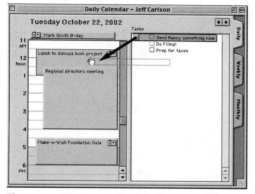

Figure 4.52 Attach to-do items in the Tasks pane to events in the Day and Week views by dragging-and-dropping them. Existing links can be viewed by clicking the folder icon that is created after linking.

Figure 4.53 Create repeating events by setting up event banners, which can be assigned categories and sub-categories.

To create and edit events:

◆ Double-click in one of the calendar views to bring up the Appointment dialog box.

◆ Click and drag on the event's time. Unlike the Windows version of Palm Desktop, the Mac software allows you to create an event with one click that spans its full duration (**Figure 4.51**).

◆ Choose Appointment from the Create menu, or press Command-Option-A.

To edit an existing event, double-click it in any calendar view, or single-click it and select Edit Appointment from the Edit menu.

You can also attach related records to other records (such as to-do items attached to events, or contacts attached to events—the Mac equivalent of phone lookups).

To attach records to events:

◆ If both records are visible, drag and drop one to the other. A link is created in both records (**Figure 4.52**).

◆ Click the folder icon (⬛▾) and choose Attach To from the popup menu.

Repeating events are known as banners in Palm Desktop for Macintosh.

To create a repeating event:

1. Choose Event Banner from the Create menu, or press Command-Option-E. The Event Banner dialog box appears.

2. Set the starting date in the Date field (or use the popup calendar to the right).

3. Specify the event's length in the Duration field (**Figure 4.53**).

4. Click the Repeat Annually checkbox to make the banner show up again next year (though it then becomes just a one-day event, like a birthday or holiday).

Attaching Notes in Mac Palm Desktop

The one truly bizarre thing about the Macintosh Palm Desktop software is the roundabout manner of attaching notes to records. Although you can attach records to events (see previous page), that's not the same as adding a note to a record (as discussed at the beginning of this chapter). Fortunately, there is a way to attach notes to events so they show up properly on the handheld device.

To attach notes in Mac Palm Desktop:

1. Attached notes are considered memos just as if you had written them into the Memo Pad. So, create a new memo (which is called "note" in Mac Palm Desktop, making things a bit more confusing), and write your text.

2. In the Title field, type "Handheld Note: Date Book" exactly (**Figure 4.54**).

3. Locate the calendar entry to which you want to add your note. Drag the note's gripper (the icon in the upper-left corner of the message window) to the calendar entry (**Figure 4.55**).

✔ Tips

■ There's a faster way of making attachments that will appear on the handheld. With a blank note visible, write "Handheld Note: Date Book" in the Title field as you did above. Now, choose New Template from the Create menu, and enter a name; if you want, choose a Command-key number from the ⌘ popup menu. From now on, choose one of the templates from the Create menu or press the Command-key to display a new formatted note window (**Figure 4.56**).

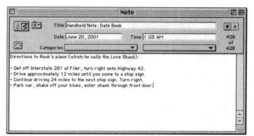

Figure 4.54 To create an attached note, you must first create the note separately (unlike in the Palm OS).

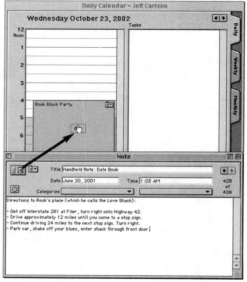

Figure 4.55 Drag the note's gripper icon to an event to attach the note.

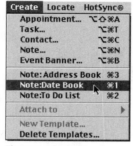

Figure 4.56 Create notes easily with templates.

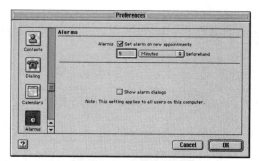

Figure 4.57 Though helpful, turn off the Show alarm dialogs option to avoid interruptions on your Mac.

Drag tasks to the calendar

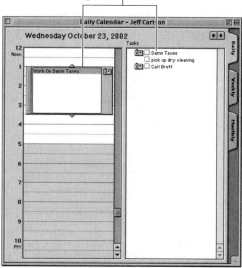

Figure 4.58 Quickly schedule tasks by dragging them from the Tasks pane to the calendar.

■ In the Palm OS Date Book, performing an address lookup puts a person's name and phone number in the title of an event. On the Mac, however, dragging a contact to an event only creates a link between the two on the desktop. Instead, you'll have to manually cut and paste the person's phone information for it to appear in the title.

■ In the calendar's Daily view, double-click the date to bring up the Go To dialog.

■ The Daily view also displays the day's active tasks in the right-hand pane; click the word "Tasks" to send completed tasks to the bottom of the list.

■ In the Daily and Weekly views, pressing Command and the right or left arrow key advances or goes back one day. Hold down option or Shift to move in one-week increments.

■ In the Monthly view, you can choose to display Appointments, Tasks, or both (or none). Go to the View menu, then choose the options under the Calendar submenu.

■ Palm Desktop for Macintosh has a feature for displaying an alarm onscreen, but be careful: since it's a non-modal dialog box, it stays up until you dismiss it, potentially halting operations in your Mac's background applications. So, I recommend turning off the alert in the preferences (**Figure 4.57**).

■ You can create scheduled to do items easily in the Daily or Weekly views. Simply drag a task from the Tasks pane to a time in the calendar. The item's title becomes the appointment's title, and any attached notes are copied over as well. The text "Work on" appears in the title, and an attachment link is created between the task and the new calendar item (**Figure 4.58**).

DateBk4: The Supercharged Date Book

The Palm OS's built-in applications haven't changed much over the past few years, in accordance with Palm's mandate to keep its handhelds simple and useful. As long as appointments are scheduled, tasks recorded, and phone numbers easily looked up, most users don't require more than the basics. But we don't all qualify as "most users." For the most full featured calendar application on the Palm OS, look to Pimlico Software's DateBk4 (http://www.pimlicosoftware.com/).

DateBk4 essentially adds all the features that you've wanted (or didn't know you've wanted) in Date Book. DateBk4 sports six calendar views, displays to-do items as well as events, and features a daily journal, floating events, and templates. In addition, DateBk4 adds categories, icons, time zone support, color, and the ability to set font styles for any record, not just the entire application (**Figure 4.59**).

But that's not all. You can split the Day view screen and choose the contents for the new window pane. To do items are usually listed, but you can also view your Address Book records, or memos, and then filter the lists based on any text you specify. Color device owners have good reason to install DateBk4: unlike the built-in applications, this program enables you to color-code categories or individual records, making it easier to quickly differentiate between events (**Figure 4.60**). And if that's not enough, you can also link records between the built-in applications (though you have to view them within DateBk4).

What's the dark side to this miracle application? The only serious criticism is its size: around 460K, which is huge by Palm OS standards. For users who don't have that much free space available, Pimlico also offers the previous version, DateBk3, which weighs in at 247K. Of all the applications I've installed on my Palm devices, DateBk4 (and DateBk3 before that) remains a permanent fixture.

DateBk4 costs $24.95 (all of which goes to the developer's organization, Gorilla Haven, a non-profit preserve that provides a secure temporary holding facility for gorillas awaiting permanent zoo housing, and helps ensure the welfare and genetic diversity of the species).

Figure 4.59 DateBk4 adds more features to the built-in Date Book database than any three programs combined.

Figure 4.60 This is the reason to buy a color handheld: events can be categorized and displayed in different colors for easy recognition—a capability missing from the initial color implementation from Palm.

5

Address Book

My first attempt at organizing the contact information I had collected over several years was a slick (I thought at the time) system involving a Personal Information Manager (PIM) program on my desktop computer and a cheap little three-ring notebook. I would print my addresses onto standard copy paper, cut the pages into 6.5-inch by 8.5-inch sections, and punch holes in the sides with a hole-punch I had modified to accommodate the binder's rings. This was my low-cost, no-hassle method of keeping my contacts handy.

Well, my system had more holes than its resulting pages. Whenever an address changed, or I added someone to my list, that information would get written in barely-legible pen in the margins. Every week or so, I'd update the PIM and have to print out fresh copies of the whole thing.

The Palm's built-in Address Book, by comparison, is such a dramatic improvement that I can only look back and blame the inexperience of my youth. With Address Book, you can store more than just names and addresses: office and home phone numbers, email addresses, driving directions, birthdays, and more.

Viewing Addresses

The Address List is another example of how Palm devices can store and present a great deal of information without cluttering up the limited screen.

Address List and Address View

◆ Contacts are listed alphabetically either by last name or by company name down the left side of the screen (**Figure 5.1**).

◆ The right-hand column lists each person's primary contact information; the letter at the end of each line indicates which type of information is displayed (for example, W equals Work, H equals Home, and E equals E-mail).

◆ A note icon (▯) at the far right indicates that the record includes an attached note.

◆ The triangular arrows in the lower-right corner scroll up and down the contact list. You can also use the scroll buttons on the handheld's case, which move through the list one screen at a time.

◆ When you tap a record to view it, the Address View shows you that contact's details (**Figure 5.2**). Scroll up or down to view the details by tapping the arrows or pressing the scroll buttons.

✔ Tip

■ If you use the physical scroll buttons to move up and down within a record in the Address View screen, you can jump to the previous or next record by pressing the buttons when you're at the beginning or the end of the current record.

Figure 5.1 The Address List displays names and preferred phone numbers— you may not even have to tap a name to get the number you need.

Figure 5.2 Tapping a name brings up the contact information; fields left blank (such as Fax number) are hidden to conserve space.

Figure 5.3 Two options are available for sorting the Address List, depending on whether you're looking for companies or people's names.

Figure 5.4 Sorting by Company, Last Name reorders the list alphabetically by company, and truncates longer names to show more information.

Figure 5.5 Specify a preferred number by using the Show in List popup menu.

Changing the Sort Order

Since there isn't much space on the screen, you can't tell if, for example, Thomas Silvestri was the guy you met at last month's conference, or if he's your genius financial adviser. Fortunately, you can choose how you want the records listed.

To change the sort order:

1. Select Preferences from the Options menu.

2. Choose either Last Name, First Name or Company, Last Name from the List By box, then tap OK (**Figures 5.3** and **5.4**).

Specifying a Preferred Number

Suppose you want to view someone's home number instead of their work phone in the Address List. The Address Book provides a way to do it, although it's slightly buried.

To specify a preferred number:

1. Tap the record you wish to change. This takes you to the Address View screen.

2. Tap the Edit button, or tap anywhere within the Address View to go into the Address Edit screen.

3. Tap Details.

4. Choose the field you want to appear in the main list by tapping the Show in List popup menu (**Figure 5.5**). Tap OK to return to the edit screen, then tap Done.

✔ Tip

■ If you know ahead of time which field you want to appear in the Address List, write that number first when you're entering the address. By default, the contact information shown in the Address List is the first contact field entered.

Changing the Display Font

You have three options for changing fonts: within the Address List, within the Address View, and within the Address Edit screen (**Figures 5.6a** and **5.6b**).

To change the display font:

1. Select Font from the Options menu.

2. Tap one of the three font styles in the Select Font window (**Figure 5.7**). Tap OK.

Figure 5.6a Choose the font to display contact information. The large font is more readable, but shows less data.

Figure 5.6b The smallest font is easier on my eyes, though probably not as readable at arm's length.

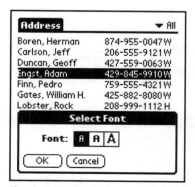

Figure 5.7 The font styles are also available separately for the Address View and Address List screens.

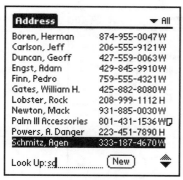

Figure 5.8 No more rustling through pages of contacts to find a number. Begin writing the last name of your contact in the Look Up field to jump to the closest match.

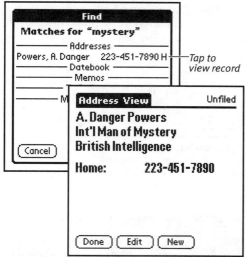

Figure 5.9 The Find function can be helpful when searching for text located within a record.

Looking Up Contacts

There's a better way to find the person you're looking for than scrolling through the list.

To search using Look Up:

1. In the Look Up field, write the first letter of the last name (or company name, depending on the sort order) you're looking for using Graffiti; the first match will be highlighted (**Figure 5.8**).

2. If the first letter doesn't match the intended name, keep writing letters until you get a match. If you know you're close, use the arrows in the lower-right corner to scroll through the list by individual record, or the plastic buttons on the case to scroll by screen.

To perform a find:

1. If you're looking for a word located within a record or a record's attached note, tap the silkscreened Find icon.

2. Enter the text you're searching for, then tap OK. The results (including matches in other programs) appear in a new window. Tap the match you want (**Figure 5.9**).

✔ Tips

■ Find will begin its search within the application you're currently running.

■ To quickly clear the Look Up field, press the up or down scroll button.

■ My work phone has Caller ID to let me know who's calling before I answer it. If there's an unfamiliar number displayed, I do a quick Find for part of the number to see if it's someone in my Address Book.

■ Unimpressed with the built-in Find? Install FindHack, a HackMaster utility that greatly expands Find's capabilities (see Chapter 8).

Entering and Deleting Address Records

Graffiti is a great method for entering text into a handheld, but I won't pretend it's always the best option. If you need to create lots of new records, you're better off typing them into Palm Desktop on your PC. But for one or two, here's how to enter them quickly (I *hate* asking people to repeat things when I can't keep up with them on my spiffy gadget).

To create a new record:

1. From the Address List or the Address View screen, tap the New button.

2. Fill in the fields using Graffiti or the built-in keypad (**Figure 5.10**). Tap Done.

✔ Tips

- Write the next field Graffiti character (❶) to go to the next field without moving the stylus from the Graffiti area.

- You can enter more than one line of text into each field. Write a carriage return (✓) and add another line of information; it stays in the same field (**Figure 5.11**).

To create a new record using Palm Desktop (Windows):

1. Click the Address button, or press F3 to view the Address Book (**Figure 5.12**).

2. Click the New Address button, select New Address from the Edit menu, or press Control-N.

3. Enter the text in the appropriate fields, then click OK.

✔ Tip

- To quickly switch between tabs, press Control-Tab.

Figure 5.10 After tapping New, write the contact's information in the fields.

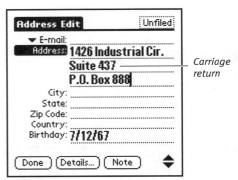

Carriage return

Figure 5.11 Don't worry if there aren't enough fields (such as a second address field): simply write a carriage return to make a new line.

Figure 5.12 With more screen space available, Palm Desktop is able to display a contact's information in the window's right pane.

ENTERING AND DELETING ADDRESS RECORDS

Figure 5.13 The Macintosh Palm Organizer features information areas that pop up entry fields when you click on them.

Figure 5.14 Sometimes we lose track of people who were once dear to us. Check Save archive copy on PC to save deleted records at the next HotSync.

To create a new record using Palm Desktop (Macintosh):

1. Click the View Contact List button from the toolbar, or press Command-Shift-C.

2. Click the Create Contact button, select Contact from the Create menu, or press Command-Option-C (the keyboard shortcut works anywhere in the program, not just with the Contact List viewed).

3. Click on an information area to access the entry fields (**Figure 5.13**). When you're finished, close the window or press Command-W.

✔ Tips

■ You can jump between the information fields by pressing the Tab key.

■ If you're typing something that's been entered before, such as a city name, Palm Desktop will automatically complete the word for you.

To delete a contact (Palm):

1. Tap the contact to select it.

2. Select Delete Address from the Record menu, or write ╱-D.

You can also tap Edit, then Details, then the Delete button—but who has that kind of time?

3. If you want to store the record in the PC's Palm archive files, be sure to check Save archive copy on PC. Click OK to delete (**Figure 5.14**).

ENTERING AND DELETING ADDRESS RECORDS

Duplicating Records

Palm OS 3.5 introduced a welcome change to the Address Book: the ability to duplicate existing records.

To duplicate an existing record:

1. Select an Address Book record from the Address List or tap it to open the Address View screen.

2. Select Duplicate Address from the Record menu, or write ✓-T (**Figure 5.15**). The new record adds the word "Copy"at the end of the text in the First name field (**Figure 5.16**).

✔ Tip

- Need to duplicate a record but aren't running Palm OS 3.5 or 4.0? You can make a copy by beaming it to yourself! In any text field, write ⅄- • -T (shortcut stroke, period, T). Then, select the record to duplicate and select Beam Address from the Record menu. Write ⅄- • -T again to deactivate the beaming feature.

Dialing Phone Numbers

Palm OS 4.0 includes built-in support for connecting to an infrared-equipped cellular phone (see Chapter 2). You can have Address Book dial a contact for you. Some devices, like the Kyocera PDA phone, include a similar command under other Palm OS versions.

To dial a phone number:

1. Tap a record to open it.

2. Choose Dial from the Record menu, or write ✓-I.

3. Select a number to dial, or edit it manually on the field provided.

4. Tap Dial to send the number to your phone.

Figure 5.15 Palm OS 3.5 added the capability to duplicate records.

Figure 5.16 When a record is duplicated, Address Book adds the text "Copy" to the First name field.

Figure 5.17 The popup phone label options provide for more than just work and home numbers.

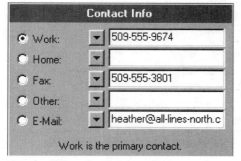

Figure 5.18 Changing the phone field names in Palm Desktop for Windows works the same as in the Palm OS.

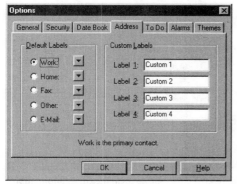

Figure 5.19 The Address tab in the Options dialog box sets the default labels for all new contacts.

Changing and Editing Phone Field Labels

Although there are five fields for contact numbers such as work and home phones, many of us have more access numbers than that. Address Book includes eight labels accessible via popup menus.

To change phone field labels:

1. Tap on a record to view it, then tap the Edit button (**Figure 5.17**).

2. Tap the popup menu next to the number you want to change. With the menu active, choose from Work, Home, Fax, Other, E-mail, Main, Pager, or Mobile.

3. Tap Done to exit the Address Edit screen.

To edit phone field labels in Palm Desktop (Windows):

1. Highlight a name and click Edit Address, or double click the name.

2. In the Contact Info area (**Figure 5.18**), click the field name next to the number you want to change, and choose the desired label from the popup menu.

3. Click the radio button to the left of the popup menu for the number you wish to appear in the Address List.

To set default phone field options in Palm Desktop (Windows):

1. Choose Options from the Tools menu.

2. Click the Address tab.

3. Change the labels in the Default Labels area as described above (**Figure 5.19**).

4. Click OK.

To edit phone field labels in Palm Desktop (Macintosh):

1. Click the Phones box within a Contact window to edit the phone fields.

2. Choose a label from the popup windows to the left of each field (**Figure 5.20**).

3. If you want that contact's name and a number to appear in the Instant Palm Desktop menu, mark the box to the far right of the desired number.

To customize phone field labels in Palm Desktop (Macintosh):

1. Choose Other from the popup menu to create a custom field name.

2. To permanently add a custom label to the menu, choose Edit Menu (**Figure 5.21**).

3. Enter a new name and click OK.

✔ Tips

- If you enter an extension into the Ext. field, it appears on the same line as the number in the Palm OS.

- Only a maximum of four fields appear in a contact's Phones section, but there are five on the handheld. The fifth field is the Email field, found in the Other Information area (**Figure 5.22**). An Email option appears on the phone field popup menu as well, giving you a way to record multiple email addresses for contacts.

- You can use any name to describe a phone field, but keep in mind that anything not matching the predefined labels will appear as Other on the handheld.

Figure 5.20 The Phones box under Palm Desktop for Macintosh features popup menus to label the fields, plus an option for adding numbers to the Instant Palm Desktop menu.

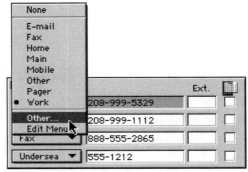

Figure 5.21 A phone field in Palm Desktop for Macintosh can have any name, though it appears as Other on the device if it's not one of the existing labels.

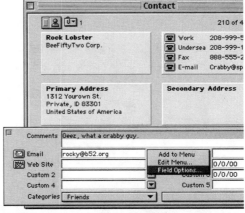

Figure 5.22 Email shows up in the Other Information field instead of in Phones like on the Palm OS and under Windows.

Figure 5.23 Name the custom fields according to the information that's most important to you.

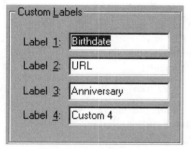

Figure 5.24 Changing these labels applies them to every record in the Address Book.

Figure 5.25 Change the field names from within an active record by selecting Field Options from a field's popup menu.

Renaming the Custom Field Labels

In addition to standard fields like Address and City, four custom fields are available for text input. Since "Custom 1" is a boring label, you can change the names to anything else.

To rename custom field labels:

1. Choose Rename Custom Fields from the Options menu to display the Rename Custom Fields dialog box (**Figure 5.23**).

   In Palm Desktop for Windows, select Options under the Tools menu, then click the Address tab to view the Custom Labels area (**Figure 5.24**).

   If you're using Palm Desktop for Macintosh, getting there is a little more tricky: open a contact by double-clicking on it, then click in the Other Information area. Choose the field you want to edit, click the popup menu to the right, and select Field Options (**Figure 5.25**).

2. Type the words or phrases you'd like to use. I find that Birthdate, Web, and Anniversary are essential labels; other possibilities include Spouse, Children (remember, you can type more than one item in the fields by writing a return character in the edit screen), or even Known Allergies.

3. Tap OK to exit.

✔ Tip

■ Remember that if you beam a contact to another Palm device, your custom label names won't transfer with the record. So, any data in these fields might confuse someone who uses different labels.

Attaching and Deleting Address Book Notes

The Palm OS's notes feature gives you a blank slate to add all sorts of information about a person or company, from a favorite movie to invaluable driving directions.

To attach a note to a contact:

1. Tap a contact to select it.

2. Tap the Edit button to bring up the Address Edit screen, then tap Note (**Figure 5.26**). Or, select Attach Note from the Record menu, or write ╱-A.

3. Compose your note using Graffiti or the onscreen keyboard.

4. When you are finished, tap Done.

✔ Tips

■ To edit the attached note later, follow the steps above to access the note. If you want a quicker method, however, tap the note icon (▯) to the right of the contact's preferred phone number.

■ You don't have to open the note separately to view it. The text appears at the bottom of the contact's Address View, and can be read using the scroll arrows (**Figure 5.27**).

■ A quick way to scroll, though harder to navigate, is to "select-scroll" through long notes. Position your cursor somewhere in the text and, without lifting the stylus from the screen, drag down the screen.

Figure 5.26 From the Address Edit screen, attach a note by tapping the Note button.

Figure 5.27 An attached note appears in the record as if it was a regular field. Use the scroll arrows to read more.

Figure 5.28 When you delete a note, you will be asked to verify your action.

Figure 5.29 On the Mac, create a new attached Note by dragging the gripper to the intended contact.

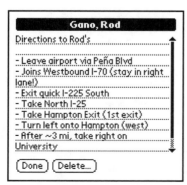

Figure 5.30 Attach driving directions to contacts and impress your relatives.

To delete a note:

1. In the Address View or Address Edit screens, select Delete Note from the Record menu, or write ╱-O.

2. If you're on the note editing screen, tap the Delete button.

3. You will be asked to confirm your choice. Click Yes or No (**Figure 5.28**).

To attach a note (Windows):

1. Double-click a contact or click the Edit button to view the Edit Record screen. Or, click the blank space to the right of the record (where the note icon normally shows up) to bring up the Note Editor.

2. If you accessed the Edit Record screen, click the Note tab, or press Control-Tab to switch to it.

3. Type the text of your note, then click OK.

To attach a note (Macintosh):

1. Create a new note by clicking the Create Note button, or pressing Command-Option-N.

2. Write "Handheld Note: Address Book" in the Title field.

3. Type the text of your note.

4. Link the new Note record to the desired Contact by dragging the gripper (▣▣) to the Contact window (**Figure 5.29**). (See later in this chapter for information on linking records.)

✔ Tip

■ I'll never be lost again! I used to keep a tattered library of paper scraps containing driving directions to people's homes and businesses in my car. Now, I store directions in notes attached to their addresses (**Figure 5.30**).

Setting Up Custom Categories

The categories that are preset in the Palm OS barely hint at the value of organizing records by category. In addition to preventing data confusion, it makes it easier to view your data in comprehensible chunks, rather than one big list.

To create a custom category:

1. Select Edit Categories from the category popup menu in the upper-right corner of the screen (**Figure 5.31**).

2. Tap New and give your category a name (**Figure 5.32**).

3. Tap OK to return to the list.

To specify the last category viewed:

1. Select Preferences from the Options menu, or write ╱-R.

2. Mark the Remember last category box, then tap OK (**Figure 5.33**).

✔ Tips

■ To quickly switch to the next category, press the Address Book button on the handheld's case. If you've created a category that currently has no records assigned to it, Address Book skips to the next category containing records. Highly annoying, however, is that the Unfiled category is skipped using this method.

■ Create several records that share the same category by displaying that category and tapping New from the Address List; each new record will remain assigned to the current category.

■ The Macintosh Palm Desktop doesn't store categories for each built-in application, so you can only have a total of 15 categories shared among those programs.

Figure 5.31 The option to edit your categories is strategically placed at the bottom of the popup category list.

Figure 5.32 Create or rename categories using up to 15 characters.

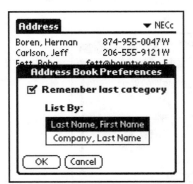

Figure 5.33 Address Book prefers to show you every contact whenever it's launched, unless you select Remember last category in the Preferences dialog.

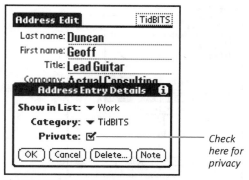

Figure 5.34 It takes a few taps to get to the Address Entry Details dialog, but it's worth it if you want to ensure that your private records are hidden or masked.

Check here for privacy

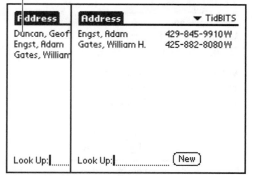

Private record

Figure 5.35 When you set the Security application's settings to Hide Records, private records disappear in the Address List.

Figure 5.36 Change the Security setting from within any application.

Marking Contacts as Private

It's fun to show off your handheld sometimes, but you don't want everyone to have unlimited access to your private information. It's easy to hide records from wandering eyes.

To mark contacts as private:

1. Tap the record you wish to mark as private, then tap the Edit button.

2. Tap the Details button.

3. Mark the Private checkbox, then tap OK (**Figure 5.34**).

4. Tap Done when finished (**Figure 5.35**).

Changing the Security Setting

Palm OS 3.5 introduced a new way of displaying private data: masking. Although the procedure below changes the display option throughout the system, you can change the Security setting from within any of the built-in applications.

To change the security setting:

1. Select Security from the Options menu, write ∕-H, or tap the Security icon in the command toolbar.

2. Select an option from the Current Privacy popup menu: Show Records, Mask Records, or Hide Records (**Figure 5.36**).

3. Tap OK.

✔ Tip

- For more information about protecting the data on your device, see Chapter 12.

Beaming Addresses

Every Palm device includes an infrared (IR) port for beaming data from one device to another. The most common usage of IR is to swap electronic business cards directly into other people's Address Books. If you've ever returned from a conference or trade show with a stack of business cards (and then lost them), you'll appreciate how useful beaming can be. Simply create a record for yourself and be prepared to amaze onlookers.

To specify your business card:

1. Find yourself (in the Address List—we can talk more about philosophy later). Tap the record to select it.

2. Choose Select Business Card from the Record menu (**Figure 5.37**).

3. If you're sure, tap Yes in the confirmation dialog. A special icon appears next to the Address View and Address Edit tabs (**Figure 5.38**).

To beam your business card:

Choose Beam Business Card from the Record menu, or just press and hold the Address Book button on the handheld's case.

To beam an Address record:

1. Tap the record you wish to beam.

2. Choose Beam Address from the Record menu, or write ╱-B. Private records become public when beamed individually.

To beam a category:

1. Make your chosen category visible in the Address List.

2. Choose Beam Category from the Record menu. All records in that category, except Private records, will be transferred.

Figure 5.37 Choose the record you want for your business card (preferably the one with your name on it), then activate it from the Record menu.

Figure 5.38 The record designated as your business card displays a "beaming file card" icon next to the Address View tab. The best way to zap it to another IR-equipped Palm device is to just hold down the Address Book button on the front of the handheld.

BEAMING ADDRESSES

Figure 5.39 Find a record and beam it from the Address List using the Beam Address icon on the command bar.

Figure 5.40 You can choose to keep the Beam Receive option turned off, knowing that there's a shortcut for turning it on without coming back to Preferences.

✔ Tips

- You don't have to view a record before beaming it. Use the Look Up field to find a record, which highlights the match in the Address List (**Figure 5.39**). Write the command stroke (╱) to view the command toolbar, then tap the Beam Address icon (☎).

- When you transfer a category, the category's name does not appear on the recipient's Palm device. However, if they're running Palm OS 3.5 or later, they can choose which of their categories to assign to the group of incoming records, or they can create a new category.

- Some people prefer to leave the Beam Receive option off in the Preferences application to conserve battery life (see Chapter 2). If you fall into that camp, but need to receive beamed business cards from other Palm users, there are two ways to activate Beam Receive without making a side trip to the Preferences application (**Figure 5.40**).

  In a text field, write ℓ- · -I to temporarily enable Beam Receive for five seconds.

  The other option is to press and hold the plastic Address Book button as if you were going to beam your business card. After you beam your information (or tap Cancel), you'll be asked if you want to turn Beam Receive on.

- It's possible to "spread-beam" records to multiple handhelds at once. This is great if you're in a small group of Palm users and exchanging business cards; as long as the recipients are in range of the IR beam, they will all receive your business card even if you send it only once.

BEAMING ADDRESSES

Importing Contacts into Palm Desktop

There's a good chance that you already have a stash of contact information stored in a desktop PIM program, or maybe even a customized database or Excel spreadsheet. If so, you should be able to transfer your records into Palm Desktop with a minimum of fuss.

To import contacts from a PIM:

1. In your existing PIM, select the export function—most programs include something like Export under the File menu.

2. Export the file as a tab-delimited text file; if you are presented with the option to include field names (such as "Last Name" or "City"), go ahead.

3. In Palm Desktop, choose Import from the File menu.

4. Click and drag the field labels in the left-hand pane of the Specify Import Fields (Windows) or Import (Macintosh) dialog box to match the data in the right pane (**Figures 5.41** and **5.42**).

5. When the data looks right to you, click OK to begin the import process. After a few seconds, the records will be available to use.

✔ Tips

- If you have the option of including field names when you export the data from your original PIM, do it—you can save some time by matching the label names instead of guessing the order.

- If you select a category from the Contact List's category popup menu before you import, the new records will belong to that category after being imported.

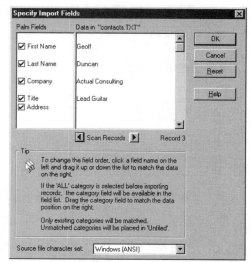

Figure 5.41 In Windows Palm Desktop, drag the field labels to match the record's field-mapping order.

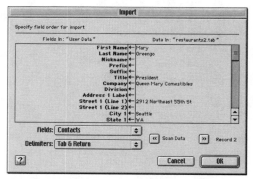

Figure 5.42 The Mac Palm Desktop takes a similar approach to Windows. This step can be slightly monotonous, but you'll appreciate it later on.

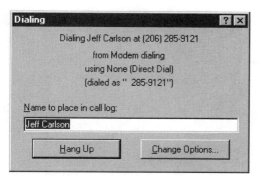

Figure 5.43 Let the computer do the work for you — never memorize a phone number again!

Select which records to print
Choose how much information will be printed

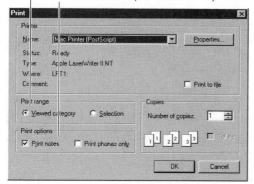

Figure 5.44 Printing Address Book records requires only two specialized fields in the standard Print dialog.

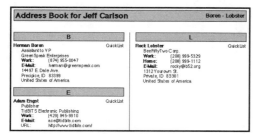

Figure 5.45 Printing from Address Book yields a readable (but not exciting) page of contact information.

Palm Desktop Special Features

In general, the desktop software mirrors the Palm OS in functionality. However, there are also a few features of Palm Desktop that add functionality, such as dialing phone numbers (if your PC is connected to the phone line you use for making calls), printing records, and sharing data with other applications.

To dial phone numbers:

1. In the Address List, click the contact you wish to call.

2. Choose Dial from the Edit menu, or right-click the contact and select Dial from the popup menu that appears. The Dialing dialog box opens (**Figure 5.43**). Under Palm Desktop for Macintosh, open the contact's information and click the dial button ([☎]).

3. Pick up the phone after the number begins dialing, and press the Talk button (Windows) or the Release button (Mac).

To print records:

1. Choose which records you want to print. If you want only a few, select them by Control/Command-clicking their names. To print an entire category, select it from the category popup menu. To print all records, select the All category.

2. Choose Print from the File menu, or press Control/Command-P. The Print dialog box appears (**Figure 5.44**).

3. Set the print range to either Viewed category or Selection, and specify full records or just phone numbers printed (**Figure 5.45**).

To share data with other desktop applications using Drag to/Send to (Windows):

1. Select the records you wish to copy.

2. In Palm Desktop 4.0, go to the Edit menu and choose an option from the Send To submenu. You can also right-click the seelction to access the same submenu.

   If you're running Palm Desktop 3.1, drag the selected records to the Drag To icons in the lower-right corner (**Figure 5.46**).

   Palm Desktop runs a set of instructions (called macros) that copy and format the data.

   If you send to Word, you're presented with a dialog box asking in which format you'd like the data: Formatted Addresses, Form Letters, Mailing Labels, Envelopes, or Leave Data as a Table (**Figure 5.47**). Click the button to choose, then click OK.

3. Word or Excel will create a new file formatted with your data. If you copied the records to the Clipboard, go to your selected program and paste the contact information (**Figure 5.48**).

✔ Tip

- In Palm Desktop 4.0, there is no icon or command to send contacts information to the clipboard. Simply select the names you want and choose Copy from the Edit menu, then paste the data into another application.

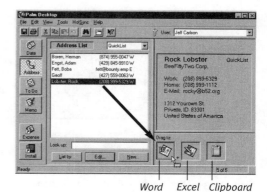

Word   Excel   Clipboard

Figure 5.46 The Drag To/Send To feature copies the selected addresses to Microsoft Word, Microsoft Excel, or to the Clipboard for use with other programs.

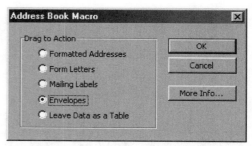

Figure 5.47 Sending records to Word lets you choose the format of the final data.

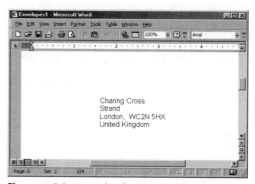

Figure 5.48 A contact has been copied into Envelopes format using the Drag To/Send To Word feature.

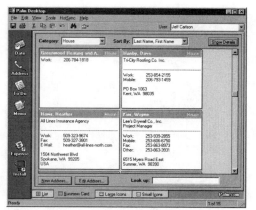

Figure 5.49 Some people find it easier to use the Business Card view to browse contact information.

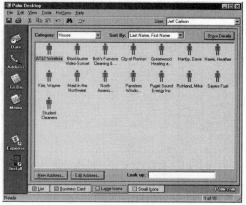

Figure 5.50 Using the Large Icons (shown here) and Small Icons views means you never have to feel left out of the crowd.

To create vCards:

If you use an email program that supports vCards (a method of attaching contact information to an email message), select a contact and choose Forward as vCard from the Edit menu. A new message is created with the vCard information attached.

You can also create a standalone vCard file (.vcf) by choosing Export vCard from the File menu.

To change the Address Book view:

With the Address Book visible, click the tabs at the bottom of the screen. The default view is the List view, but you can also arrange your contacts in the easier-to-read Business Card view (**Figure 5.49**) or the Large Icons and Small Icons view (**Figure 5.50**).

The Hide Details button displays more contacts by removing the details pane, and becomes the Show Details button when the pane is hidden.

Macintosh Palm Desktop Special Features

Palm Desktop for Macintosh includes several features not found in the Windows software. For example, it offers the ability to attach not only notes to records, but also to create links between related records. Unfortunately, the links don't transfer over to the handheld, but they do save time and effort on the Mac.

To link records:

1. Open a Contact record by selecting it and pressing Return, or double-clicking it.

2. Grab the gripper ( ) in the upper-left corner and drag it to the contact you wish to link. You can drag contacts onto events, to do items, and memos as well (**Figure 5.51**). You can also just drag one record in the Contact List onto another without viewing the details of either.

   Alternately, click the attachment popup menu ( ) and choose an item from the Attach To submenu.

To set Contacts preferences:

1. Choose Preferences from the Edit menu. The Preferencecs dialog box appears (**Figure 5.52**).

2. Click the Contacts button on the left.

Notable preferences here include:

◆ **Phone popup menu.** No matter how you type the number, it will be formatted according to this selection.

◆ **Auto-capitalization.** Similar to the Palm OS, Palm Desktop capitalizes information within Contacts fields.

◆ **Auto-completion.** Palm Desktop stores lists of field contents; when you're entering information, it searches for a match and displays the likely result as you type.

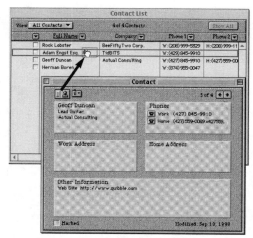

Figure 5.51 Create relational links between records by dragging them onto one another.

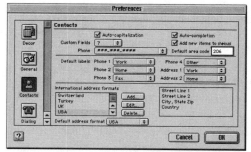

Figure 5.52 Palm Desktop offers several options for working with Address Book (Contact) data.

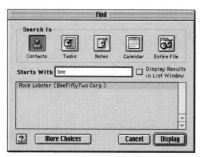

Figure 5.53 The Find command displays matches containing the entire text in the Starts With field. Type more letters to narrow the search if several items appear.

Click name to sort...   ... or choose popup menu item.

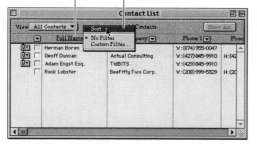

Figure 5.54 Sort the list by any column's contents by either clicking on the column's name, or choosing Sort from the popup menus.

Click and hold here

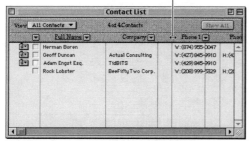

Figure 5.55 Click in the title area and drag to change the order of the visible columns.

To find contacts:

1. Choose Find from the Locate menu, or press Command-F to display the Find dialog box (**Figure 5.53**).

2. Begin typing the name you're searching for. If you're looking for text within a contact, but it isn't a name or company name, click Display Results in List Window.

3. Click Display when it's found.

To sort records:

◆ To sort each list according to a column's contents, click the column's title (it will become underlined to indicate it's the active method) or choose Sort from each title's popup menu (**Figure 5.54**).

◆ You can also edit the columns to customize your display. Click and drag a column's right border to change its width. To rearrange the columns' order, click and hold in the area next to a column name, then drag left or right to position it (**Figure 5.55**). To choose which columns are displayed, select Columns from the View menu and mark the ones you want.

✔ Tips

■ Palm Desktop has the added ability to sort using secondary criteria as well. For example, if you want to sort a list of people within a specific company, click the Company column title, then Shift-click the Full Name column title.

■ The Mark checkbox (**Figure 5.56**, next page) enables you to mark records from multiple categories, then quickly view them without creating a filter by choosing Marked from the popup menu in the column head. When printing, you can opt to print only the marked records without first locating them in the Contact List.

MACINTOSH PALM DESKTOP SPECIAL FEATURES

To filter specific data:

You can also configure the sorting method by choosing Custom Filter from the popup menus, which displays only the items that meet the filter's criteria. For example, if you want to list only the phone calls you need to make, set up a filter that searches for the words "call" or "phone" (**Figure 5.56**).

To save memorized views:

When you've set up a sort order and specific filters, choose Memorize View from the View popup menu to save it. This way, you can see related tasks and notes without repeating the sorting steps above. To see the full list again, click the Show All button.

To create a pre-addressed email message:

1. In a record's Contact window, click the Other Information area.

2. Click the email button ([🖃]) beside the Email field. A blank email message is created in your email program with the contact's email address in the To: field.

✔ Tip

■ You can change the email client that's tied into the Email field's button. Choose Field Options... from the field's popup menu, then choose your email client from the Script File popup menu (**Figure 5.58**). (If you use Qualcomm's Eudora Pro, you should download the Create Eudora Pro Message AppleScript, found at http://www.palmgear.com/.)

Figure 5.56 Mark records that you use frequently to view and print them quickly, without creating a filter.

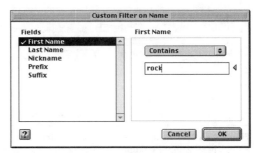

Figure 5.57 Create custom filters to display only the contacts matching specified criteria.

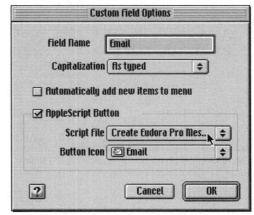

Figure 5.58 The custom fields can be customized even further. Here, the Email field is set to create a pre-addressed message in Eudora Pro.

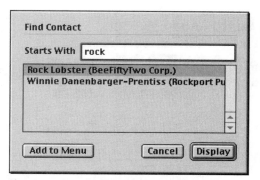

Figure 5.59 Search your Address Book using the Instant Palm Desktop's Find Contact feature.

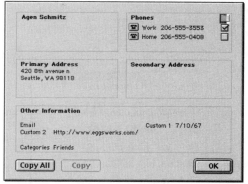

Figure 5.60 All the information of Palm Desktop—without the RAM overhead—is available when you select a record from the Instant Palm Desktop menu.

Using the Instant Palm Desktop Menu

The Instant Palm Desktop menu resides in the upper-right corner of your screen, next to the Mac OS's Application menu, and allows you to access contacts and other records without having to launch Palm Desktop.

To access contact information using the Instant Palm Desktop:

◆ Click the menu and highlight a contact to view or edit its details; or, choose Open Palm Desktop to launch the program.

◆ Search for an address by selecting Find Contact (**Figure 5.59**). To make a contact appear permanently on the menu, click the Add to Menu button. You can also dial phone numbers directly from the contact detail window (**Figure 5.60**).

◆ Create new addresses, events, To Do items, memos, and event banners from the Create submenu.

To add contacts to the Instant Palm Desktop:

In a record's Instant Palm Desktop contact view, or the Contact window within Palm Desktop, check the box to the right of the phone number you want to appear in the Instant Palm Desktop menu.

To remove contacts from the Instant Palm Desktop:

In the Contact window, uncheck the box to the right of the phone number.

✔ Tip

■ If you find yourself writing your address frequently in letters or email, put yourself in the Instant Palm Desktop menu, then click the Copy All button to get the info.

Alternatives to Using the Built-In Address Book

The Address Book offers a lot of power in a svelte package, but what if you want to supercharge your contact list? Although there are plenty of alternatives, the two I'm most impressed with are Super Names (http://www.standalone.com/) and PopUp Names (http://www.benc.hr/popnames.htm). Both programs use the Address Book's database as their data source, which means your contacts are still synchronized with your PC.

Super Names

I was dubious of Super Names at first, mostly because I respond strongly to interfaces. A quick look at the Super Names main screen shows how crowded it can be (**Figure 5.61**). But notice what's there: categories appear as tabs across the top of the screen; an alphabet running beneath the tabs lets you tap a letter to jump to that range of contacts; an optional panel below the Address List previews the highlighted name, with icons to specify which info appears.

In addition to cramming a lot of useful information on one screen, Super Names lets you link contacts to other contacts, or even to records from Date Book, the To Do List, or the Memo Pad (**Figure 5.62**). Linked records can be displayed by tapping a paper-clip icon at the top of the screen.

PopUp Names

PopUp Names shows more contact information on its main screen, but it has the distinction of being viewed from within any application on your handheld. PopUp Names is actually a system hack (see Chapter 8); when enabled, write a stroke in the silkscreened area (the default is to draw a line from the Calculator icon to the Find icon) to bring up the PopUp Names window (**Figure 5.63**).

You can even perform Address Book functions like beaming your business card or other contacts just as if you've launched the Address Book application itself.

Figure 5.61 Once you get the hang of the Super Names interface, you'll like how easy it is to view contact info.

Figure 5.62 Link contacts or other records to view them quickly next time.

Figure 5.63 PopUp Names is available from any application on your Visor.

To Do List & Memo Pad

When I tell people about Palm handhelds, most seem to get excited about the Date Book and Address Book, two applications that can greatly decrease the amount of paper they carry. But when I was first considering whether to buy a handheld, it was the To Do List that thrilled me. I need to *see* tasks that must be accomplished, or else I risk forgetting about them until it's too late. A digital to-do list that keeps reminding me of tasks not yet finished was irresistible.

The Memo Pad, on the other hand, was low on my list of required features. I mean, it's a necessary element (what's the point of having a palmtop device if you can't jot down quick notes?), but light bulbs are also necessary elements, and you don't see me drooling over the latest 100-watt GE soft-white bulb.

Now, both applications are essential to me: I can track my tasks with the To Do List (and make them disappear when completed), and I can use Memo Pad to store information that I had never considered before.

Viewing Options

The To Do List (**Figure 6.1**) can be as sparse or as detailed as you want. Tap the Show button to access the To Do Preferences window, which provides the following options (**Figure 6.2**).

◆ If you prefer to see the items you've accomplished, mark the Show Completed Items checkbox.

If you uncheck this option to hide completed items, the records are still held in the device's memory until you manually purge them (see "Purging Records" later in this chapter).

◆ The To Do List, by default, displays all upcoming tasks, even if they're several years away. If you would rather live for today, mark Show Only Due Items.

◆ Marking Record Completion Date changes an item's due date to the date it was checked off when finished.

◆ Show Due Dates, when marked, adds a date column to the right of the task names; items with no due date specified are represented by dashes.

◆ Marking Show Priorities displays a column of numbers, representing the importance of each task (1 is highest, 5 is lowest), between the checkboxes and item names.

◆ As with the Address Book and Memo Pad, To Do List records can be assigned to categories. Show Categories adds a category column to the right side of the screen.

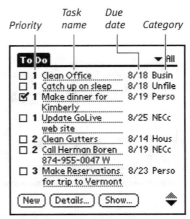

Figure 6.1 The To Do List, with all aspects visible, includes each task, plus its priority, due date, and category.

Figure 6.2 Depending on your tolerance for visual clutter, you may want more options visible.

Figure 6.3 Choose how your private records are displayed.

Figure 6.4 The Sort by popup menu organizes tasks to fit your preferences.

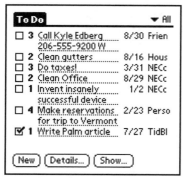

Figure 6.5 Sorting by Category, Due Date can do funky things with dates: the task for "Invent... device" is really set for January 2, 2002, eleven months after "Make reservations..." because they belong to different categories.

Changing Security View

Beginning with Palm OS 3.5, private records can be displayed, masked (grayed out), or (as in previous versions) hidden from within the To Do List.

To change the Security view:

1. Select Security from the Options menu.

2. Tap the Current Privacy popup menu to choose from one of three methods: Show Records, Mask Records, or Hide Records (**Figure 6.3**).

3. Tap OK to exit.

Setting the Sort Order

Once you've decided which elements will be visible, you need to figure out how to sort the To Do records. Feel free to experiment with each setting for a few days to get a sense of what works best for you.

To set the sort order:

1. Tap Show to bring up the To Do Preferences window (**Figure 6.4**).

2. Tap the Sort by popup menu to choose from one of four methods: Priority, Due Date; Due Date, Priority; Category, Priority; or Category, Due Date (**Figure 6.5**).

3. Tap OK to exit.

✔ Tip

■ I can't stress how much I love to check off a To Do item and have it *disappear*. In college, I carried spiral notebooks filled with to-do lists—or rather, I carried notebooks filled with scribbles and marked-out scribbles. Ick. I can understand that people like to see what they've accomplished, but to me it's all just clutter. Show Completed Items is therefore never marked on my handheld.

Entering To Do Items

Creating new To Do items takes more than just having someone say, "Do this!" over your shoulder. But not much more.

To create a new To Do item:

1. Tap the New button. A flashing cursor will appear on a blank line.

2. Write the name of your task—feel free to use multiple lines (**Figure 6.6**). Tap anywhere in a "null" area of the screen (such as the lower-right corner) to deselect your new task.

✔ Tips

■ You don't have to tap the New button to create a new To Do item. With nothing selected, start writing in the Graffiti area; a new record will be created automatically (**Figure 6.7**).

■ The default settings for new To Do items are Unfiled, no date, with a priority of 1. If you want a new task to share attributes of an existing item, you can maintain category, priority, and/or due date by highlighting an existing record and then tapping New.

■ If one category is displayed (versus viewing All), any new records are assigned that category.

Figure 6.6 Tapping the New button creates a blank record for you to name.

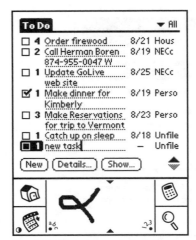

Figure 6.7 If you know what you want to add, just write it! Entering Graffiti characters with nothing selected creates a new To Do List item.

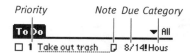

Figure 6.8 You can edit most aspects of a task without leaving the To Do List by tapping these areas.

Figure 6.9 Tap the Details button to bring up a dialog box where you can change any aspect of a To Do item.

Figure 6.10 The only aspect of a task you can't edit from the main list is an item's privacy state.

Editing To Do Items

Depending on which options you've chosen to show, almost every aspect of a To Do item can be changed from the main To Do screen. However, if you prefer a cleaner window, the options are no more than two taps away (**Figure 6.8**).

To prioritize a task:

1. If visible, tap the priority column to the left of the task name and choose a different priority level. Or, tap the To Do item, then tap the Details button.

2. Choose a priority from the buttons at the top of the To Do Item Details window. Tap OK to make the change.

To change a task's category:

1. If visible, tap the category column at the far right of the screen and choose a new category. Or, tap the To Do item, then tap the Details button.

2. Tap the Category popup menu and select a new category (**Figure 6.9**). To add or edit categories, see "Categorizing To Do Items and Memos" later in this chapter. Tap OK.

To make a task private:

1. Tap the To Do item, then tap the Details button.

2. Mark the Private checkbox (**Figure 6.10**). If you've chosen Hide Records or Mask Records from the Security application, the record's text will not be visible when you tap OK. (See Chapter 2 for information on hiding and showing private records.)

To change a task's due date:

1. If visible, tap the due date column and choose a new date. Otherwise, tap the To Do item, then tap the Details button.

2. Tap the Due Date popup menu. The frequently used commands Today, Tomorrow, and One week later make it easy to reschedule tasks (**Figure 6.11**).

3. If you need to switch to a specific date, tap Choose Date and select a new day (**Figure 6.12**). Tap OK.

To mark a task completed:

The moment you've been waiting for—tap the checkbox at left to mark the task completed (**Figure 6.13**).

✔ Tips

- The To Do application indicates a missed deadline by displaying an exclamation point (!) in the due date column (see "Take out trash" in Figure 6.13).

- Despite my best intentions, sometimes I don't complete all of today's tasks by the end of the day. (See Chapter 15 for strategies to avoid this type of situation.) Rather than manually tap the Due Date popup menus on the past due items to reflect today's due date, I use the shareware utility Plonk (http://www.alcita.com/palmpilot/) to update them all for me with one touch.

Figure 6.11 Your handheld knows how you work: four common date options are included in the popup menu.

Figure 6.12 If you select Choose Date from the popup menu, you can tap your intended date on the calendar.

Completed task

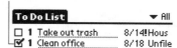

Figure 6.13 Tap the checkbox to mark a task completed. Feels good, doesn't it?

EDITING TO DO ITEMS

Figure 6.14 Tap the Note button to add important information to a task.

Figure 6.15 Navigating a note attached to a To Do item is identical to notes in the other built-in applications (unless you're running Palm OS 3.5 or later).

Adding and Deleting Notes to To Do Items

To attach a note to a task:

1. Tap an item to select it.

2. Tap the Details button, then tap the Note button (**Figure 6.14**).

   Alternately, select Attach Note from the Record menu, or write ╱-A.

3. Compose your note using Graffiti or the onscreen keyboard. Tap Done when you are finished.

✔ Tip

- To edit the attached note later, follow the steps above to access the note. If you want a quicker method, tap the note icon (▯) to the right of the task's name.

To navigate a note:

Use the scroll bar on the right side of the screen or the physical scroll buttons to move through the text.

If you're using Palm OS 3.3 or earlier, select Go to Top of Page or Go to Bottom of Page from the Options menu to jump quickly to the beginning or end (**Figure 6.15**).

To delete a note (from main list):

1. Tap the To Do item to select it.

2. Select Delete Note from the Record menu, or write ╱-O. Confirm its deletion by tapping Yes or No.

To delete a note (standard method):

1. Tap Details, then the Note button.

2. Tap Delete in the Note window. Confirm whether you want to delete it by tapping Yes or No.

Purging Records

It may bring you a measure of satisfaction to know there are dozens, maybe hundreds, of completed tasks in your handheld. Unfortunately, that means they're also taking up RAM. To free up some memory, purge those aging To Do items (**Figure 6.16**).

To purge old records:

1. From the To Do List, select Purge from the Records menu, or write ✓-E.

2. If you want to remove the items from your handheld, but keep them stored on your computer's hard drive, mark the Save archive copy on PC checkbox (**Figure 6.17**). They will be transferred at the next HotSync operation, and removed from your handheld.

3. Tap OK.

Figure 6.16 You can see how much space your completed and pending To Do items are filling by going to the Applications screen and selecting Info from the App menu. Here, the amount of free memory has increased dramatically following a purge.

Figure 6.17 The urge to keep all those successfully completed To Do items can be overpowering, but at some point you'll need to free up some memory on your handheld. Mark the Save archive copy on PC to ensure that the tasks aren't lost forever.

Figure 6.18 Memo Pad lets you store all those random scraps of information.

Figure 6.19 The text on the first line of your memo becomes its title. From there, write your memo, or paste the text in from the clipboard.

Creating and Editing Memos

The Memo Pad is straightforward, yet surprisingly useful. Imagine all of your Post-it notes—plus the crumpled papers discovered in last week's laundry—stored in one location (**Figure 6.18**). The power here is not in the number of features the Memo Pad offers, but in its overall utility.

To create a new memo:

1. Tap the New button.

2. Start writing. The first line of your memo will become its title, so don't write something generic like "Note" (**Figure 6.19**).

3. Tap Done when you're, well, done.

✔ Tip

■   With nothing selected from the Memo Pad list, begin writing in the Graffiti area. A new memo will be created containing what you've written.

To edit a memo:

1. Tap once on the title of the memo you want to edit.

2. To change the memo's category, select one from the category field in the upper-right corner. Or, tap the Details button.

3. Tap Done.

To make a memo private:

1. After tapping the memo you want, tap the Details button to display the Memo Details dialog box.

2. Mark the Private checkbox. If the Security preferences are set to hide private records, the memo will not appear in any of the Memo Pad category lists.

3. Tap Done.

Sorting Memos

Information, unlike dark socks, begs to be sorted. Some prefer alphabetical listings, while others are quite content with chaos. Although the Memo Pad doesn't claim to be the storehouse of the world's information, its sorting capabilities—though limited—can appeal to both extremes.

To sort memos:

1. Select Preferences from the Options menu, or write ✐-R, to display the Memo Preferences dialog box (**Figure 6.20**).

2. Choose a sorting method from the Sort by popup menu. Alphabetic lists items based on their first letters; Manual gives you the power to list items randomly, or by your own secret sorting code. Tap OK.

Note that you must first select Manual sorting before you can begin moving items within the Memo List (**Figure 6.21**). If you've been manually sorting and want to switch back to Alphabetic, you will lose your sort order. Unfortunately, the sorting method you choose applies to all memos, so you can't have some categories sorted manually and others sorted alphabetically.

✔ Tips

- Several utilities have been written to make it easier to manipulate text. Drag and Drop Hack (http://www.wakuwaku.ne.jp/shuji/) lets you move text without using Copy and Paste. Under Palm OS 3.1, SelectHack (http://www.jeffjetton.com/) lets you tap twice to select a word, and three times to select a sentence.

- If you want to type on the road, consider two keyboard solutions: Landware's GoType! Pro (http://www.landware.com/), or the Palm Portable Keyboard (http://store.palm.com/). See Chapter 1 for more on these keyboards.

Figure 6.20 The Memo Pad gives you two options for sorting the Memo List.

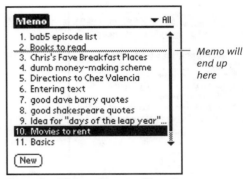

Memo will end up here

Figure 6.21 With sorting set to Manual, tap and drag a memo to a new location. A gray line indicates where it will end up when you lift the stylus.

Figure 6.22 Jump quickly within a memo using the Options menu (Palm OS 3.1 only).

Is Memo Pad Good Enough for Taking Notes?

You'd think that having a palm-sized device to write with would make people want to ditch paper forever. Although there are some people who use their handhelds as note-taking machines, I've found that writing longer texts takes more effort and headache than regular ink and wood pulp.

The advantage of writing longhand is that you can write several letters with one stroke (depending on your handwriting style, of course), whereas Graffiti requires that each character be a separate entity. Plus, extended Graffiti writing tends to aggravate my hands and wrists,

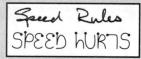

Figure 6.23 Longhand text is a little easier on the hands and wrists than Graffiti.

which have had their share of repetitive strain injuries (RSIs) in the past (**Figure 6.23**). I prefer to use the Memo Pad as a great place to store information, not necessarily create it.

Navigating Memos

Moving around in memos isn't much different than navigating notes (see "To navigate a note" earlier in this chapter), but a few aspects do stand out.

To navigate memos:

◆ Use the scroll bar at right (if the memo extends past one screen length) to move up and down the text.

◆ Press the plastic up and down buttons on the handheld's case. One added benefit of this approach is that you can jump to the next or previous memo, without returning to the main Memo List.

◆ If you're running Palm OS 3.1, jump quickly from the top to the bottom (and vice-versa) by choosing either Go to Top of Page or Go to Bottom of Page from the Options menu (**Figure 6.22**). Unfortunately, this capability was removed in Palm OS 3.5.

✔ Tip

■ Although the Go to Top of Page and Go to Bottom of Page commands were removed in Palm OS 3.5, there's still an easy workaround to zap through your text: tap and drag up or down to select the text and quickly go to the top or bottom. It may not be the most elegant solution, but it's easy and it works.

Categorizing To Do Items and Memos

To assign a To Do List category:

1. If Show Categories is selected in the To Do Preferences, tap the category name to the right of a record and choose a new category from the popup menu that appears (**Figure 6.24**).

   If categories are not visible, select the record and tap Details.

2. Select a name from the Category popup menu. Tap OK to return to the list.

To assign a category to a memo:

1. Tap a memo to open it.

2. Select a category name from the popup menu in the upper-right corner of the screen. Or, tap Details and choose an item from the Category popup menu there.

To set up custom categories:

1. In both the To Do List and the Memo Pad, tap the category popup menu in the upper-right corner. Select Edit Categories from the bottom of the list to bring up the Edit Categories dialog box.

2. Tap the New or Rename button and write the category name (**Figure 6.25**) or tap a name and Delete to remove a category.

✔ Tips

■ To create multiple records sharing the same category, go to that category's screen, then create your records there.

■ You can merge categories without changing each record individually. Simply rename the categories so they share the same name; you will receive a dialog box confirming your action (**Figure 6.26**).

Figure 6.24 Assign categories quickly by tapping the category column.

Figure 6.25 You can specify up to 15 categories for each of the four built-in applications.

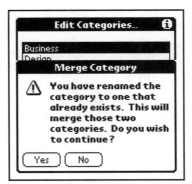

Figure 6.26 Instead of manually reassigning a category to multiple records, merge two existing categories into one.

CATEGORIZING TO DO ITEMS AND MEMOS

Figure 6.27 Selecting a font changes the setting for all memo records, not just the one currently viewed.

Figure 6.28 Tap the Beam icon in the command bar under Palm OS 3.5 or later.

Changing the Font

In the To Do List and Memo List, you can set a different font for list and record views.

To change the font:

1. In either the list view or the record view, select Font from the Options menu, or write ╱-F. The Select Font dialog box appears.

2. Choose the font from the boxes provided, and tap OK (**Figure 6.27**).

Beaming Records

Save a friend some writing time and transfer your to do items or memos via infrared.

To beam a To Do item or memo:

1. Tap the record that you want to beam. The Memo Pad will display the entire memo; the To Do List will position your cursor in the record's text.

2. Select Beam Item (To Do List) or Beam Memo (Memo Pad) from the Record menu, or write ╱-B; you can also choose the Beam icon (🖅) from the command toolbar under Palm OS 3.5 or later (**Figure 6.28**).

To beam a category:

1. With no records selected, select the category you wish to beam from the category popup menu at the top-right corner. To beam all categories, choose All.

2. Select Beam Category from the Record menu. Note, however, that your categories will appear as Unfiled on the recipient's Palm device. (Starting with Palm OS 3.5, they can choose a category for the received records.)

Working in Palm Desktop for Windows

Using the To Do List and the Memo Pad within Palm Desktop is, for the most part, the same as working on the handheld (**Figure 6.29**). There are also a few features that can only be accessed on your PC.

To print records:

1. Choose the items you want to print, or choose the category to print.

2. Choose Print from the File menu, or press Control-P.

3. Specify how you want the data to appear in the Print Options box. Click OK to create a printout (**Figure 6.30**).

To share To Do items with other applications using "Drag to":

1. Select the to do items to transfer.

2. In Palm Desktop 4.0, go to the Edit menu and choose an option from the Send To submenu. You can also right-click the seelction to access the same submenu.

   If you're running Palm Desktop 3.1, drag the selected records to the Drag To icons in the lower-right corner.

3. If you chose Word, you are given the option to format the data as a Task Progress Report, a Task Delegation Form, or just Leave Data as a Table. When the transfer is complete and the data is formatted, it will be available in Word.

Figure 6.29 The To Do List within Palm Desktop presents all of your options on one main screen.

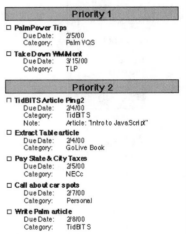

Figure 6.30 Printing from Palm Desktop isn't sexy, but it works. The layout of tasks depends on the sort order you've specified using the Show button.

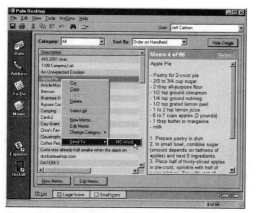

Figure 6.31 Memo contents are displayed in the pane at right. The contextual menu offers the Send To command.

Figure 6.32 The Send To MS Word action activates a set of macros that formats your data using handy templates.

To share memos with other applications using Drag To/Send To:

1. Select the memos you wish to transfer.

2. In Palm Desktop 4.0, go to the Edit menu and choose an option from the Send To submenu. You can also right-click the seelction to access the same submenu (**Figure 6.31**).

   If you're running Palm Desktop 3.1, drag the selected records to the Drag To icons in the lower-right corner.

3. Format your information in the program you chose (**Figure 6.32**).

✔ Tips

■ In addition to clicking the application buttons at left, you can press the F4 key to view the To Do List, and the F5 key to bring up the Memo Pad. F1 launches the Palm Desktop online help.

■ In Palm Desktop 3.1, you can quickly access the Note Editor from the To Do List by clicking either a note icon (🗋) to the right of a task, or the blank space where the icon would appear, which will take you to the Note Editor. Palm Desktop 4.0 has unfortunately removed this handy shortcut.

■ When adding records in Palm Desktop 3.1, you can press the Apply button to deactivate the current record. If you're adding multiple records, however, forget about the Apply button and instead just press New to begin the next record—your previous entry will be added automatically to the list.

Working in Palm Desktop for Macintosh

In essence, the To Do section of Palm Desktop for Macintosh (referred to as the Task List) provides the same functionality and features as its Windows counterpart, even though it looks quite a bit different. However, because of the program's lineage as Claris Organizer, the Mac Palm Desktop works a bit differently.

To view the Task List or Note List:

◆ Select Task List or Note List from the View menu, or press Command-Shift-T or Command-Shift-N.

◆ Click the View Task List or View Note List button on the Toolbar (**Figure 6.33**).

To create new To Do items and memos:

◆ Double-click an unused portion of the Task List window or Note List window (**Figure 6.34**). You can also double-click the Task pane of the Daily calendar view.

◆ Choose Task or Note from the Create menu, or press Command-Option-T (To Do item) or Command-Option-N (memo).

◆ You can also click the Create Task or Create Note button on the Toolbar.

✔ Tips

■ The Daily calendar window also displays tasks for that day only. The only time I ever need the full Task List is if I'm looking ahead at future To Do items.

■ In the Daily calendar window, set aside a block of time to work on a task by dragging it to the day's schedule. Palm Desktop adds "Work on" to the task name—or "Celebrate" if it's a birthday reminder created by Palm Desktop!

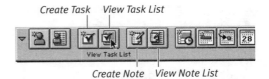

Create Task   *View Task List*

Create Note   *View Note List*

Figure 6.33 The Toolbar offers quick access to the Task and Note controls.

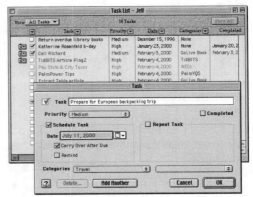

Figure 6.34 Double-clicking in the Task List brings up a new Task window.

Click name to sort... ...or choose a popup menu item.

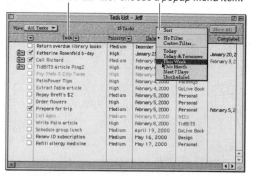

Figure 6.35 Sort the list by any column's contents by either clicking on the column's name, or choosing Sort from the popup menus.

Click and hold here

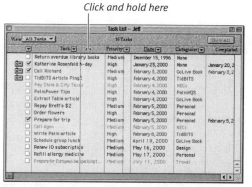

Figure 6.36 Click in the title area and drag to change the order of the visible columns.

Figure 6.37 Create custom filters to display only the tasks or memos that match specified criteria.

To sort records:

◆ To sort each list according to a column's contents, click the column's title (it will become underlined to indicate it's the active method) or choose Sort from each title's popup menu (**Figure 6.35**).

◆ You can also edit the columns to customize your display. Click and drag a column's right border to change its width. To rearrange the columns' order, click and hold in the area next to a column name, then drag left or right to position it (**Figure 6.36**). To choose which columns are displayed, select Columns from the View menu and mark the ones you want.

To filter specific data:

You can also configure the sorting method by choosing Custom Filter from the popup menus, which displays only the items that meet the filter's criteria. For example, if you want to list only the phone calls you need to make, set up a filter that searches for the words "call" or "phone" (**Figure 6.37**).

To save memorized views:

When you've set up a sort order and specific filters, choose Memorize View from the View popup menu to save it. This way, you can see related tasks and notes without repeating the sorting steps above. To see the full list again, click the Show All button.

✔ Tips

■ You can sort a list according to multiple criteria. Click a column name to perform the first sort, then Shift-click another column name to then sort the sorted results.

■ In the Daily calendar view, sort the day's Task List according to completion by clicking the word "Tasks" above the list.

WORKING IN PALM DESKTOP FOR MACINTOSH

You can attach related records to other records (such as memos attached to To Do items or records). Although this linkage does not carry across to the handheld, it can be a valuable way of working with your data on the desktop.

To attach records to To Do items and memos:

◆ If both records are visible, drag and drop one to the other. A link is created in both records (**Figure 6.38**).

◆ Click the folder icon (📁▾) and choose Attach To from the popup menu.

As I mentioned in Chapter 1, the biggest confusion arising from Macintosh Palm Desktop is the way it handles notes belonging to records (such as in the Date Book or Address Book). Whereas the Windows Palm Desktop treats attached notes as separate entities, the Mac software uses its Notes feature to handle attached notes.

Each note attached to a To Do item exists as a separate record in the Mac Palm Desktop Note List, and each is titled, "Handheld Note: To Do List." It is then linked to its associated record using the Palm Desktop's attachment feature explained above. With that in mind, it becomes relatively easy to attach new notes on the desktop.

To attach notes to To Do items:

1. Click the Create Note icon or press Command-Option-N.

2. Type "Handheld Note: To Do List"exactly as shown in the Title field.

3. Write the text of your note.

4. Link the note by dragging its Gripper (📝) to its associated task (**Figure 6.39**).

Figure 6.38 Drag and drop records onto each other to create links, indicated by the folder icon that appears to the left of records.

Figure 6.39 Be sure to use the title "Handheld Note: To Do List" to ensure that your note will appear as an attached note on your handheld.

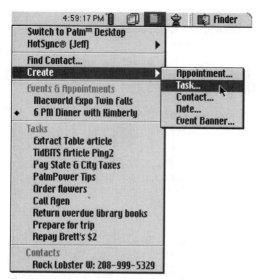

Figure 6.40 You don't even need to open Palm Desktop to access its features; the Instant Palm Desktop menu is a quick method of accessing or creating records.

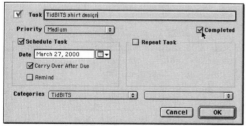

Figure 6.41 Experience the joy of completing a task without even launching Palm Desktop to mark it done.

Instant Palm Desktop menu

The day's current tasks are also listed in the Instant Palm Desktop menu (**Figure 6.40**). From here you can edit or create tasks—without even launching Palm Desktop.

◆ Highlight an item to view or edit its details, or choose Open Palm Desktop or Switch to Palm Desktop (if it's already running) to launch the program.

◆ To mark an item as done, highlight it to open the Task dialog box. Click the Completed checkbox and click OK (**Figure 6.41**).

◆ Create new To Do items by selecting Task from the Create submenu.

Using Note Pad

Palm m100 and m500 series models include Note Pad, a handy way to jot messages in a Post-it note fashion. Unlike Memo Pad, the records in Note Pad are simple drawings; a separate Note Pad application displays the pictures on your Mac or Windows PC.

To create a new note:

1. Launch Note Pad from the Applications screen, or press the Note Pad button on the handheld (it's the rightmost one, usually reserved for the Memo Pad). A new blank record is created and named according to the date and time.

2. Write on the screen. Tap the pencil icon at lower-right to change the thickness of the line, or select the eraser icon to remove what you've drawn (**Figure 6.42**).

3. If you want a more descriptive title than the timestamp, highlight the title field and write a title using Graffiti.

4. Tap Done when you're finished. Tap New to immediately create a new note. Or, of course, you can destroy your masterpiece by tapping Delete.

   When you HotSync your device, you can view or copy your notes using the Note Pad application on your computer (**Figure 6.43**).

To set Note Pad alarms:

1. With a Note Pad record open, choose Alarm from the Options menu, or write ╱-A. The Set Alarm dialog appears.

2. Select a day and time. Unlike the Date Book, where you specify a lead time before an event, the time chosen here is the actual time the alarm will sound.

3. When the alarm goes off, the note is displayed; tap OK (**Figure 6.44**).

Figure 6.42 Select a line weight and then draw words or pictures.

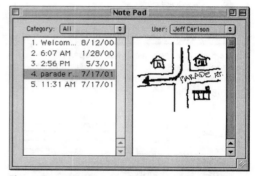

Figure 6.43 View your notes on the computer using the basic Note Pad application.

Figure 6.44 Note Pad is a quick and easy method of creating simple alarms.

USING NOTE PAD

CALCULATOR, EXPENSE, & CLOCK

7

Remember when having one of those calculator watches was the coolest? Imagine! A whole calculator on your wrist—and if you could just sneak it into math class without anyone suspecting....

The screen is now bigger than the old calculator watches (and the buttons are certainly larger!), but the utility of having a calculator on my handheld has been helpful for those times when this former English major has found himself awash in numbers.

The number fun doesn't stop at the calculator, though. If you have to keep track of expenses for work, the included Expense application should save you a headache at month's end when you're trying to explain to your boss where that $100 went in Las Vegas.

CALCULATOR, EXPENSE, & CLOCK

157

Using the Calculator

Admittedly, the Palm OS's built-in calculator isn't what you'd call comprehensive (especially if you're a real number cruncher). It adds, subtracts, multiplies, and divides. It has big buttons so you can use your finger instead of the stylus if you want to. And it reinforces the Palm philosophy that something doesn't have to be complicated and bloated with features in order to be useful.

Still, there are several things lurking just below the surface of the Calculator application that make it better than a cheapo math machine hiding somewhere in the back of your desk drawer.

To perform calculations:

1. Launch the Calculator application by tapping the silk-screened icon, or the Calculator icon from within Applications (**Figure 7.1**).

2. Tap the buttons to enter numbers and basic mathematical operations.

3. Tap the percentage button to convert a number to a decimal percentage (for example: **2** **5** **%** = 0.25).

4. Tap the **+/-** button to make a number either positive or negative.

To clear the results field:

1. Tapping **C** clears the entire calculation.

2. Tapping **CE** clears the last number you entered without wiping out everything.

✔ Tip

■ You can operate the calculator by writing in the Graffiti area (**Table 7.1**). I'm not sure why exactly you'd want to, but at the very least it's good Graffiti practice!

Figure 7.1 There's no mistaking that this is a calculator, right down to the finger-friendly buttons. (Just to note, devices running Palm OS 3.5 and earlier feature rounded buttons.)

Table 7.1

Graffiti Calculator?

Yes, it's true! Use the Calculator without tapping any buttons by writing numbers and symbols in the Graffiti area.

Button	Graffiti	Button	Graffiti
1	|	CE	Ɛ
2	2	C	C
3	3	MC	m
4	L	MR	R
5	5	M+	P
6	6	%	./
7	7	+/-	.\
8	8	÷	\⅛
9	9	×	.⋈
0	O	−	.⁻
.	..	=	\Z
		+	\∝

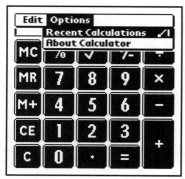

Figure 7.2 View the last several steps in an operation by bringing up the Recent Calculations screen.

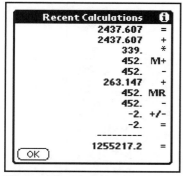

Figure 7.3 The Calculator's "tape" makes it easier to see where mistakes are made, although it only stores one screen full of information.

To memorize calculation results:

1. Tap the ![M+] button to store the current result in memory; a small "m" will appear in the number field. If you tap the button again later, the new result is added to the stored number, instead of replacing it.

2. Tap ![MR] to display the stored number; you can use it as part of a calculation in progress.

3. Tap ![MC] to clear the contents of the stored memory.

To view "the tape":

1. You can access a list of the most recent numbers in a calculation by choosing Recent Calculations from the Options menu, or by writing ╱-I (**Figure 7.2**).

2. You'll see the numbers of the current calculation in a list running down the right side of the screen (**Figure 7.3**). Note that only what you see is stored; you can't scroll up to an earlier number.

USING THE CALCULATOR

Copying and Pasting Calculations

Being able to take your calculation results to another application is one of the reasons I said that Calculator is more useful than most calculators. Sure, you can write the numbers on paper, but that's just *so* 1995.

To copy and paste calculations:

◆ On the main screen, choose Copy from the Edit menu (or write ╱-C) to copy the current number to the Palm OS's Clipboard for pasting into other programs. Similarly, you can copy a number from another application and choose Paste (or write ╱-P) to add it to your calculation.

◆ In the Recent Calculations screen, choose Copy from the Edit menu (or write ╱-C) to grab the visible list of calculations for pasting elsewhere (**Figure 7.4**).

✔ Tips

■ If you make a calculation, then switch to another application, the calculation result is held in memory. However, the last set of operations normally viewed by the Recent Calculations screen gets erased! If you're going to need the full transcript of a calculation later, copy it first before exiting the Calculator. You may want to set up a Memo Pad record to paste in your results before moving on to the next task.

■ There are several calculators you can download that should be able to handle whatever you throw at them (**Figure 7.5**). For example, RPN (http://www.nthlab.com/) is an advanced calculator that also accepts plug-ins written by other developers. FCPlus Professional (http://www.infinitysw.com/) specializes in financial calculations.

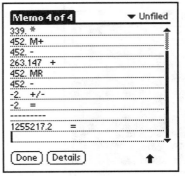

Figure 7.4 Paste calculations or results into other applications, like Memo Pad, shown here.

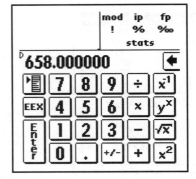

Figure 7.5 Other calculators, such as RPN (top) and FCPlus Professional (bottom) take over where the built-in Calculator leaves off.

Figure 7.6 Expense records are shown in a basic list that's easy to read and quick to access.

Figure 7.7 Choose from 28 different expense types when creating records.

Using Expense

Business people who are continually on the move have adopted the Palm OS platform in droves. Not only can they retrieve their valuable information quickly, they can manage one of the most dreaded aspects of modern business: expense reporting. Keeping track of charges that will be reimbursed by your company is often no more involved than three or four Graffiti strokes. At the end of the month, the data can be easily transferred to a Microsoft Excel file.

To create new Expense items:

1. Launch Expense from the Applications screen by tapping its icon.

2. Tap the New button (**Figure 7.6**). A new record is created with today's date, the temporary title "-Expense type-", and a field for entering the expense amount.

3. Write the amount in the numbers section of the Graffiti area. Expense will automatically enter ".00" after the number if you don't specify a cent value.

4. Tap a title to acccess the type popup menu, then select from a list of 28 expense types (**Figure 7.7**). If none of them match your expense, select Other; unfortunately, you can't edit the type list. Don't just leave "-Expense type-" as the type—the record won't be saved!

5. Tap on a blank area of the screen to deselect the record.

USING EXPENSE

✔ Tips

■ Once Expense is launched, you can avoid the New button entirely by writing the expense amount in the Graffiti area. A new record will be created automatically with the numbers in place.

■ Additionally, you can begin writing the name of an expense type in the Graffiti area. If you have the automatic fill feature turned on (see below), the first match will be selected (**Figure 7.8**).

To edit Expense records:

1. Tap a record to select it; the date will become highlighted to indicate your selection.

2. To modify the date, expense type, or amount, tap those elements and make the change directly (**Figure 7.9**).

3. Tap a blank area of the screen to deselect the record.

To toggle the "automatic fill" feature:

1. Choose Preferences from the Options menu, or write ╱-R. The Preferences window appears.

2. Mark or unmark the Use automatic fill when entering data checkbox, then tap OK (**Figure 7.10**).

Figure 7.8 The automatic fill feature lets you create records by writing the first letter of an expense type in Graffiti.

Consider making a donation to the Online Authors' Fund.

Figure 7.9 The amount fields can hold a maximum of seven characters. (And if that's not enough, why do you have to expense it?)

Figure 7.10 The automatic fill feature can dramatically decrease the time it takes to enter an expense record.

USING EXPENSE

Figure 7.11 The Receipt Details screen is where you find the bulk of your expense information. Taxi rides and plane trips are good times to flesh out your expense information.

Editing Expense Details

The Receipt Details screen lets you specify more information about an expense (**Figure 7.11**)—but don't feel compelled to fill in everything if it doesn't apply (such as the City field if you never travel).

To edit Expense details:

1. With a record selected, tap the Details button to bring up the Receipt Details window.

2. Select a category from the Category pop-up menu. Choose Edit Categories to set up new ones.

3. If you didn't select an expense type in the main screen, tap the Type popup menu to choose one.

4. Select the method of payment from the Payment popup menu.

5. Select other currencies from the Currency popup menu.

6. Write the name of the payee in the Vendor field. With automatic fill activated, Expense will display previous vendors that match letters alphabetically as you write them (for example, writing D would bring up "Dan's Café," but writing Di would switch to "Diva Espresso").

7. Write the city name in the City field. The automatic fill feature works here as well.

Recording Attendees and Notes

Expense offers the ability to easily add notes, such as who was present at a lunch.

To record attendees:

1. In the Receipt Details window, tap the dotted box beside Attendees (if no attendees are listed, the box reads Who).

2. Write the names of the people present. If their names are located in your Address Book, tap the Lookup button (only contacts with data in the Company field are shown). Selecting a person copies the name, title, and company information to the Attendees screen (**Figure 7.12**).

To add and delete notes:

1. Tap the Note button on the Receipt Details screen to open a Memo Pad-like window where you can jot down miscellaneous details about the expense (**Figure 7.13**).

2. Change the typeface by selecting Font from the Options menu (or writing /-F).

3. You can record a person's name and phone number by choosing Phone Lookup from the Options menu (or writing /-L).

4. Tap the Delete button to kill the note, or tap Done to complete your edits.

✔ Tips

■ Although you can specify a separate note for each expense record, you can also write notes in the Attendees screen as well, consolidating some of your information in one place.

■ Put a space in the Company field to make a record show up in the Lookup list.

Figure 7.12 Use the Lookup button on the Attendees screen to quickly record the participants of a meeting.

Figure 7.13 The Note feature is very much like Attendees, but sticks closer to a Memo Pad record.

Figure 7.14 Sort your list of expenses by Date or Type. If you drive often, note whether you want to use Miles or Kilometers to record your travel.

Figure 7.15 Mileage is the only expense type that doesn't show a currency indicator next to the amount.

Viewing Options

One problem with keeping track of expenses is that they all tend to blur together at a certain point (specifically, just before you need to compile them and turn them in). As you're reviewing expenses, choose to view them chronologically or by type, as well as display distance and currency indicators.

To change the sort order:

1. Tap the Show button on the main Expense screen to display the Show Options window (**Figure 7.14**).

2. Tap the Sort by popup menu to sort by Date or Type.

To change the distance measurement:

1. Tap the Show button on the main Expense screen to display the Show Options window.

2. Tap the Distance popup menu and choose either Miles or Kilometers.

3. When you choose Mileage as the type, either mi or km appears instead of a currency symbol, depending on your choice (**Figure 7.15**).

Specifying Currency

The default currency type is set to dollars ($), but Expense also includes English pounds (£), German deutschemarks (DM), and the Euro (¤) on its Currency popup menus (you can add others).

To set the default currency:

1. Choose Preferences from the Options menu, or write ✒-R.

2. Tap the Default Currency popup menu to choose a currency type, then tap OK.

To add countries to the Currency popup menus:

1. Choose Edit Currencies from any Currency popup menu (found in the Preferences and Receipt Details windows).

2. Specify countries for up to five currency list items by tapping the popup menus to the right of each currency slot (**Figure 7.16**). Tap OK when finished.

To create custom currencies:

1. Choose Custom Currencies from the Options menu, or write ✒-Y.

2. Tap a dotted box to specify a new country (**Figure 7.17**).

3. In the Currency Properties window that appears, write the name of the country and its symbol (**Figure 7.18**). Tap OK.

4. You can create up to four currencies. Tap OK to return to the main window.

✔ Tip

■ If you use only one type of currency, or you're just tired of seeing that dollar sign on every record, you can opt to hide the currency symbol. Tap the Show button on the main Expense screen and unmark the Show currency checkbox. Press OK.

Figure 7.16 View up to five countries in the Currency popup menu by specifying them here.

Figure 7.17 Is the currency list missing a few countries? Enter them at the Custom Currencies screen.

Figure 7.18 Be omnipotent! Create countries out of thin air and...assign them currency symbols.

Click here to "launch" Expense

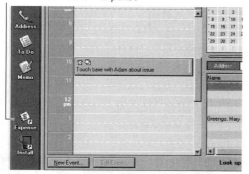

Figure 7.19 It looks like just another Palm Desktop application, but Expense actually directs you to a Microsoft Excel macro.

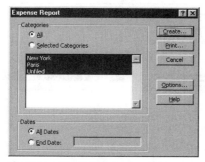

Figure 7.20 The first dialog box asks you to specify the categories and dates you want included on the report.

Figure 7.21 The options screen is where you choose a template for the data, as well as other information.

Exporting to Excel

When you click the Expense button in Palm Desktop, don't worry if your computer suddenly launches Microsoft Excel instead. The desktop implementation of Expense is accomplished using Excel macros that format your data into a spreadsheet.

Unfortunately, this only applies to Palm Desktop for Windows. There is no built-in support for Expense in the Mac software.

To export Expense data to Excel:

1. In Palm Desktop, click the Expense button at left (**Figure 7.19**). (If you don't see an Expense button, is Excel installed on your machine? If it is, run the Palm Desktop software installer again, making sure the Expense module is selected.)

2. Excel will launch (if it isn't already open), and you will be presented with the Expense Report dialog box. Choose the categories and the date range you want to appear on the report (**Figure 7.20**).

3. Click the Options button. In the Expense report Options dialog box, enter your name, department, phone number, the project name, and the person to bill to, if applicable.

4. Click the Template popup menu to choose the report's final formatting (**Figure 7.21**). Palm Desktop includes four sample layouts, plus a version called "DATALIST.XLT" that simply lists the information in a readable form.

5. Select a country from the Local Currency popup menu.

6. Click OK, then click the Create button in the Expense Report dialog box. The formatting spreadsheet will open with all of the data in place.

✔ Tips

- In addition to the spreadsheet, you'll see a small floating palette containing a button labeled with a dollar-sign icon (**Figure 7.22**). This is your link to the Expense data from Palm Desktop. Click it to generate a new report.

- An error on my part led to an interesting discovery: you can view the raw expense data from a tab-delimited text file using Notepad or any word processor. The dialog box in **Figure 7.23** resulted because I had not yet installed Excel, pointing me to the file where Palm Desktop stores the expense data (it's called "expense.txt" and is located in the "expense" folder within your Palm user folder). It's not pretty, but you can extract information from it if you have to (**Figure 7.24**).

- I said that there's no built-in support for extracting Expense data on the Macintosh, but that doesn't mean it can't be done. WalletWare's ExpensePlus for Palm (http://www.walletware.com/) offers more expense features than Palm's Expense application, plus conduits for Macintosh and Windows.

- Since Palm Desktop uses a macro file to generate reports in Excel, you may receive a dialog box warning that macros can contain viruses. Click the Enable Macros button to proceed.

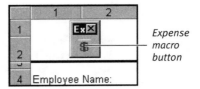

Figure 7.22 To create a new expense layout, click the floating dollar-sign button to run the Excel macro again.

Figure 7.23 My failure to install Excel before clicking the Expense button in Palm Desktop led me to the location of Expense's data file.

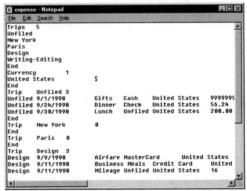

Figure 7.24 This is how Palm Desktop stores your raw expense data—not pretty, but useful.

Figure 7.25 Clock shows you the current date and time, without having to launch the Date Book application.

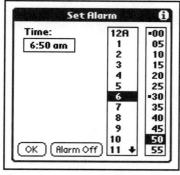

Figure 7.26 Unlike Date Book, the alarm in Clock occurs at the time specified, not at a time prior to an event.

Figure 7.27 The Alarm Preferences works independently of the volume controls in the Palm OS preferences.

Using Clock

Palm m100 and m500 devices include Clock, a simple application that gives you quick access to the current date and time (**Figure 7.25**). It can also be used as an alarm clock.

To view the time with Clock:

◆ Launch Clock from the Applications screen.

◆ Tap the Clock icon in the upper-left corner of the silkscreen area, next to the Applications icon.

◆ On the m100 and m105, press the scroll up button on the device's case when the power is turned off.

To set an alarm:

1. Tap the field next to Alarm to bring up the Set Alarm dialog box.

2. Choose a time by tapping the hour and minute columns (**Figure 7.26**).

3. Tap OK to finish. If you're cancelling an alarm, tap the Alarm Off button.

✔ Tips

■ On the main Clock screen, the Set Date & Time button takes you to the Preferences application (see Chapter 2).

■ Choose Alarm Preferences from the Options menu to change the alarm sound and volume (**Figure 7.27**).

■ After an alarm occurs, the alarm feature is turned off. For repeating alarms (such as a meeting that happens each day at the same time), use Date Book to schedule a repeating event (see Chapter 4).

SYSTEM EXTENSIONS

It was bound to happen. When Palm chose to create an open programming environment, they invited ordinary people (not just established third-party developers) to produce applications for the Pilot. One result is that the Palm OS platform boasts a developer community of over 150,000 registered developers—another result is system enhancements like HackMaster (`http://www.daggerware.com/hackmstr.htm`), TealMaster (`http://www.tealpoint.com/`), and X-Master (`http://www.linkesoft.com/`).

These programs enable programmers to build extensions, called "hacks," that enhance the functionality of the Palm OS. With these system enhancements, you can solve some of the minor irritations of the Palm OS (like the limited Find function, or the small clipboard), and add features previously unavailable.

Powerful stuff, which is why you should keep in mind that some of the hacks deal with low-level elements of the OS, and could potentially require you to reset (though not necessarily erase) your organizer.

I consider a system extension program one of the essential applications for any Palm OS device.

Important System Extension Notes

These extension-controlling programs (**Figures 8.1**, **8.2**, and **8.3**) are extremely easy to use, but it's good to be aware of a few things before you start hacking away at your handheld.

◆ Hacks are installed using the same steps as normal files (see Chapter 2), but they don't show up as application icons; instead, they all reside in the controlling application. Installing a hack file without the program present makes it inaccessible (but it remains in memory).

◆ If you want to remove a hack, make sure it has been deactivated first in the controlling program, then delete it using the Application program. Ugly things can happen when deleting activated hacks.

◆ Always be sure to read the ReadMe files that accompany extensions; some hacks work only under certain versions of the OS, some may conflict with other hacks, and some may require that the device be soft-reset in order to run. Know exactly what you're installing before you install it.

◆ The controlling programs are polite. If your handheld should happen to crash or be reset at any point, the application asks if you want to reinstall (reactivate) the hacks that were previously active.

For clarity's sake, I'm going to use the original, HackMaster, as the example program in this chapter. If you're using one of the others and don't see a feature I mention, check the program's menus for something similar (for example, the Uninstall All command is a button in HackMaster, the All on button in TealMaster, and the Deactivate All menu item in X-Master).

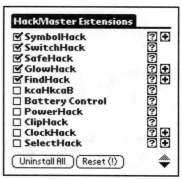

Figure 8.1 It may not look like much, but HackMaster provides plenty of added functionality to the Palm OS.

Figure 8.2 TealMaster's interface is similar to HackMaster, but adds the capability to create extension sets.

Figure 8.3 X-Master is further simplified, but just as useful.

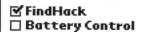

Figure 8.4 The checkboxes to the left indicate whether a hack is activated or is disabled.

Figure 8.5 Tapping the question-mark icon displays information about a HackMaster extension.

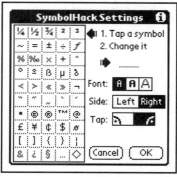

Figure 8.6 Tapping the plus-sign icon (when available) brings up configurable settings for hacks.

Working with Hacks

Once you have loaded a few hacks into your handheld, they appear in a bare-bones list within the application. As you activate each one, it moves to the top of the list. Tapping the Uninstall All button turns them all off.

To activate and deactivate a hack in HackMaster:

Mark the checkbox to the left of the hack's name to activate it; tap the checkbox again to deactivate it (**Figure 8.4**). Yes, it really is that simple.

To get information about a hack in HackMaster:

Tap the question-mark icon to the right of the extension's name for information, including the version number, the developer's contact info, and tips for use (**Figure 8.5**).

To change preferences for a hack in HackMaster:

If a hack is configurable, a plus-sign icon will appear to the right of the question-mark icon. Tap here to change its options, then tap OK to return to the main screen (**Figure 8.6**).

To soft-reset your handheld within HackMaster:

Next to the harmless Uninstall All button in the main HackMaster screen is the more alarming Reset (!) button. Tapping it initiates a soft reset of your handheld. Don't worry, you won't lose any information; this is just a convenient location to reset your organizer without digging into the device's reset hole with the stylus reset pin (see Appendix A for more information about resetting your handheld). After the Palm OS restarts, you will be asked if you want to enable the previously active extensions.

WORKING WITH HACKS

Essential Hacks

These are, in my view, the hacks that I would not leave the house without. Some provide basic added functionality; a few elicit that "Of course!" reaction in people.

SwitchHack

SwitchHack (http://www.deskfree.com/) is, palms down, my favorite hack. It offers two quick ways to move between your programs.

To use SwitchHack:

1. To switch directly to the last program you were running, place your stylus on the silkscreened Applications icon and drag to the Graffiti area. Repeat the same gesture to switch back.

2. To view a popup list of the last ten programs you've used, place the stylus on the Menu icon and drag to the Applications icon. Tap the name of the program you want to jump to (**Figure 8.7**).

SymbolHack

If you want to write characters such as ¼, ±, or ©, but don't want to memorize the Graffiti combinations, install SymbolHack (http://perso.wanadoo.fr/fpillet/). It displays a popup window of common symbol characters when you tap either the lower-left or lower-right corner of the Graffiti area (**Figure 8.8**). Tap on a symbol to insert it into your text.

MultiClipHack

The Palm platform has come a long way, but you're still limited to storing only 1,000 characters in the clipboard. To correct this annoying oversight, install MultiClipHack (http://www.fatal-error.com/), which expands the clipboard up to 32K, and stores up to 16 clipboard items at a time.

Figure 8.7 To access SwitchHack's popup menu of applications, drag from the Menu icon to the Applications icon.

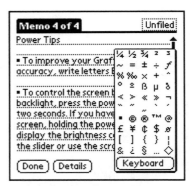

Figure 8.8 Why memorize obscure Graffiti combinations? SymbolHack displays a palette of symbol characters—tap one to insert it into your text.

Figure 8.9 FindHack replaces the Palm OS's limited Find feature, adding Wildcards and a list of recent finds.

Figure 8.10 TealEcho draws the character you're currently writing.

FindHack

The built-in Find feature is effective, but limited. For example, you can only search for the beginning of a word (searching for "dear" yields "dearly," but not "endearment"). FindHack (http://perso.wanadoo.fr/fpillet/) provides the Find features that should have been built into the Palm OS.

To use FindHack:

1. To perform a search in any application, tap the silkscreened Find icon.

2. Write the text you wish to find; a popup menu to the right of the Find field lists the last six searches you performed, plus four permanent search terms that you can define (**Figure 8.9**).

3. Select whether you want the search to be performed in all applications, the four built-in applications, or only the current program.

4. Tap the Use Wildcards checkbox to access advanced options. A question mark (?) or period (.) will substitute for any character ("?ell" will find "bell" and "well"). An asterisk (*) matches character sequences ("dark*road" finds "dark road" and "dark and winding road").

5. Tap OK to begin the search.

TealEcho

Most of us are used to direct feedback when we write; for example, a pen's ink shows us what we're writing. TealEcho (http://www.tealpoint.com/) provides "digital ink" by displaying Graffiti characters as you write them, which often improves your Graffiti legibility (**Figure 8.10**).

ESSENTIAL HACKS

SafeHack

The ability to show and hide private records (see Chapter 2) is often helpful, but it does not take into consideration that humans are operating the machine—if you forget to hide your visible private records and your handheld is lost, then your secrets are exposed. SafeHack (http://www.waterworld.com.hk/) takes on this responsibility for you by automatically toggling the Palm OS security setting when the device is turned off. The next time you (or a thief) turns the handheld on, your private records are hidden or (in Palm OS 3.5 and higher) masked.

Swipe

A great Palm shortcut is to configure an action for drawing a stroke from the bottom to the top of the screen (you'll find this in the Buttons section of the Palm OS Preferences). Swipe (http://www.doublebang.com/) extends that functionality by adding six other configurable screen strokes (**Figure 8.11**). For example, use the bottom-to-top stroke to activate backlighting, but also configure the lower-right-to-upper-left stroke to beam a selected event.

GadgetHack

GadgetHack (http://ourworld.compuserve.com/homepages/mcdan/) displays most of the important controls in every application, borrowing space from the title bar (**Figure 8.12**). Tap once to get the time, twice for your battery level, and a third time to display a row of buttons representing functions such as Lock & Turn Off, backlight control, and even an option to invert the screen's pixels for better readability under some lighting conditions.

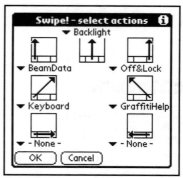

Figure 8.11 Swipe gives you six more options for activating commands with a single pen stroke.

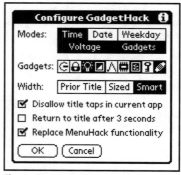

Figure 8.12 GadgetHack puts most of the Palm OS's frequently used commands in the title bar.

Figure 8.13 GlowHack activates the handheld's backlight automatically during preset hours.

Figure 8.14 BackHack's usefulness is mirrored only by its cleverness.

Noteworthy Hacks

System extensions are designed to customize your Palm device usage, so here are some other hacks worth mentioning.

GlowHack

If you're the type to wake up in the middle of the night to jot down an idea, GlowHack (http://www.dovcom.com/) will help you by automatically turning on the handheld's backlight. You can specify the time range for when GlowHack is activated (late evening hours, for example) (**Figure 8.13**).

MenuHack

The only truly bizarre user-interface element of the Palm OS before version 3.5 is the need to tap the Menu icon at the bottom of the Graffiti area to activate a menu at the top of the screen. MenuHack (http://www.daggerware.com/mischack.htm) lets you tap the title bar of a program to access its menus.

BackHack

Okay, so BackHack (http://www.jeffjetton.com/backhack/) isn't really useful, but it was worth including for the entertainment value alone (**Figure 8.14**). If your coworker goes to lunch without taking her handheld, sneak this little hack into her system and... on second thought, maybe that's not such a good idea. Install it on your own device, and think of your own clever schemes!

LightHack

If you would prefer that the handheld's backlighting is reversed (so that inactive pixels are illuminated), install LightHack (http://www.quartus.net/products/lighthack/).

Palm V Contrast App Hack

The contrast button on many devices (often located in the lower-left corner of the silkscreen area, or as a separate button like on the Palm V) rarely gets used once you've adjusted the contrast level. Palm V Contrast App Hack (http://www.synsolutions.com/) gives you the option of launching an application by tapping the contrast button (**Figure 8.15**). To bring up the contrast control, double-tap the button.

Figure 8.15 Elegant and useful, Palm V Contrast App Hack turns the contrast button into a fifth application button.

LeftHack

If you're left-handed, you know what a pain it can be to try to scroll text while reading on your handheld: your hand obscures the text! Install LeftHack (http://www.quartus.net/products/lefthack/) to move the scroll bar and scroll buttons to the left side of the screen (**Figure 8.16**).

ClockPop

Some people just don't like to wear watches. You can still keep track of the time, and maintain that full-arm tan, with ClockPop (you can find it at http://www.palmgear.com/). Similar to Palm's Clock application on its new devices, ClockPop displays a screen with the time, date, and other information when you push and hold an application button of your choice (**Figure 8.17**).

Figure 8.16 LeftHack puts the scroll bar on the left side of the screen, so the text isn't obscured when you're reading or writing.

Figure 8.17 Check the time quickly with ClockPop: just hold down one of the application buttons for a few seconds.

Figure 8.18 If your Palm V is clicking at you because it was inadvertantly turned on in your pocket, use PalmVHack to control its buttons.

Figure 8.19 Change the functionality of lifting the Palm VII's antenna with Antennae Hack.

Palm V & Palm VII Essential Hacks

Each device has its own quirks and advantages, and the Palm V and Palm VII families are no exception.

PalmVHack

The Palm V designers deserve kudos for the sleek metallic handheld, but also deserve a thump on the head for the scroll button. If the Palm turns on (by accidentally pressing an application button or when an alarm goes off) and the unit is in your pocket, the Palm V cover can press against the scroll button and continue to send button clicks until the battery goes out. PalmVHack (http://www.rgps.com/) features the ability to power down the Palm after the application buttons have been pressed (though not a good option if you use them to turn on the device) or following alarms (**Figure 8.18**).

AntennaeHack

By default, lifting the Palm VII's antenna activates Palm.net and establishes a wireless connection. Using AntennaeHack (http://www.palmgear.com/), you can use the antennae to launch applications, or perform actions such as immediately check and send email using the iMessenger application (**Figure 8.19**).

Part 2
Communicating

Extending Your Handheld's Reach

Palm OS devices were designed as extensions of the personal computer, not replacements for it. And despite the fact that handhelds are immensely portable, your data is really only being transported from one computing box to a smaller box. Now, with the addition of a modem or network connection, you can have the world's information literally in the palm of your hand using electronic communication hardware and software.

Chapter 9, **Email**, covers what you need to access your email from Palm OS handhelds, plus an overview of modem options for getting you there (note, however, that a modem isn't necessarily required in some cases).

Chapter 10, **Web Access**, gets you surfing the World Wide Web on a tiny screen—but the screen size is less limiting than you may think.

Chapter 11, **Pages, Faxes, Newsgroups, Telnet**, explores other options for sending and receiving electronic data.

Chapter 12, **Protecting Your Data**, looks at the darker side of being able to share important data—unintentionally sharing it with the wrong people. You'll find information on password protection, encryption, and tips for keeping your handheld's contents secure.

9

EMAIL

As a freelance writer and designer, I've learned the value of "flexible portability." I alternate my working time between my office at home, an office space I share with several colleagues, and an assortment of coffee-houses in the Seattle area. A large part of that portability (both in importance and size) is my laptop, an invaluable tool that allows me to work just about anywhere. However, it can be heavy and awkward to lug around.

My Palm organizer, on the other hand, is easily the most portable device I own. It fits into my shirt pocket, weighs almost nothing, runs for months on the same battery charge, and continues to spark spontaneous conversations from nearby gawkers. Yet despite these advantages, it remained—until recently—a second-class citizen to my laptop because it lacked the ability to connect directly with two of the lifebloods of my business: email and the World Wide Web.

Now, with several alternatives on the market for expanding my handheld's communications abilities, I can often leave my laptop at home or on my desk at the office, and still be connected to the information I need.

Modem Hardware

Before you can retrieve email, you'll need a modem of some sort to connect to the Internet.

Palm modems

Snap one of these portable add-ons to your Palm device, connect a phone line, and you're ready to get online or perform a Modem HotSync with your computer back at the office (**Figure 9.1**). The modems are powered by their own pair of AAA batteries and operate at speeds of up to 56Kbps—not as fast as the DSL connection at the office, but acceptable when you consider that 98 percent of the data being transmitted is straight text. The HotSync button on the front initiates a Mode HotSync by default, but you can remap it to launch applications—such as Mail—if you choose. Since it's a standard modem, you can also use it to send faxes, pages, or dial-up bulletin-board systems (BBSes); see Chapter 11.

Novatel Wireless modems

Novatel Wireless makes wireless modems (http://www.novatelwireless.com/) that attach to several Palm organizer models like a flat version of the HotSync cradle. The Minstrel and OmniSky (http://www.omnisky.net/) modems support data rates as high as 19.2 Kbps over the Cellular Digital Packet Data (CDPD) network. Check the Web sites for service availability in your area.

Cellular phones

A growing number of cellular companies are offering Internet-access services with their phones via infrared or cable connections to the Palm device. Using Palm's Mobile Internet Connection Kit (http://www.palm.com/software/mik/), I'm able to get online using a Nokia 8290 cellular phone (**Figure 9.2**).

Figure 9.1 The Palm V Modem clips to the back of a Palm V or Palm Vx, retaining its curvy form without adding much bulk.

Figure 9.2 Many newer cellular phones include infrared receivers, which you can use to dial your ISP from the handheld.

Palm VII and Palm VIIx

Using the Palm VII's built-in wireless circuitry and swivel antenna, you can grab email and information from the Web without requiring a single phone line. Someday, every handheld device will offer built-in wireless communication (and we'll wonder what the big fuss was about way back when), but until then the Palm VII and Palm VIIx remain the darling devices of people who need their information long before they get back to the office (**Figure 9.3**).

Phone/PDA combinations

The Palm OS devices from Kyocera and Samsung herald the day when Palm and phone will become one multifaceted device. Since you're sending data out over the airwaves anyway, why not put it to good use? You can use these handhelds to act as modems in addition to making phone calls (see Chapter 1).

Your PC and modem

That's right, your computer is actually the Palm OS method of choice for sending and receiving email (I doubt that the concept of Web browsing was high on the list of features during the original PalmPilot's development; remember, Palm OS devices are geared toward simplicity). See the next page for details.

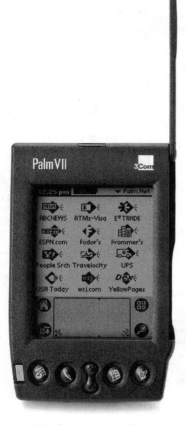

Figure 9.3 Raising the Palm VII's built-in antenna automatically initiates a connection with the Palm.net wireless Internet service.

Getting Online: Two Approaches

Connecting via HotSync

If you've opened up the built-in Mail application, you've noticed that it's noticeably lacking email-related commands like Connect, Check Mail, or Receive. There is a Send button, but it's misleading—it doesn't actually send anything. What's going on?

In keeping with the philosophy of simplicity, the built-in Mail program acts as an extension of your desktop email software.

When you perform a HotSync operation, the data in Mail and in your desktop application are synchronized (**Figure 9.4**); the next time you check your email, you send out what was composed on the handheld. A few Web browsing applications, such as AvantGo (see Chapter 10), use HotSync to transfer content to your handheld for later viewing.

Modem connection

The second method, which is probably more familiar, is to establish an active Internet connection directly from the handheld, avoiding the need to HotSync the data before any action can be taken (**Figure 9.5**).

A direct connection can be more convenient, but it also requires modem hardware, and in some cases, a free phone line. If you have those, you can use email packages like Multi-Mail Pro (http://www.actualsoft.com/), Eudora (http://www.eudora.com/), and One-Touch Mail (http://www.jpmobile.com/jpmdevice.asp) to send and receive mail on the fly.

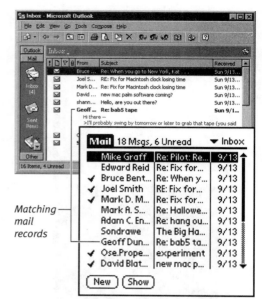

Matching mail records

Figure 9.4 Palm's Mail synchronizes with your Windows email application during each HotSync operation.

Figure 9.5 Direct-dial makes connecting easier, though you may lose the ability to synchronize your mail with your desktop email program.

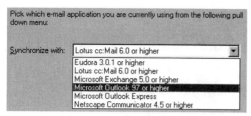

Figure 9.6 You can synchronize email with your PC if you use one of the programs in the Mail Setup list.

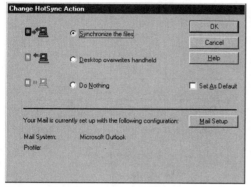

Figure 9.7 Specify the action of the mail conduit from the Custom item of Palm Desktop's HotSync menu. If you want to specify a new desktop email program to link to, click the Mail Setup button.

Mail on the Macintosh

The Palm Desktop software has never supported synchronizing Mail with the Macintosh, leaving many Mac users with another icon to ignore in the Applications screen. However, developers have written their own links to the Mail application. Actual Software (http://www.actualsoft.com/) sells a conduit that will sync with their MultiMail Pro application, and also works with Palm's Mail application. Other programs, like Eudora, now offer HotSync options as well.

Email via HotSync: Palm Mail

If you want to print a record that's on your handheld, you have to transfer that information to your PC and print from there. Using the built-in Mail application works the same way: any emails you create on the handheld must first pass to your desktop email application to be dispatched out to the Internet.

To configure Mail on your PC:

1. If you didn't set up Mail when you were installing the Palm Desktop software the first time, open the Palm Mail Setup application (click the Windows Start button, then navigate to the Applications submenu, then the Palm menu).

2. At the Mail Setup window, select your preferred email application from the Synchronize with popup menu (**Figure 9.6**). Click Next.

3. When the installer is done, click the Finished button. If you ever change your primary email application, running the Mail Setup program again will let you easily reconfigure the Mail link.

4. Choose Custom from the HotSync menu in Palm Desktop, or the HotSync icon in the Taskbar to configure the conduit action for Mail.

5. At the Change HotSync Action window, choose Synchronize the files, Desktop overwrites handheld, or Do Nothing to specify how the mail is handled during a HotSync (**Figure 9.7**). You can also reconfigure your email setup by clicking Mail Setup.

Using Mail

When you open Mail, you're presented with the contents of your Inbox (**Figure 9.8**). The left column displays the senders' names, the center column lists the message titles, and the right column (if visible) notes the date received. Emails that have been read are marked with a checkmark to the left. Use the scrollbar or the plastic up and down buttons to scroll through messages.

Mail includes five built-in mailbox folders: Inbox, Outbox, Deleted, Filed, and Draft. Tap the popup menu in the upper-right corner of the screen and select the one you want to view. Note that the Deleted folder is functionally equivalent to the other folders until you perform a HotSync, at which point its contents are removed.

You can also change the font displayed in the folder list view by choosing Font from the Options menu (✓-F).

By default, messages are listed according to the date they were received.

To change the sort order and date column visibility:

1. Tap the Show button in any folder view. The Show Options dialog box appears.

2. Tap the Sort by popup menu to organize the list by Date, Sender, or Subject (**Figure 9.9**). This setting applies to all folders, not just the active one.

3. If you want to hide the date column in list views, unmark the Show Date checkbox.

Figure 9.8 Mail lists your incoming messages along with their dates and sender's names.

Figure 9.9 Use the Sort by popup menu to organize messages in all folders (not just the visible one).

Figure 9.10 Signatures can be added to each outgoing message, giving you space to list contact information or even a favorite quote.

Figure 9.11 Write your message's text and addresses in the New Message window. If you need more room to write, tap the name of the field for a full-screen, Memo Pad-like interface.

Most people who use email specify a block of text that appears at the bottom of every message they write, known as a signature. This is good for including contact information, quotations, or even as a substitute for signing their names at the end of each email.

To specify a signature:

1. Choose Preferences from the Options menu, or write ╱-R.

2. Write your signature text on the lines provided (**Figure 9.10**). A blank line will automatically be inserted between a message's body text and signature. Tap OK.

To create a new Mail message:

1. From any folder view, tap the New button; you can also choose New from the Message window, or write ╱-N.

2. Write the email address of the email's recipients in the To field, separated by commas.

   To make entering addresses easier, choose Look Up (╱-L) from the Options menu, or tap the Lookup button on the full-screen field. Contacts from your Address Book that have email addresses specified will appear; begin writing a person's last name in the Look Up field, or scroll through the list. Select a name and tap the Add button.

3. If you want to CC ("carbon copy") other recipients, write their email addresses in the CC field, or perform a lookup.

4. Write a descriptive title in the Subj field.

5. In the Body field, write the text of your message (**Figure 9.11**).

✔ Tip

■ If you're sending to more addresses than are visible, tap a field's title (such as To or Subj) to view it in a full-screen.

Setting message details:

Tap the Details button to specify other options (**Figure 9.12**). The Priority and BCC ("blind carbon copy") features must be set for each message, whereas the others will apply to all subsequent emails.

◆ The Priority popup menu lets you choose between High, Normal, and Low.

◆ The BCC checkbox adds a BCC field to the New Message screen, where you can specify a recipient whose address won't be seen by the people in the To or CC fields.

◆ Mark the Signature checkbox to automatically add your signature text to the outgoing message.

◆ Marking the Confirm Read and Confirm Delivery checkboxes requests that you be notified when the recipient receives and reads your email, depending on whether your desktop email program supports it.

To "send" a message:

When you've written your message and specified its options, tap Send. This saves it in the Outbox, awaiting the next HotSync.

If the message isn't quite ready to be sent, choose Save Draft (✓-W) from the Message menu to store it in the Draft folder.

To edit a saved outgoing message:

1. Tap the folder popup menu and choose Outbox or Draft.

2. Tap the message you want to modify.

3. Tap the Edit button.

4. If you've edited a draft message, tap the Send button to move it to the Outbox when it's ready to be sent.

Figure 9.12 Only the Priority and BCC options need to be set for each message; the others apply globally.

Figure 9.13 The Reply to options save you the trouble of retyping each address of the people who received the original. Although not technically a "reply," you can also tap Forward to send the message to a new recipient.

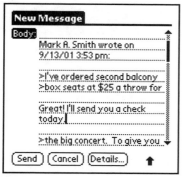

Figure 9.14 Replying gives you the option of including a copy of the original message, so your recipient can view your comments in context.

To read messages:

1. Tap an email's subject or author to read its contents.

2. Use the scrollbar at right to scan down the full text of the message.

3. The arrows in the lower-right corner take you to the previous (left arrow) and next (right arrow) emails in the list, without having to return to the main screen.

Due to the limited screen space, only the sender's name and the subject line are shown at the top of each message you read.

To view email header information:

Tap the Complete Header icon (the right-most one) in the upper-right corner. To return to the shorter view, tap the Abbreviated Header icon. The option you choose applies to all messages, not just the current email.

To forward or reply to a message:

1. After you've read a message, tap the Reply button to respond to the author.

2. The Reply Options window will appear (**Figure 9.13**). Choose whether you want to reply to the Sender of the message, or to All recipients who received it (including the sender). You can also tap Forward to direct the message to a new recipient.

3. Mark the Include original text checkbox to send the full message in your reply.

4. If you've chosen to include the text, mark Comment original text to automatically add greater-than symbols (>) before each line of the existing message to differentiate between the original author and your remarks (**Figure 9.14**).

5. Specify the recipients in the To and CC fields, write your message, then tap Send.

To file a message:

1. To store a message in the Filed folder, choose File from the Message menu, or write ✁-I.

2. If you want to store a copy in the Filed folder (instead of moving the original), tap the No button on the Message Filed Options screen (**Figure 9.15**).

To delete a message:

1. Tap the Delete button after reading a message to send it to the Deleted folder.

2. You will be asked if you really want to delete the message. To turn off the confirmation dialog box in the future, choose Preferences from the Options menu (or write ✁-R), and unmark the Confirm deleted message checkbox.

Deleted messages remain in the Deleted folder until you HotSync, at which point they're gone for good. This lets you go back and pull them out if you inadvertently killed the wrong messages. That means, however, that the ones you really wanted erased are still taking up memory until you HotSync.

To purge deleted messages:

If you need to free some space, select Purge Deleted from the Message menu (✁-E). Tap Yes to confirm your action.

✔ Tips

■ There's no easy way to delete all messages in Mail; they must be deleted individually. However, on the desktop, set the HotSync mail conduit to Desktop overwrites handheld. In your desktop mail program, move the Inbox items to a temporary folder, then HotSync.

■ Another option: use Mail Cleaner (http://www.wakuwaku.ne.jp/shuji/) to bulk-move messages between folders.

Figure 9.15 Mail includes only one custom message mailbox, Filed, but it's good for keeping your Inbox clean.

Figure 9.16 Too many email messages can quickly eat up your memory. Use the HotSync options to control which ones are transferred.

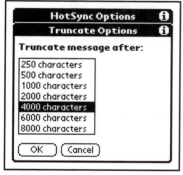

Figure 9.17 Another method of minimizing your email's memory use is to truncate incoming messages.

If you get as much email as I do, your handheld could fill up pretty quick. Fortunately, the settings in the HotSync Options dialog box help control the flow of email between the desktop and your organizer.

To configure HotSync options:

1. Choose HotSync Options from the Options menu, or write /-H. The HotSync options dialog box appears.

   Tap the All button to transfer everything between the two devices. Tap Send only to transfer only the messages in the Outbox folder to the desktop; no new messages are added to the handheld. Tap Unread to download only unread messages to your device (**Figure 9.16**).

2. Tap the Truncate button to specify a maximum character length per message to transfer from the desktop (**Figure 9.17**). This can be effective if you receive a lot of lengthy unsolicited bulk emails.

To filter incoming messages:

1. In the HotSync Options dialog box, tap the Filter button. This feature lets you set certain criteria for which emails get transferred from your desktop based on message content.

2. Mark Retrieve All High Priority to transfer messages tagged as top priority, regardless of their contents.

3. The popup menu in the lower half of the screen controls the filtering action based on the information you provide in the fields below. The Ignore Messages Containing item will not copy emails that meet the criteria you specify; the flipside is the Retrieve Only Msgs Containing item, which transfers emails only if they meet the criteria, ignoring the rest.

continues on next page

4. Enter the filter strings that Mail will use when analyzing the incoming messages. You can enter more than one entry per field (separated by commas), so entering billg@microsoft.com, sjobs@apple.com in the From field would catch a message that's written by either sender, not both (this is known as an implicit OR).

However, if you also add data to another field, Mail will only catch messages containing information in both fields (an implicit AND); entering billg@microsoft.com in the From field, and Newton in the Subj field will filter a message about Newton by billg@microsoft.com, but will ignore any other messages by the same sender (**Figure 9.18**).

Figure 9.18 Filters can either keep unwanted messages out, or only allow messages you deem important.

✔ Tips

■ You can assign different filter settings for local and remote (modem) HotSync connections. A more stringent set of filters for when you're on the road, for example, can save you money if you're paying hotel phone rates or using a calling card to connect to your desktop computer at home.

■ Although Mail has been set up to work in conjunction with your PC via HotSync, there's a way to use Mail by connecting directly from your handheld. Top Gun Postman (http://www.isaac.cs.berkeley.edu/pilot/TGpostman/) features Send mail, Get mail, and Both buttons to dial up your Internet Service Provider (ISP) and transfer email to Mail. Plus, it can optionally let you preview the sender, recipient, and subject information of each email, and it lets you decide if you want to download the entire message. The only downside is that the software is no longer supported...but it does work. You'll need a modem and much of the connection information described in the next section.

Direct-Dial Email

Sending and receiving email with the help of your PC is a great way to have it available for browsing and answering later. But suppose you're sitting in a taxi, stuck in the rush-hour crush of vehicles, and you realize that the most important email of your career is sitting dormant on the computer at the office? You could jump out of the cab in a rage and run screaming into the night—but that still does not solve the problem (and, depending on the city you live in, might not draw much attention). If you have a wireless modem and your handheld, however, you could compose and send the email, save your job, and catch up on the personal letters you haven't had time to write lately. It's not science fiction; the capability to send and receive email almost anywhere is very real.

In this section, I'm going to cover some of the basic elements required for setting up direct-dial email connections, rather than try to hit every feature of every email client. I'm using MultiMail Pro as the sample program to keep things simple, but note that the following features are available in other applications. Once you have a grasp of the basics, you'll be able to pick up the specifics of each program (many of which share features with Mail, described earlier) with no problems.

Which Email Client to Use?

Choosing an email program can be as personal a decision as choosing a flavor of Palm device. I rely on email, so it's important that the software works the way I do. Two examples include MultiMail Pro and Eudora.

MultiMail Pro (http://www.actualsoft.com/) supports SMTP/POP3 connections, and also interfaces with IMAP4 (Internet Message Access Protocol) servers, which store messages permanently on the mail server. It also sports a Quick Sync option, which lets you work offline, then synchronize your handheld mailboxes with the server's IMAP mailboxes. MultiMail Pro can also send and retrieve some types of file attachments.

Eudora (http://www.eudora.com/), has a clean interface, supports limited styled email (such as colors that are encoded using HTML markup), and synchronizes with the desktop versions of Eudora.

Depending on how you access the Internet, your choice may be initially made—most modem hardware vendors include versions of email software with their modem.

As with any hardware or software decision, consider the option that best suits your needs, rather than which bells and whistles are available.

Direct-Dial Modem and Network Setup

The first thing you'll need is a modem (see the beginning of this chapter). Since I tend to split my time among three main locations during business hours, I prefer to connect with a wireless modem where available, avoiding the hassles of finding a phone line and dialing into my ISP's bank of modems.

The next essential task is to configure your Modem and Network preferences (accessed via the Prefs application). (See Chapter 2.)

To check email, you'll need a POP or IMAP server: the machine that you connect to when checking for new incoming email. Check your desktop email application for these settings, or contact your ISP.

To send email, you need to access an SMTP (Simple Mail Transport Protocol) server that directs your messages through the complicated paths of the Internet. This server is often the same machine that you specified in the POP or IMAP setup, but not always (as you can see, it's worth setting up a good relationship with your ISP to handle questions).

To set up POP:

1. In MultiMail Pro, choose Server from the Options menu, or write /-M.

2. Most modern email clients support more than one mailbox, so you can manage multiple email accounts using the same program. Tap the number (1–8) of the mailbox you want to set up.

3. Write the name or IP number of the server in the Server field (**Figure 9.19**).

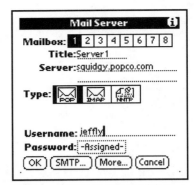

Figure 9.19 POP is the protocol that handles your incoming email. If you don't assign a password, you will be asked to enter it each time you connect.

Figure 9.20 Direct-dial connections require you to specify an SMTP server that will route your outgoing mail.

4. Enter your user name in the Username field. In many cases, this is the same user name you entered in the Network preferences screen (see Chapter 2). However, if you use several different addresses that point to one core address, enter the main one here. You only have to enter the user name, not the server name ("jeffers" instead of "jeffers@necoffee.com").

5. Tap the Password button to enter the password used to access your mail. If you don't specify a password, you will be prompted for it each time you connect.

6. When you're finished, tap OK.

To set up SMTP:

1. In MultiMail Pro, select Server from the Options menu, or write ✐-M.

2. Tap the mailbox number (1–8) of the configuration you want to edit.

3. Tap the SMTP button (**Figure 9.20**). The SMTP Options dialog box appears.

4. In the Server field, write the outgoing server's name or IP number.

5. Enter your name in the Name field as you wish it to appear in recipients' emails.

6. Write your email address as it will appear to others in the Email field. Note that this may not match the user name you use to connect with. Tap OK.

DIRECT-DIAL MODEM AND NETWORK SETUP

Connecting to Your ISP

Dial-up email clients rely on the Network preferences screen to establish an initial connection with your ISP's servers. If you want to open a connection before working in your email program, tap the Connect button (**Figure 9.21**).

If you don't connect manually, the clients will automatically initiate a connection when you send or retrieve mail if you've properly specified the settings. Most of the programs also include a link, such as Network Panel (✓-W) under the Options menu in MultiMail Pro, that takes you directly to the Network preferences screen.

Also, some programs, like MultiMail Pro, include the capability to filter incoming mail. This helps block unwanted spam, or mailing list messages that you don't want to download to your handheld.

To retrieve mail headers and/or messages:

1. Tap the Get or Both buttons to initiate a connection.

2. Tap the Headers Only button to download only the incoming message headers. This lets you preview the sender and subject of an email, then decide if it's something you want to download (**Figure 9.22**).

3. Tap the Headers+Bodies button to download all pending emails without reviewing them first.

To filter email:

1. Choose Filters from the Options menu.

2. Tap the Add button.

3. Name the filter and specify conditions to scan for (**Figure 9.23**). Tap OK, then the Done button.

Figure 9.21 The Palm OS's Network preferences panel controls dial-up Internet access. Here, I've accessed it from within MultiMail Pro, which is why you see a Done button (which takes you back to the email application).

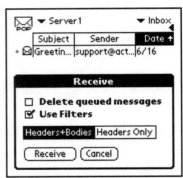

Figure 9.22 If you're on a speedy connection, consider using Headers+ Bodies to download full messages; otherwise, Headers Only quickly grabs the address and subject information.

Figure 9.23 Don't let spammers win. Set up filters to block unwanted email.

Figure 9.24 MultiMail Pro supports a variety of email attachments, ranging from Memo Pad records (shown here) to JPEG images.

To attach files to outgoing emails:

1. After tapping the New button to create a new message, tap the paperclip-icon button, then tap Attach. The Attachments dialog box appears.

2. Choose a file format from the Select popup menu (**Figure 9.24**).

To send or save mail:

1. After composing your outgoing mail, tap the Send button to dispatch it immediately. If you have a connection established, that message will be sent; if not, MultiMail Pro will dial your ISP.

2. Tap Send Later if you want to store it in the Outbox for sending later (switch to the Outbox and tap Send when you're ready).

✔ Tip

■ MultiMail Pro can send and receive Palm OS database files (.PDB) and applications (.PRC). This means that you can share a file with someone by sending it to them via email. If they receive it using Multi-Mail Pro on their handheld, they have the option of installing the file from the email message, rather than installing via a Hot-Sync operation.

The Palm.Net Network

Even with its built-in transmitter, the Palm VII and VIIx would be just regular organizers without the Palm.Net network that supports its access. Palm.Net piggybacks on Bell South's Mobitex Network, a nationwide (covering about 260 highly populated areas of the U.S.) wireless network used for shuttling data for pagers and similar devices. When you lift the Palm VII antenna, the transceiver finds the nearest broadcast tower and relays your data requests to the rest of the Palm.Net network.

As you can see in **Table 9.1**, Palm.Net service isn't cheap. However, although 300K doesn't sound like much data, Palm's engineers have gone to great lengths to maximize every byte (see Chapter 10). You can always view the status of your account using the Palm.Net application (**Figure 9.25**), or by going to http://wireless.palm.net/.

Diagnostics

To determine the current strength of the incoming Palm.Net signal, plus view the location of the nearest radio tower, launch the Diagnostics application. A display of five stair-stepped bars indicates how strong the wireless signal is.

✔ Tip

■ The network identifies you online by your Palm VII's serial number and the location of the nearest relay tower. That means, however, that you can easily be pinpointed. If you're uncomfortable with broadcasting your location, go to the Preferences application and choose the Wireless screen from the popup menu in the upper-right corner. Mark the Warn when sending ID or location information checkbox to get the option of cancelling any transaction that would send this info.

Figure 9.25 Launch the Palm.Net application to access your account to see how much data you've transferred.

Table 9.1

Palm.Net Pricing (as of August 2001)				
PLAN	MONTHLY COST	KILOBYTES INCLUDED	ADDED KILOBYTE	APPROX. SCREENS
Basic	$9.99	50K	$0.20/K	150
Expanded	$24.99	150K	$0.20/K	450
Volume Unlimited	$44.99	Unlimited	n/a	Unlimited

Figure 9.26 iMessenger resembles the bare-bones Mail program; only those three little lines in the Check & Send button indicate a wireless email client.

Figure 9.27 Tap the message status icon to display a contextual menu with options for acting on the message.

Email with iMessenger

As we become more connected via email, it can be a necessity (or a luxury) to flip up the antenna and check our messages. When you register for the Palm.Net service, you're given an email account that works with the Palm VII's built-in email client, iMessenger. Functionally, iMessenger is almost a clone of the built-in Palm Mail program; reading and writing messages is the same (**Figure 9.26**).

The downside to iMessenger is that it only checks your Palm.Net email, and the mail doesn't synchronize with your desktop mail application. However, iMessenger is tied into the Palm VII so well that email becomes truly effortless. You don't even need to configure any basic mail server settings; it's already set up for the Palm.Net service.

To check and send email using iMessenger:

1. Launch iMessenger. Be sure the Palm VII antenna is raised.

2. Tap the Check & Send button.

✔ Tips

- In the main window, tap the icon to the left of a message to activate a contextual popup menu containing commands for performing actions on the message (**Figure 9.27**).

- By default, lifting the antenna connects to the Palm.Net network and displays the Palm.Net category in the Applications screen. AntennaeHack (http://www.palmgear.com/) adds the ability to launch programs or even check and send your messages automatically when the antenna is raised.

- Choose Show Log from the Options menu to view a list of transferred emails.

Checking other email accounts

Although iMessenger only transfers email using your Palm.Net account, third-party options enable you to check your existing POP or IMAP email accounts. ThinAirMail (http://www.thinairapps.com/) and iPopper (http://www.corsoft.net/) store your account information on their servers, which are used to grab your email from your regular mail server when you check your mail from the Palm VII (**Figures 9.28** and **9.29**).

The advantage to these programs is that the email coming to you still shows up in your desktop mail client (since you're just reading the mail from another source, not redirecting it entirely). Be aware, though, that you may use up your monthly kilobyte quota faster by accessing multiple email accounts.

There are also PQAs available to access Web-based email services such as Yahoo, Hotmail, and Excite. See http://www.palm.net/email_solutions/ for more information.

Storing Palm.Net email on your desktop

It's impractical to store all your iMessenger email on the Palm VII, so getting the messages to the desktop becomes a high priority. Unfortunately, there's no easy way to do that, but there are two workarounds.

◆ To have outgoing messages automatically sent to your POP account, go to the Palm.Net Web page (http://wireless.palm.net/), click the My Account link, and enter an address for the iMessenger Blind Carbon Copy feature.

◆ You can open the iMessenger data file on your PC (called iMessengerDB.prc, in your user folder) with a word processor or text editor to view the contents of your emails.

Figure 9.28 ThinAirMail checks your POP or IMAP mailboxes from a Palm VII.

Figure 9.29 iPopper includes the ability to filter incoming messages from your POP account.

Figure 9.30 Write quick notes that are sent immediately.

Figure 9.31 Messages can be sent immediately, or saved for editing later.

SMS Text Messaging

I don't mind a good long conversation now and then, but sometimes I need to keep things short. Using SMS (included in the Palm Mobile Internet Kit), you can send brief text messages to GSM-capable phones or to Internet email addresses.

To send an SMS text message:

1. Launch the SMS application. It acts much like the Palm Mail program, with mailboxes for new, sent, deleted, archived, and draft messages.

2. Tap the New button to create a new message. Enter the recipient's phone number in the To field, or tap the To button to perform an Address Book lookup.

3. Write your message in the lines provided (**Figure 9.30**).

4. Tap the Send button to dispatch the message immediately, or tap Outbox to store it for later (**Figure 9.31**).

✔ Tip

■ You can insert a signature to your messages. Choose Add Signature from the Options menu or write ╱-Z.

WEB ACCESS

When someone first suggested that I could access the World Wide Web using my handheld, I thought he was out of his mind. What, take the graphics-rich Web and compress it onto that little screen? *Right.*

Shows how much I knew at the time. With a modem and the right software, getting onto the Web from your Palm device is now no big deal (and quite luxurious compared to most Web-enabled cellular phones). You can even use Palm Query Applications (PQAs), the miniscule Web-clipping programs first popularized on the wireless Palm VII handheld on nearly any device.

If you don't have a modem, you can still download Web content during the HotSync process using AvantGo. I find that I read articles from a handful of sites on my handheld that I normally wouldn't remember to look up when I'm at my computer—which is perfect for the times that I'm waiting in line, stuck in traffic, or otherwise stalled.

Browse the Web via HotSync: AvantGo

Of all the cool things a handheld can do, the most fun to demonstrate to people is browsing the Web, which can often work faster over a 14.4 Kbps connection than their expensive multimedia-tricked PCs at home.

As with email, there are two approaches to getting Web content on your handheld: HotSync and direct-connect. Using HotSync to connect is great for saving news stories and other longer documents to be viewed later; having a direct connection is helpful when you need to look up information on the spot.

Using AvantGo (http://www.avantgo.com/), you download content from various channels when you perform a HotSync, then view it on your handheld (**Figure 10.1**).

Figure 10.1 AvantGo offers news stories from several key content providers.

To set up AvantGo:

1. Download the AvantGo client software from the company's Web site, and run the installer.

2. After the desktop software is installed, the AvantGo QuickStart process will open in your default Web browser (**Figure 10.2**). Follow the directions to choose the channels you wish to subscribe to; you'll have to perform a HotSync twice before you're finished.

✔ Tip

■ The AvantGo installation software may have been included with your device. Check the CD-ROM that came with your handheld before downloading AvantGo from the Web.

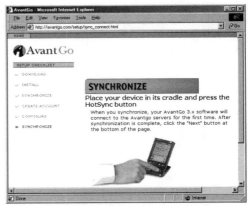

Figure 10.2 Although the process of setting up AvantGo involves multiple steps, the Web-browser interface makes the process easier. From here, choose the content channels you'd like to subscribe to.

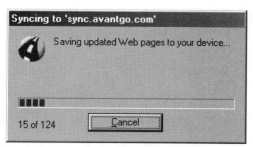

Figure 10.3 When you perform a HotSync, AvantGo downloads the most recent headlines and articles from the channels you specified during setup.

Figure 10.4 Tap a channel name to view the contents that were downloaded during HotSync.

Figure 10.5 AvantGo acts like the Web browser on your desktop, with back, forward, and home buttons in the upper-right corner of the screen.

To connect to the Web:

Once you've chosen your channels and installed the software, HotSync the handheld—that's it. When the AvantGo conduit springs into action, it will connect to the Web and download the most recent news and information (**Figure 10.3**).

To view AvantGo content on your handheld:

1. Tap the AvantGo program icon to launch AvantGo.

2. Tap a channel from the list on the home screen to view its content (**Figure 10.4**). The home icon (🏠) takes you back to the main list, while the arrows beside it move back and forward as in most Web browsers (**Figure 10.5**).

3. Tap an article title to read its full contents.

✔ Tip

■ AvantGo does its best to format a Web page's content to suit the small Palm device screen. For this reason, table cells aren't displayed by default. However, if you want to get a better feel for how a page is laid out (since designers often use tables as page structure), or just want to view tabular data coherently, choose Preferences under the Options menu (or write ✏-R), and mark the Show Tables checkbox. You'll find yourself scrolling horizontally as well as top to bottom, but the contents may be more readable.

BROWSE THE WEB VIA HOTSYNC

To add new channels:

1. On your PC, connect to the AvantGo site (http://www.avantgo.com/).

2. Browse the selection of available channels grouped into several categories (**Figure 10.6**). Click the Add Channel icon to add it to your list of channels.

3. HotSync your device.

To remove channels:

1. In the AvantGo application, choose Channel Manager from the Channels menu (**Figure 10.7**).

2. Check the channels you wish to delete, then tap the Clear button.

3. HotSync your device.
   You can also remove channels from your account at the AvantGo Web site.

✔ Tips

■ You can add any Web site to your list of active channels. Click the Custom Channel link at AvantGo's Web site and enter the URL for a site.

■ AvantGo supports active loading of Web sites if you have a modem connection. Use the Connect option in the Channels menu to initiate a connection (if you're not already online), then choose Modem Sync from the same menu.

■ Try not to go crazy when adding AvantGo channels to your profile—having too many can substantially increase your download times, and in a worst-case scenario, cause the HotSync process to time out before completing.

Figure 10.6 Edit, add, or delete channels using the AvantGo Web site.

Figure 10.7 Mark the channels you no longer wish to read and they'll be deleted at the next HotSync operation.

Figure 10.8 I'm tired of typing these common characters on my desktop's Web browser, much less writing them in Graffiti, so it's nice to see shortcuts for them in Blazer's Open Page dialog.

Figure 10.9 Blazer displays Web images and text. To scroll around the page, tap the stylus and drag.

Direct-Dial Web Browsing

Before I launch into the wonders of handheld Web access, let me first say that if you're used to browsing the Web using a PC, you might be underwhelmed. We've grown accustomed to highly visual Web pages, with multiple graphics and scrolling Java whatsits. You're not going to get the same experience on a 160 by 160-pixel screen.

What you will get is extremely portable access to information anywhere in the world—not all of it just text-based, either. Using Blazer (http://www.handspring.com/software/blazer_overview.jhtml), you can view 16-bit grayscale images without any extra software. For this discussion, I'll be using Blazer as the sample program, though other programs such as EudoraWeb (http://www.eudora.com/) are also available.

To connect to a Web site:

1. Choose Open from the Page menu, write ╱-O, or tap the open icon (🗁). The Open Page dialog box appears.

2. Write the destination address in the field provided. Choose an item from the buttons to insert commonly used URL text (**Figure 10.8**). If you previously visited a site, the address is inserted as you write it.

3. Tap the Go button to access the site.

Navigating Blazer

◆ Blazer's interface is wonderfully minimal. Tap the scrollbars at the right edge of the screen to scroll vertically. Better yet, tap anywhere on the screen (except on a link, of course) and drag—the contents move under your stylus (**Figure 10.9**).

◆ Links are marked with dotted underlines in the text; tap them to jump to their destination URLs.

To save a bookmark:

1. To keep a page location in memory for accessing later, choose Add Bookmark (✓-A) from the Save menu. The Bookmarks dialog box appears.

2. Assign a category, or change the name or URL of the bookmark.

3. Tap OK.

To edit bookmarks:

1. Choose Bookmarks (✓-B) from the Edit menu, or tap the Bookmark icon (📄), to access the Bookmarks dialog box (**Figure 10.10**). You can edit a bookmark's name and URL by highlighting it and tapping the Edit button. Also available are buttons to create a new bookmark (New), or jump to (Go) bookmarked URLs.

2. Tap Done to exit.

✔ Tips

■ Blazer can display images in up to 16 shades of gray or thousands of colors, depending on your device. That takes more processing power, though. To speed up image rendering, go to Blazer's preferences (choose Preferences from the Options menu, or write ✓-R) and change the setting in the Images popup menu.

■ The only thing I don't like about Blazer is that it immediately assumes that you have an Internet connection when you launch it. If you don't, you get an error. To prevent Blazer from trying to make a connection right away, go into Preferences and mark the checkbox labeled Ask before establishing Internet connection (**Figure 10.11**).

Figure 10.10 Bookmarks make it easy to access frequently viewed Web sites.

Figure 10.11 Keep Blazer from attempting an Internet connection whenever it's launched.

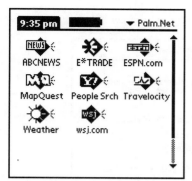

Figure 10.12 Palm Query Applications appear in a new Palm.Net category. PQAs are identified by three "energy burst" lines in their icons.

Palm Query Applications

If you have a Palm VII or the Palm Mobile Internet Kit, you can run Palm Query Applications (PQAs). Each of these small programs is, in effect, a customized Web form that interacts with servers on the Internet to deliver specific information (**Figure 10.12**).

Web clipping

In order to minimize the amount of data passing over the network (and thereby costing you money), PQAs employ a technique called "Web clipping."

Unlike Web browsing, which involves kilobytes of images and code designed to make a Web page appear on a regular computer screen, Web clipping delivers only the essentials. The images all reside within the PQA, so when you submit a query using an application, the only data going out are the few bytes required to process your request and the bytes to deliver the response. When you're searching for driving directions, for example, only the beginning and ending addresses are sent over the network, and only the text result returns.

The Web clipping interface

Web clipping essentially works as one application, with PQAs acting as individual components. For that reason, all PQAs share the same interface elements (**Figures 10.13** and **10.14**).

◆ **Status indicator.** When a query is in progress, the title bar changes to indicate what's happening (such as "Sending" or "Receiving").

◆ **Stop button.** Tapping the Stop button during a query aborts the action. The button also pulses as a visual indicator of an active network connection.

◆ **Back button.** Like in a Web browser, the Back button takes you to the last Web clipping screen.

◆ **Signal strength indicator.** The stair-stepped icon displays the current signal strength.

◆ **Network access indicator.** Three lines beside a link or within a button indicate that tapping it will initiate a network connection to retrieve the information.

◆ **Key icon.** Tapping a button with a key icon indicates that the data transfer will be securely encrypted.

Status indicator *Stop button* *Back button*

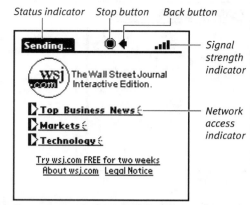

Signal strength indicator

Network access indicator

Figure 10.13 Web clipping applications share the same interface elements.

Figure 10.14 Secure transactions are marked with a key icon and encrypted.

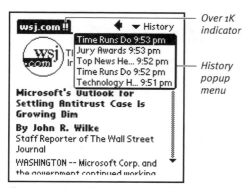

Over 1K indicator

History popup menu

Figure 10.15 Jump back to recent Web clipping pages with the History menu.

Figure 10.16 Tapping a PQA's title bar expands it to display the number of bytes transferred to access the page.

◆ **History popup menu.** Tap this menu to quickly go back several screens' worth of Web clippings (**Figure 10.15**).

◆ **Bytes received.** After a screen has loaded, tap the title bar to see how many bytes were received (**Figure 10.16**). If the number exceeds 1K (1,024 bytes), two exclamation points (!!) appear in the title.

✔ Tips

■ Since PQAs are all smaller components of the larger Web clipping feature, the Back button works between PQAs, and can even be used to get back to the Applications screen.

■ If you want to store lots of PQA applications, but only use a few on a regular basis, recategorize the lesser-used ones to a new category such as "Palm.Net2." That way, the most frequently used ones will appear when you lift the antenna, without the clutter of the rest.

Recommended PQAs

Like any other category of Palm software, developers are hot to create new PQAs. Here are a noteworthy few.

MapQuest

MapQuest (http://www.mapquest.com/) is one of my favorites. If I misplace my directions, or just end up completely lost, I can enter starting and ending addresses and find my way (**Figure 10.17**). It also includes some U.S. traffic reports.

Moviefone

How many times have you wanted to see a movie but didn't have a newspaper or telephone at hand to look up show times? With moviefone (http://www.moviefone.com/), enter your zip code to find the closest theaters and schedules.

Weather.com

The Weather Channel (http://www.weather.com/services/) was one of the first to release a PQA, in this case a nifty application for getting the latest weather conditions.

Starbucks Coffee Store Locator

Okay, this isn't an "essential" PQA (http://www.starbucks.com/), but it's come in handy a few times when I'm staying at a hotel that serves particularly bad coffee (**Figure 10.18**).

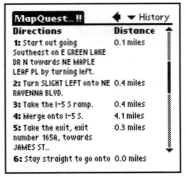

Figure 10.17 People will think that you finally know your way around town.

Figure 10.18 It's the sign of the apocalypse, but good to the last drop. They could have made this simpler by just displaying, "At the next corner."

PAGES, FAXES, NEWSGROUPS, TELNET

11

Although email and the World Wide Web garner much of the attention these days, they aren't the only outlets for communicating with the outside world. Using your Palm device, you can send faxes, read newsgroup messages, or interact with Internet servers or private bulletin board systems (BBSes) using a Telnet command-line interface. In some cases you'll need a modem to connect directly to these services, which may just be the incentive for buying one if you were undecided before.

Sending Pages

If you have a modem connected to your handheld, you can send alphanumeric pages directly from it using PageNOW! (http://www.markspace.com/)—handy if you're on the road and don't want to haul out your laptop. (Isn't it amazing how laptops are starting to sound like large and bulky items now?)

To send a page using PageNOW!:

1. Select Users from the popup menu in the upper-right corner to enter the information for each person you would page. If their paging service isn't listed in the Service popup menu on the Users screen, select Services from the upper-right popup menu and enter that information.

2. Return to the Send Page screen (again, from the popup menu at the upper-right corner), and use the Send To popup menu to choose a recipient.

3. Compose your message in the Message field. PageNOW! keeps track of the character count, and how many pages (screens) will be displayed on the person's pager (**Figure 11.1**).

4. Tap Send to transmit, or Send Later to store the message in your Out box until you're ready to send it (**Figure 11.2**).

✔ Tip

■ PageNOW! 2.0 supports using GSM and PCS cellular phones with integrated modems, and sending pages over TCP and SNPP protocols.

Figure 11.1 The Message field tracks how many characters you've used to avoid sending a truncated page.

Figure 11.2 Tapping the Send button in the main screen dials the paging service and sends your message.

Figure 11.3 Fax Memo Pad documents directly from your handheld.

Figure 11.4 Tapping the Preview button displays a rendition of what the page will look like. The letters are chunkier than they will appear due to the handheld's screen resolution.

Figure 11.5 When you're ready to fire off your masterpiece, hit Send.

Faxing

Although email is often more convenient for transmitting electronic data, sometimes it can be easier to send a fax. Mark/Space's Fax (http://www.markspace.com/) lets you turn Memo Pad items or Clipboard text into printed pages.

To send a fax using Fax:

1. Select Memo Pad, Clipboard, or Saved Fax (see step 3 below) from the Source popup menu. If grabbing a memo, scroll through the list and highlight the one you want to send (**Figure 11.3**).

2. Specify a recipient by entering their information in the To and Number fields. Or, tap the Lookup button to scan your Address Book for fax numbers.

3. To see what the page will look like, tap the Preview button prior to sending. To save the fax for sending later, tap the Save button (**Figure 11.4**).

4. Tap Send to dispatch the fax (**Figure 11.5**).

✔ Tips

- Fax's preferences allow you to specify the resolution (normal or fine), plus set parameters such as the margin measurements and character size. Choose Page Setup from the Options menu.

- Fax includes settings for use with cellular GSM modems, so you may not even need a standard modem. However, it currently won't work with a Palm VII or an Omni-Sky modem, which doesn't produce regular modem tones (which communicates with its wireless network directly via TCP/IP).

Reading Newsgroups

Newsgroups are essentially large bulletin board systems (BBSes) covering nearly any topic you can imagine, where participants post public messages and discussions. For people who subscribe to newsgroups, reading and replying to them on a Palm device is a great method of staying current on discussions. PalmReader (http://www.mindspring.com/~lior/PalmReader.html) works through a conduit on the PC; Yanoff (http://yanoff.sourceforge.net/) connects directly if you have a modem. I'll use PalmReader as an example.

To access newsgroups using PalmReader:

1. After installing the desktop conduit, launch the PalmReader application (**Figure 11.6**) and tap the Settings button to specify your news server and which groups to subscribe to.

2. Tap the Add button to subscribe to a group, like alt.comp.sys.palmtops.pilot.

3. HotSync your organizer.

4. Launch PalmReader on the handheld, and tap the name of the newsgroup to view a list of messages (**Figure 11.7**).

5. To read a message, tap its subject title. Unread messages are marked with a dot to the left of the name.

6. Choose Reply from the Commands menu to write a response to a message; choose Post to create a new message. Both will be transferred at the next HotSync.

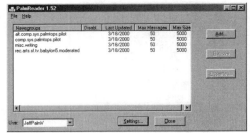

Figure 11.6 PalmReader downloads newsgroup messages on your PC and transfers them at HotSync.

Figure 11.7 Keep up with the latest gossip and discussions.

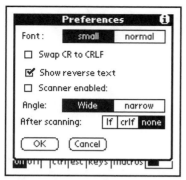

Figure 11.8 Telnet connections often assume that you're using a screen much larger than a Palm screen. Use the preferences in Mocha Pocket Telnet to make it more readable for you.

Figure 11.9 Mocha Pocket Telnet gives you a command-line interface for communicating with Internet servers. The proxy box in the lower-right corner scrolls the screen.

Telnet

Telnet opens a direct TCP connection to a remote host computer, and is often used to open a command-line "shell" session (a minimal text-based interface to the stored data) on a system running Unix or another multi-user operating system. Telnet is also often used to connect to a dedicated device like a network router.

I'm going to use Mocha Pocket Telnet (http://www.mochasoft.dk/) as an example, but you can also find Online (http://www.markspace.com/).

Using Mocha Pocket Telnet:

1. Configure Mocha Pocket Telnet's settings by choosing the topics under the Options menu. There isn't enough space here to cover them all; essentially, they control how the text is displayed onscreen, and how the data transferred between your Palm and the server interacts (**Figure 11.8**).

   Choose Network from the Options menu, or write ╱-N to specify the name of the server you wish to contact. Fill in the Host field and tap OK.

2. To connect, tap the On button at the lower left (**Figure 11.9**). You will be prompted with a login; write your user name, then the carriage return character (╱). Alternately, you can select Keyboard from the Edit menu, or write ╱-K, to bring up the Palm OS onscreen keyboard. Write your password in a similar manner (some servers don't display the password as it's being written, but don't worry—the data is being sent).

3. Write your commands instead of typing them based on the options you are given. Use the Ctl and Esc buttons at the bottom to simulate those keys.

TELNET

PROTECTING YOUR DATA

At a conference I attended, one of the keynote speakers lost his handheld during the event. Tragic, yes, but not because he was missing a cool gadget. As a colleague mentioned to me, "There are people in this room who would *kill* for the phone numbers in that PalmPilot."

Most of us probably don't carry the private contact information of industry leaders and heads of state in our organizers, but there are plenty of phone numbers, appointments, and memos that we'd rather not share with just anyone. The solution is to implement a security system to safeguard your data.

Palm's Built-In Security

The Palm OS provides two methods of securing the data on your handheld, accessible through the Security application (see Chapter 2 for instructions on how to use Security).

Current Privacy setting

You can mark records from the built-in programs as Private. When the Current Privacy setting is set to Hide, private records are invisible. To view them, you need to return to the Security application, tap the Show button, and enter your password (**Figure 12.1**).

Under Palm OS 3.5 and higher, private records can also appear masked, so that you don't forget about private records entirely (**Figure 12.2**). (You don't want to know how often I've re-created an appointment or contact that already existed but was hidden.)

This system is simple and, for the most part, effective. A password-protection scheme won't keep out someone intent on getting your data, but it will likely deter most people.

However, there are a couple of things about private records that bother me: if you make them visible, then forget to hide them again, even your most ingenious password won't make the data secure; plus, I just don't like the process of changing the setting in earlier versions of the operating system, where you have to navigate to the Security application each time you want to make a change (**Figure 12.3**). Fortunately, Palm OS 3.5 and 4.0 features the ability to change the global security setting from within any application that supports the new Security menu item.

Figure 12.1 The Security application uses password-protection to hide private data and lock the handheld (Palm OS 3.1 shown).

Figure 12.2 Palm OS 3.5 offers a third security viewing option, Mask Records.

Figure 12.3 You have to jump between applications to activate and deactivate the feature if you're not running Palm OS 3.5 or later.

Figure 12.4 The Owner screen (which you set up in the Preferences program) is used when powering on your handheld after using the Lock & Turn Off feature.

Figure 12.5 LockMe! provides more control over the Palm OS lock feature.

The good news is that there are a few good alternatives that make Security less cumbersome. SafeHack automatically hides or masks private records when your Handheld powers off. Although not directly related to security, SwitchHack avoids jumping in and out of Applications by providing program launching shortcuts (see Chapter 8 for more on both utilities). TealLock (covered later this chapter), provides SafeHack's functionality, in addition to a host of other security settings.

Locking the Handheld

The other built-in security feature is the ability to lock your device by requiring users to enter the Security password before they can access anything (**Figure 12.4**). This is invoked by tapping the Lock & Turn Off button in the Security application.

However, like the Current Privacy setting, this feature's usefulness is somewhat diminished by the number of taps it takes to actually activate it. Under Palm OS 4.0, you can use the Auto Lock Handheld feature to specify when to lock the device (such as when powered off, or at a specific time).

But if you own an older handheld, third-party software saves the day. Most of the "launcher" utilities that replace the Applications program (see Chapter 2) include an option to power off and lock the handheld.

For more control, turn to LockMe! (http://wwwipd.ira.uka.de/~witte/pilot/lockme/), a small freeware utility that lets you specify a time to periodically engage the locking mechanism; tap the Lock every popup menu to choose the duration, and then choose a beginning time from the Starting at popup menu (**Figure 12.5**).

PALM'S BUILT-IN SECURITY

Custom Security Options with TealLock

One reason I like TealLock (http://www.tealpoint.com/) is that it extends the Palm OS's security capabilities—sort of like the Security application on steroids. At the same time, it centralizes many of the functions offered by other utilities in one application.

To set up and activate TealLock:

1. Launch TealLock from the Applications screen (**Figure 12.6**).

2. Tap the User Password button to assign a password. Enter it again when prompted to confirm your choice.

3. Tap the TealLock Status On button to activate TealLock. The device will reset to load TealLock's features at startup.

Tapping the Lock and Off button turns off the handheld; when you power it on again, you're presented with a customizable screen where you enter your password to gain access to the device (**Figure 12.7**).

To change the Lock Screen image:

1. From TealLock's main screen, tap the Change Settings button to display the TealLock Settings window.

2. Tap the Image button under Owner/ Lock Screen.

3. Tap the Select button or write the name of a TealPaint database containing images you'd like to use for the lock screen (see Chapter 13 for information about TealPaint).

4. Mark the Use Image checkbox to activate the custom screen feature. Tap OK.

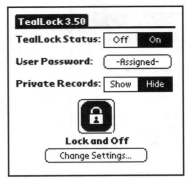

Figure 12.6 Similar to the Security application, TealLock offers more settings by tapping Change Settings.

Figure 12.7 TealLock's locked screen includes the date and time, a custom image, and the option to show or hide private records after tapping OK.

Figure 12.8 Enter the text that you would like to be displayed on Teal-Lock's lock screen.

Figure 12.9 TealLock's activation settings are the heart of its usefulness.

To change the Lock Screen text:

1. Tap the Change Settings button if you're not already on the TealLock Settings screen.

2. Write the text as you'd like it to appear. Use carriage return characters (⁄) to move the text down the screen and avoid overlapping your image (**Figure 12.8**).

3. Mark the checkboxes below the text field to specify the text style.

4. Tap OK.

To configure when to hide private records:

1. From the TealLock Settings screen, tap the Hide When button under Private Records to display the Activation Settings dialog box.

2. Mark the checkboxes of the features you'd like to use. You can choose to hide records depending on a time range, when the handheld turns off, or when you write a ShortCut; specify the character to use by writing it in the Shortcut field (**Figure 12.9**). Tap OK when you're done.

To configure when to show private records:

1. From the TealLock Settings screen, tap the Show When button under the Private Records heading.

2. Specify a ShortCut character that will display hidden records by writing it in the ShortCut field. Tap OK when you're done.

To set up a locking schedule:

1. From the TealLock Settings screen, tap the Lock When button under the Locking Screen heading. You'll find the same variables here as in the Hide When/Show When activation settings windows (see previous page).

2. Specify a time period to automatically lock the handheld, specify a ShortCut, or set the lock to engage when the power shuts off (**Figure 12.10**).

3. Tap OK when you're done.

Advanced TealLock settings

TealLock includes more security settings than I have room to detail here. Tap the Advanced button on the TealLock Settings screen to set options such as disabling the silkscreen buttons or the serial port, specifying a time to expire the current password, and others (**Figure 12.11**). You can also encrypt certain record databases when the device is locked for yet more security (**Figure 12.12**).

✔ Tips

- A security flaw was found in Palm OS 3.5 and earlier that lets someone access a locked handheld using a serial cable and debugging commands. To avoid this, enable the Lock out serial port checkbox in TealLock's Advanced Settings screen.

- If TealLock doesn't provide the peace of mind you're looking for, consider more of a "scorched-earth" approach: PDABomb (http://products.asynchrony.com/PDABomb/). Using PDABomb, you can specify that if the correct password isn't submitted within a period of time or number of attempts, the handheld's memory gets completely erased! That'll teach someone to try to pinch your data.

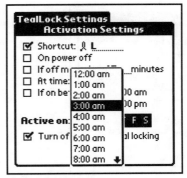

Figure 12.10 Tap the At time popup menu to configure automatic activation.

Figure 12.11 You control many aspects of how TealLock secures your data.

Figure 12.12 For even more security, encrypt databases when the handheld is locked.

When the Palm OS Security Isn't Necessarily Secure

The Palm OS's built-in security features are good enough for most of us. If you're concerned about having your handheld lost or stolen, setting up a lock screen and private records will probably keep unwanted eyes away from your data. Unfortunately, anyone with access to your desktop computer can easily read your records, whether they're marked Private or not.

Figure 12.13 You can access your records using a standard text editor or word processor.

As mentioned in Chapter 2, your data is stored in a number of folders within a user folder that resembles your organizer's device name. The bad news is that those files are not encrypted, scrambled, or otherwise protected. Try the following steps in Windows.

To read your "private" data:

1. Make sure you have some records marked private, and that Hide Private Records is selected under the View menu in Palm Desktop.

2. If you're running Palm Desktop for Windows, open a text-editing application

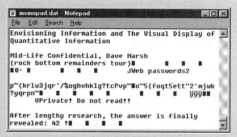

Figure 12.14 The so-called "private" record at the bottom of the screen is quite visible.

such as Notepad. (The Palm Desktop for Macintosh stores all of its records in one file, so this technique doesn't apply if you're on a Mac. Don't get smug, however: the Mac Palm Desktop doesn't support hidden records at all, so everything marked Private is visible!)

3. Choose Open from the File menu and navigate to your user folder.

4. Open your user folder (still within the text editor's Open dialog box), then open one of the folders corresponding to the built-in applications (**Figure 12.13**).

5. Make sure Files of type is set to All Files (*.*), and select a .dat file (such as memopad.dat).

6. All of your memos will be viewable, interspersed with a bit of garbage characters. Scroll down to read your "private" information (**Figure 12.14**).

Palm Desktop Security

So what can you do to protect your data on the desktop? In addition to optionally hiding and showing private records, Palm Desktop also can require a user to enter her password to gain access to her data (**Figure 12.15**).

To keep people from snooping on your hard drive, you may want to look into purchasing a professional security program that lets you encrypt your handheld files (or folders). You would have to decrypt them before you launched Palm Desktop or performed a HotSync, but that may be a fair tradeoff if you're particularly concerned about security.

To set up Palm Desktop password access (Windows):

1. From the Tools menu, choose Options. The Options dialog box appears.

2. Click the Security tab and mark the Require password to access desktop data checkbox (**Figure 12.16**).

3. Click OK.

✔ Tip

■ Macintosh Palm Desktop offers no such access security. If you're concerned, however, you can use the Apple File Security utility under Mac OS 9 to encrypt your user file. Locate the User Data file within your user folder, then drag it to the Apple File Security application, or Control-click and choose Encrypt from the contextual menu. When you launch Palm Desktop the next time, a blank user will be created because your user data will not be read. If you normally launch Palm Desktop by clicking on the User Data file (or an alias of it), you will be prompted to enter the passphrase you used to encrypt it. This isn't an ideal solution, but at least it's a step beyond what's available.

Figure 12.15 You'll have to enter your password when launching Palm Desktop, or switching between users.

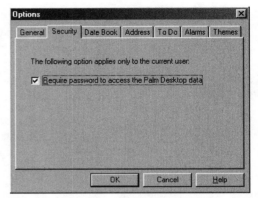

Figure 12.16 Consider using the desktop password access option if your computer is publicly available to others, or if you synchronize Palm Desktop with multiple handhelds.

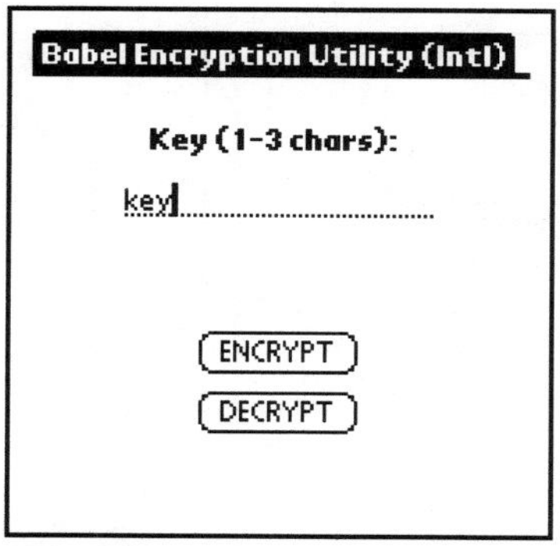

Babel Encryption Utility (Intl)

Key (1-3 chars):

key

(ENCRYPT)
(DECRYPT)

Figure 12.17 Babel encrypts and decrypts the contents of the Clipboard.

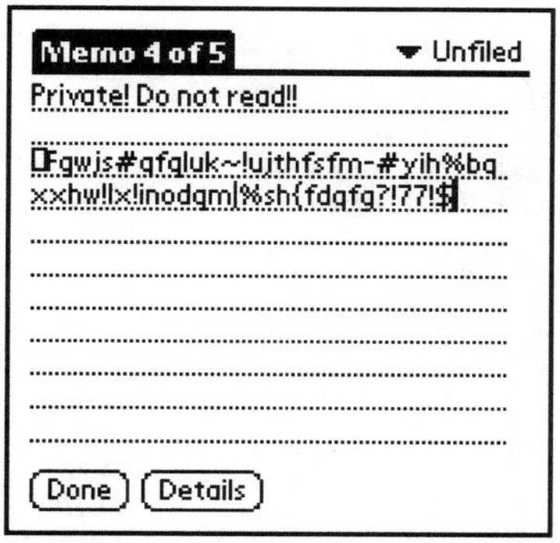

Memo 4 of 5   ▼ Unfiled
Private! Do not read!!

Fgwjs#qfgluk~!ujthfsfm-#yih%bq
xxhw!lx!inodgml%sh{fdgfg?!7?!$

(Done) (Details)

Figure 12.18 This garbage (admittedly useful garbage) results when you paste encrypted contents over the original.

Record-Level Security

Another option on the handheld is to encrypt your information on a record-by-record basis. The Babel Encryption Utility (http://www.wangner.net/babel.html) provides basic, but effective, cryptography. CryptoPad (find it at http://www.palmgear.com/) encrypts information in a Memo Pad-like listing. And ReadThis! (http://members.nbci.com/PixIL/Software/ReadThis/) makes encryption easy to use in any application.

To secure information using Babel:

1. Go to a record that you want to secure, and copy the sensitive text. This works particularly well for Memo Pad records, but can also be applied to any text field (such as parts of an Address Book record).

2. Highlight the text and choose Copy from the Edit menu (✓-C).

3. Switch to Babel, then enter a three-digit passcode. Tap the Encrypt button to continue (**Figure 12.17**).

4. Switch back to your source application (Memo Pad, in this case), and paste the encrypted information over the existing data by choosing Paste from the Edit menu (✓-P). You'll see a string of garbage representing your data (**Figure 12.18**).

5. To unscramble the encrypted text in the future, reverse the process, this time tapping the Decrypt button and pasting the normal text over the encrypted text.

RECORD-LEVEL SECURITY

To store encrypted information using CryptoPad:

1. In the CryptoPad application , open an existing Memo Pad record; or, choose New Memo from the Record menu (✓-N), or tap the New button.

2. Choose Encrypt Memo from the Record menu, or write ✓-E (**Figure 12.19**). A Password dialog appears.

3. Enter a password for this record. Each encrypted record can have its own unique password. Tap OK.

To encrypt text using ReadThis:

1. ReadThis exists as an application and a system hack; create an encryption key in the application, then activate the hack.

2. Find the text you wish to encrypt in any application. To scramble a portion of a record, highlight that text.

3. Drag the stylus from the upper-right corner of the screen; a lock icon appears beneath the stylus. Drop the icon on the text by lifting the stylus (**Figure 12.20**).

4. Repeat the last step to decrypt any block of encrypted text. Depending on your ReadThis settings, you may have to re-enter your encryption key.

✔ Tip

- A free desktop decoder is available for ReadThis-encrypted text, so you can decrypt your information while working on your PC (http://members.nbci.com/PixIL/Software/ReadThis/).

Figure 12.19 CryptoPad replaces the Memo Pad application, adding the option to encrypt individual records.

Drag your stylus from the upper-right edge of the screen to activate ReadThis.

Figure 12.20 ReadThis adds encryption to any editable text field, including partial text selections.

RECORD-LEVEL SECURITY

Storing Secure Account Information

It's amazing that we're able to keep track of all the important phone numbers, credit card numbers, and passwords that go into our heads—so amazing, in fact, that most of us can't do it. Numerous applications let you store your most important information in one secure place.

MobileSafe Account Manager (http://www.handmark.com/) stores information for credit cards, product serial numbers, access numbers, bank accounts, and more.

To store information in MobileSafe Account Manager:

1. From MobileSafe Account Manager's main window, tap New to create a record. Tap the type of entry you want from the list that appears.

2. Enter your information in the fields provided. Each record type has prespecified field labels, but you can choose other labels that reflect your data by tapping the named popup menus.

3. Choose Change Password (✓-W) from the Options menu to protect the file. The next time you launch it, the password will be required to access the list.

✔ Tips

- To double-protect a record, mark the Private checkbox on the edit screen. If you've set the Security application to Hide Records, your record will remain hidden until you elect to show private records.

- You can enter your numbers in a Memo Pad record on your PC, transfer it to your handheld, then import it into MobileSafe to save some Graffiti work.

Security Risks Most People Don't Consider

It's tempting to install some sort of security program and then rest easy. However, there are other security weaknesses you should keep in mind if you're serious about protecting your data.

Passwords

Don't use your name, birthdate, or anything else that's fairly obvious to guess as a password. Try to mix and match numbers and letters, or substitute letters for numbers (such as "s1ngs0ng"). Another technique is to think of a phrase and use the first letters of each word to create a password (such as "w2fm1" for "watch two funny movies first").

Social engineering

Gaining access to your computer or handheld doesn't have to happen over a network or via software. A colleague of mine with data security consulting experience told me about one act of "social engineering," a method of circumventing a security system's encryption, passwords, or firewalls. To test a client's security setup, he donned a telephone repair man's uniform and went to the company's headquarters. The helpful staff directed him to the phone closet, where he was able to install a device that monitored all of their network traffic, rendering their external security measures useless.

STORING SECURE ACCOUNT INFORMATION

Part 3
Your Handheld,
Your Life

Getting Control of Your Information

I first bought a Palm OS-based device based on needs: I needed to improve my organizational skills, keep track of people's contact information, and maintain a list of to do items so I could stay focused on the work at hand. This section deals with many ways a handheld can not only record your information, but also help improve the way you use it.

Chapter 13, **Images & Multimedia**, displays how you can add images to the Palm OS's predominantly text-based environment.

Chapter 14, **Long Texts**, breaks the 4,000 character barrier of the Memo Pad. Read reports, memos, or even a classic novel on the train ride home.

Chapter 15, **Managing Your Time**, points out several techniques for tracking and making the most of your time.

Chapter 16, **Managing Your Data**, covers ways to control the ever-increasing load of information that comes from all directions.

Chapter 17, **Traveling with Your Palm**, takes the handheld on the road, including how to find yourself using GPS.

Chapter 18, **Managing Your Money**, explores how you can keep your accounts up to date by tracking them on a handheld.

Chapter 19, **Games and Entertainment**—I just couldn't leave this out. Here are a few favorites that can significantly aid your efforts to facilitate a stress-free paradigm amid the ever-changing global business zeitgeist.

IMAGES & MULTIMEDIA

If the Palm OS lacks one major feature, it is built-in support for drawing (though Note Pad, which comes with Palm m100 and m500 series devices, is a late hopeful). Graffiti is useful, but sometimes I don't want to write each letter individually. Or, to use a more common example, it would be helpful to attach a quickly sketched map to a set of text directions. And of course there are those times when I just want to doodle. (Penning a brilliant idea on a napkin is novel, but not so helpful when the waiter whisks it away at the end of the meal!)

Fortunately, one of the strengths of the Palm OS platform is the way developers respond to users' needs. As a result, there are now several outlets for creating, viewing, and manipulating graphics on your organizer. You can now easily import images from your PC, or export pictures created on the handheld. Best of all, you can download these programs for free, or for a reasonable shareware fee.

There are also other options: who would have guessed a few years ago you could turn your handheld into a digital camera? Not me, but apparently someone was pondering the idea, and made good on what was no doubt a heap of scribbled notes and drawings.

Painting Basics

You're holding a stylus and a touch-sensitive screen. Doesn't it just make you want to draw a squiggly line, or a caricature of your best friend? Art historians will have a field day in the future with our creations, but there's no doubt that, given the same circumstances, most people will doodle—even just a little bit.

There are several painting programs available, but the one I'll use as an example is TealPaint (`http://www.tealpoint.com/`). In addition to basic painting tools, it offers the ability to zoom in on a picture, select elements by drawing a marquee around them, and insert text.

To sketch using TealPaint:

1. When you first launch the program, you're asked to name a new image database where your pictures will be stored. Several image databases can coexist on the same device (**Figure 13.1**).

2. Tap the New button to create a new image, appropriately named New Image.

3. Select a painting tool (such as pencil, line tool, or geometric shape) from the second button from the left at the bottom of the screen (**Figure 13.2**).

4. The third button from the left chooses the pattern. Tap it to determine what type of "ink" the painting tool will use. If you're using a color device, choose the foreground color from the color swatch next to the Undo button (**Figure 13.3**).

5. Specify the size and shape of the painting tool by tapping the fourth button from the left. Sketch away! You can undo the previous action by tapping the Un button. Tapping the Grid snap selector in the lower-left corner constrains some tools to an invisible 8 by 8-pixel grid.

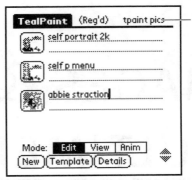

Tap the database name to open other image databases

Figure 13.1 You can store many images within multiple TealPaint databases. Tap a thumbnail to view and edit a drawing.

Figure 13.2 Using TealPaint's painting tools, you can add a few happy UFOs (or trees, or whatever) to your masterpiece.

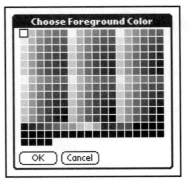

Figure 13.3 (Time to use your imagination again in my grayscale book.) Now you can paint in color if you own a color handheld.

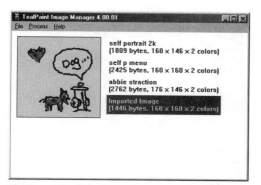

Figure 13.4 TealPaint Image Manager extracts your images from the TealPaint databases on the handheld.

Figure 13.5 Tapping Details displays the file size and image dimensions. Tap Done to go back to the drawing screen, or Delete to remove the image entirely.

Exporting and Importing TealPaint Images

TealPaint comes with a Windows desktop utility called TealPaint Image Manager, which extracts images from TealPaint databases and saves them as Windows bitmap (.bmp) image files (it lets you print images as well). A bare-bones Mac utility is also available from the TealPoint Web site.

To export TealPaint images:

1. Perform a HotSync to update the database files on your desktop.

2. Launch TealPaint Image Manager, and select Open database from the File menu.

3. Databases are stored in the Backups folder located within your Palm user folder. In the TealPaint Image Manager program, open the database file, then click OK (**Figure 13.4**).

4. Click on an image name at right, then select Export image from database to .BMP from the Process menu.

5. Name the file, choose a location on your hard drive, then click the Save button.

To import images into TealPaint:

1. Make sure the image you want to transfer to TealPaint is in Windows bitmap format.

2. In TealPaint Image Manager, choose Import .BMP image into database. Locate your image file and click the Open button.

✔ Tips

■ To remove the green coloring of a Palm image, click Yes in the dialog box asking if you want to force black and white colors when you export the file.

■ To view information about an image on your handheld, tap Details (**Figure 13.5**).

Importing Photos into Your Handheld

Soon, having a set of photographs in your wallet will be *so* passé. FireConverter, a Windows program, and FireViewer, an application that runs under the Palm OS, work together to turn your handheld into a portable portfolio (find both at http://www. firepad.com/).

To convert images:

1. Launch FireConverter and click the Open button to choose an image original (**Figure 13.6**).

2. Choose your resolution from the Color Mode radio buttons, depending on your device. See the samples at right of the available resolutions (**Figure 13.7**).

3. If it's not already selected, click the Preview Firepad Image checkbox to see what will be displayed on the handheld. Use the Resize button to scale the image.

4. When you're ready, click the Save button. If you have the Auto-Install checkbox marked, the .pdb file will be uploaded at the next HotSync.

✔ Tip

■ If you have an image-editing program such as Adobe Photoshop, lightening the original image can make a big difference in the final quality.

Figure 13.6 FireConverter's image preview updates automatically based on the settings you choose.

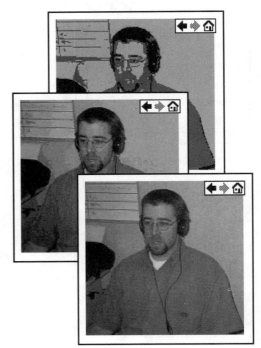

Figure 13.7 Be careful when you send me an embarrassing photo! Here, my friend Rod contemplates his role in the universe in four grays (top), 16 grays (middle), and thousands of colors (bottom).

Figure 13.8 Select the name of the image you want to view in FireViewer.

Tap anywhere and drag to scroll around the image.

Figure 13.9 Cherish photos forever (or at least until the next hard reset).

Figure 13.10 Tap anywhere and select Details from the popup menu. From the Image Details screen, you can also set its category and privacy setting.

To view images:

1. After performing a HotSync, launch the FireViewer application.

2. Tap an image name from the list of available files (**Figure 13.8**).

3. If the image is larger than the visible screen area, tap and drag your stylus to scroll around the picture (**Figure 13.9**). You can also set the four plastic application buttons on the case to navigate the image: choose Preferences from the Options menu (/-R), then select Button Assignment from the top popup menu.

4. Tap the Home icon at upper right to return to the main screen.

To edit image information:

1. With an image displayed, bring up the menu and select the Record menu.

2. The Details option lets you view the image's dimensions, file size, and type (**Figure 13.10**). You can also categorize the image using the Category popup menu, and mark whether the image is Private or not.

3. Tap Delete to remove the image from memory.

4. Beam the image to another FireViewer owner by tapping the Beam button.

5. Add comments about the image by selecting Attach Note.

6. When you're finished, tap OK, or tap Cancel to disregard any changes.

IMPORTING PHOTOS INTO YOUR HANDHELD

Taking Photos

Putting pictures onto your Palm device is a neat trick...but what about using it to take photographs in the first place? No, I'm not proposing that you strap together a Palm and a Polaroid with duct tape. Instead, take photos with the Kodak PalmPix camera (http://www.kodak.com/US/en/digital/cameras/palmPix/). The handheld acts as the viewfinder, and also stores images at pixel sizes of 320 by 240, 640 by 480, or 800 by 600.

To take photos with the PalmPix:

1. Launch the PalmPix software.

2. Tap an icon at lower left to choose an image resolution. The number to the right tells you how many shots are left at that resolution, based on the handheld's available memory (**Figure 13.11**).

3. Press the Date Book button on the handheld's case to engage the viewfinder.

4. When you have the shot lined up, press the Date Book button again to capture it.

5. Preview shots on the handheld (**Figure 13.12**), or transfer them to your computer the next time you HotSync for viewing in an image viewer (**Figure 13.13**).

✔ Tips

- The resolution on the viewfinder is surprisingly pretty rough (very blocky and pixelated), but the end result is clearer.

- Like most cameras, the PalmPix software includes an exposure timer, so you can take snapshots of yourself without seeing your arm outstretched along one side of the picture.

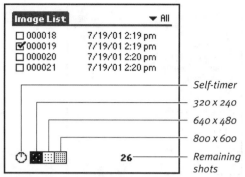

Figure 13.11 Choose from three resolutions before you snap a photo.

Self-timer
320 x 240
640 x 480
800 x 600
Remaining shots

Figure 13.12 Get a sense of what the picture looks like by viewing it on the Palm device.

Figure 13.13 This scene was shot at the 800 by 600 pixel setting (and resized to fit on this page). Kids, only take photos like this when your car is parked!

Figure 13.14 Sony bills its CLIÉ N710C as a "personal entertainment organizer," and throws in the headphones to prove it.

Playing Digital Music

Playing digital music from your handheld computer: the notion was probably less than a glimmer in most people's eyes at first, yet today the idea is becoming as natural as storing your addresses. As long as the information is digital, why not? With the rise of the MP3 music format, it's now possible to take a selection of your music collection with you, without the bulk of CDs or a separate music player.

The Sony CLIÉ PEG-N710C includes built-in software (and headphones to boot!) for playing MP3-formatted digital music stored on Sony Memory Sticks (**Figure 13.14**). It also supports ATRAC3-formatted files, a method of encrypting the files so that they can only be used on one device. If you use ATRAC3 files, you can only store them on special MagicGate Memory Stick media.

✔ Tips

- Since digital music files take up a lot of memory, plan on purchasing a 64 MB or 128 MB Memory Stick. You'll only be able to put two or three songs on the 8 MB Memory Stick that comes with the N710C device.

- I love the designers at Sony. The N710C includes a small remote control as part of the headphones that let you control the music output without turning on the CLIÉ. But in an inspired bit of usefulness, the remote also sports a stylus nub for easily using the device without withdrawing the normal stylus.

- Consider encoding your songs in a lower-quality bit rate to store more data.

- If you use a Macintosh, install The Missing Sync by Mark/Space (http://www.markspace.com/missingsync.html) to transfer files to Memory Sticks.

To transfer digital music files to the Sony Memory Stick:

1. Place the CLIÉ in its cradle and launch the AudioPlayer software.

2. Choose Transfer from the Options menu, or write ⁄-K. The Transfer Mode screen appears, indicating the status of the connection with the PC.

3. Under Windows, the CLIÉ's Memory Stick shows up as a new device (typically as an E drive). Double-click the disk to open it.

4. Copy your music files to the MSAudio folder within the Programs folder.

5. From the Windows Taskbar, click the Unplug or Eject Hardware icon and choose Stop USB Disk. This closes the connection from the PC side.

6. On the CLIÉ, tap the Exit button.

To listen to digital music:

1. Launch the AudioPlayer software (**Figure 13.15**). Tap the Play/Pause button to begin listening.

2. Switch between songs by tapping the Forward or Back buttons. Or, tap the Playlist icon (▤) to view a list of songs. Select the one you want and tap Play (**Figure 13.16**).

3. Tap the Song Information icon (♫) to view details about the current track.

✔ Tips

■ Be sure to disconnect the file transfer on the PC before doing anything on the CLIÉ to avoid possible data loss.

■ Tap the circular Jog dial image in the upper left corner to change the function of the Jog dial when listening to music (**Figure 13.17**).

Figure 13.15 The AudioPlayer software includes controls familiar to anyone who has used a portable music device.

Figure 13.16 Mix and match your own music collection. No more carrying around an entire CD just to listen to the one good song on it.

Figure 13.17 You can change the Jog dial's commands in AudioPlayer.

PLAYING DIGITAL MUSIC

14

LONG TEXTS

Like the concept of a truly paperless office, the notion of electronic books replacing traditional printed texts has been floating around for years. Instead of carrying around an armful of bound paper, you can store hundreds or thousands of books without felling a single tree or throwing out your back.

However, people haven't yet embraced a completely digital reading experience, though not for a lack of options. High profile devices like the Gemstar eBook (`http://www.nuvomedia.com/`) have garnered a lot of press for their "revolutionary" approaches to distributing long texts.

The funny thing is, Palm OS device owners have been enjoying the same capability for years. The Doc format has enabled readers to take any text file on the go, while third party options use their own formats. And recently, Adobe's Portable Document Format (PDF) has moved to the Palm OS. Publishers eager to test the waters of the digital book market now offer book-length works; Online Originals (`http://www.onlineoriginals.com/`) and Peanut Press (`http://www.peanutpress.com/`) are thriving.

Reading a lot of text on a small screen isn't an ideal task, but it's not as bad as I first thought. Plus, 400 pages of fiction are a lot lighter to carry when stored in a shirt pocket.

Reading Doc-Formatted Texts

A number of applications are available for reading documents that you install on your handheld; the grandfathers of the field are AportisDoc (http://www.aportis.com/) and TealDoc (http://www.tealpoint.com/), though most reader applications now recognize the Doc format. For the sake of example, I'll focus on TealDoc.

Doc files can contain bookmarks that jump down to main sections of the document. Bookmarks can be preformatted (see "Converting Texts to Doc Format" later in this chapter), or created by the reader.

To open Doc files:

1. After installing a Doc file into the handheld, open TealDoc. You'll see a list of available Doc files that are stored in the device's memory (**Figure 14.1**).

2. Tap the Open button at the bottom of the screen, then tap the title of the document you want to read.

To navigate a document:

◆ Tap anywhere in the lower half of the screen to scroll down; tap the upper half to scroll up. You can advance through the files without having to be precise about tapping a scroll bar or arrow.

◆ You can also move to the top or bottom of the document by choosing Go Up Page (✓-U), Go Down Page (✓-D), Go to Top (✓-T), or Go to Bottom (✓-B) from the View menu.

◆ Tap the percentage indicator to display the Scroll panel (**Figure 14.2**). Drag the horizontal slider at the bottom of the screen to scroll through the document; the percentage will change depending on the slider's location.

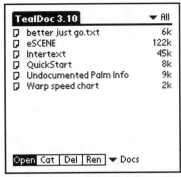

Figure 14.1 Any Doc-formatted files that you install show up in the Doc reader's list view.

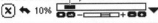

Figure 14.2 Move swiftly through your document by dragging the horizontal scroll bar in TealDoc.

Figure 14.3 Control the scroll rate by tapping the Screen Tap and Scroll buttons selectors.

Figure 14.4 Bookmarks can be set up before the file is installed, or you can add them to access your favorite passages.

✔ Tips

- You can specify that tapping advances the text by screen (the default), by partial page (a full screen minus one overlapping line), or by line. Choose Preferences from the Doc menu (✓-P) and tap the Line, Part, or Page boxes under Screen Tap. You can also specify scroll options for the physical scroll buttons on the handheld's case (**Figure 14.3**).

- If you have Line selected above, tapping and holding the stylus to the screen will scroll the text until you lift it. Depending on where you tap, the scrolling speed will be slower (closer to the middle) or faster (closer to the lower or upper edges).

- If you want to be able to select and copy text with your stylus, tap the Select button under Screen Tap in the Preferences screen.

To use bookmarks:

1. Tap the down-arrow in the lower right corner of the screen to view the bookmarks popup menu (**Figure 14.4**).

2. Tap the section name you want to access.

To add bookmarks:

1. Scroll up or down to display the section you wish to bookmark.

2. Choose New Bookmark from the popup menu, or Add New Bookmark from the Marks menu (✓-1), and enter a descriptive title. Tap OK.

✔ Tip

- To remove, rename, or scan the document for bookmarks, choose those options from the Marks menu.

To automatically scroll the document:

1. When AutoScroll is active, the screen advances automatically. Under the Special menu, choose AutoScroll Go (✓-G) to begin. AutoScroll Stop (✓-S) turns the feature off.

2. Tap the percentage indicator to display the Scroll panel, or choose Show Scroll Panel from the View menu.

3. The smaller horizontal bar at the bottom of the page indicates the scrolling speed; tap the plus (⬢) or minus (⬢) buttons to the right of the bar to adjust the speed (**Figure 14.5**).

4. Tap the go button (⬢) to start, or the stop button (⬢) to stop scrolling.

✔ Tip

- You can also control the scrolling speed using the plastic application buttons on the front of the handheld's case. Choose Preferences (✓-P), then tap one or both buttons under Autoscroll keys active on.

To perform a search within the current document:

1. Choose Show Font Panel (which also displays the search controls) from the View menu, or tap the percentage indicator.

2. To search, tap the magnifying glass icon, or choose Find from the Doc menu (✓-F) (**Figure 14.6**). Enter the text you want to find, and mark any of the four search options.

3. To search again for the same term, tap either of the arrows surrounding the magnifying glass icon; or, choose Find Next (✓-N) or Find Last (✓-L) from the Doc menu.

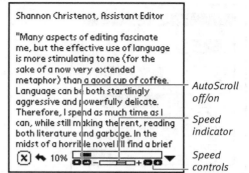

Figure 14.5 Configure the AutoScroll rate by tapping the controls at the bottom of the screen.

Figure 14.6 Tap the magnifying glass button to perform searches.

READING DOC-FORMATTED TEXTS

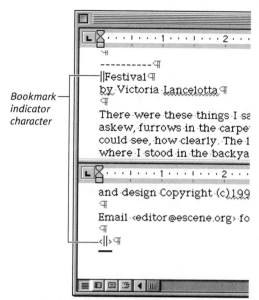

Bookmark indicator character

Figure 14.7 Specifying a unique character set at the end of the document (bottom) instructs Doc readers to add a bookmark where the characters are found within the text.

Converting Texts to Doc Format

You can create your own Doc files from existing text files using utilities such as MakeDoc (http://www.aportis.com/resources/AportisDoc/makedocutilities.html), AportisDoc Professional (http://www.aportis.com/), QEX (http://www.visionary2000.com/qed/qex.htm), and PalmBuddy (http://perso.wanadoo.fr/fpillet/).

To prepare the text file:

1. Your text is going to be viewed on the small screen, so strip out any long breaking lines of repeated dashes (----), or reduce them to about 20 characters.

2. Make sure there's a carriage return after each paragraph, not each line. This gives you more flexibility when viewing at different font sizes.

3. Save your document as a text-only file.

To specify bookmarks:

1. Choose a character combination that isn't likely to show up in your text (such as ||).

2. At the end of your document, put it between brackets (<||>) to define the file's bookmark notation.

3. Add the character combination (without brackets) before each section you wish to bookmark (**Figure 14.7**). When the Doc reader encounters the characters, it creates a new bookmark, using the text that follows as a bookmark label.

To convert the file:

Drag and drop the text file onto the conversion utility, or open the utility and use the Browse button to locate the file.

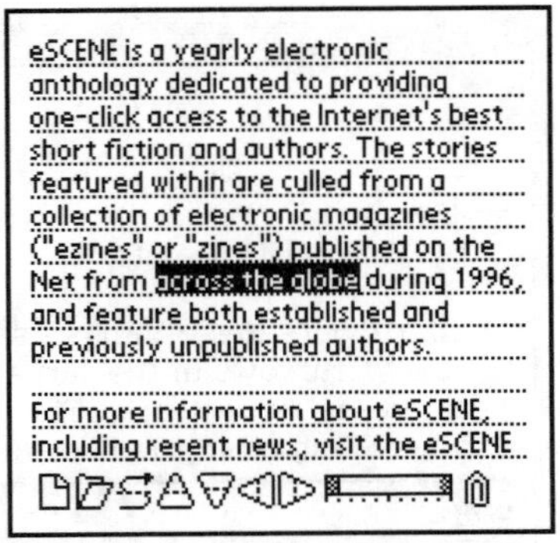

✔ Tips

- TealDoc offers the ability to embed pictures, links, and Web bookmarks into text files, similar to HTML markup. For this to be activated, though, the document needs to be converted to TealDoc format on the handheld. From the main list screen, select All to TealDoc format. To return the files to standard Doc state, select All to public format. See the documentation that comes with TealDoc for instructions on how to mark up your text to accommodate these features.

- You can also edit Doc-formatted files directly on the handheld (**Figure 14.8**) using the editor/word processor QED (http://www.visionary2000.com/qed/).

- Use MakeTeal (http://www.io.com/~bryce/maketeal.html) to convert HTML formatted text files into TealDoc document files.

eSCENE is a yearly electronic anthology dedicated to providing one-click access to the Internet's best short fiction and authors. The stories featured within are culled from a collection of electronic magazines ("ezines" or "zines") published on the Net from across the globe during 1996, and feature both established and previously unpublished authors.

For more information about eSCENE, including recent news, visit the eSCENE

Figure 14.8 QED can edit Doc-formatted files, as well as open them.

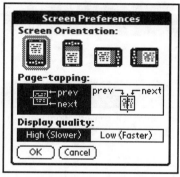

Figure 14.9 Since Peanut Press books require the purchaser to unlock titles, mainstream authors and publishers are offering books in the Palm Reader electronic format.

Figure 14.10 Palm Reader's preferences enable you to find the best method of reading the books.

Reading Books with Palm Reader

Peanut Press (http://www.peanutpress.com/) developed their own software for reading electronic books under the Palm OS. They also had another requirement: ensure that books purchased from their site could be opened only by the people who bought them. The result is Palm Reader, which includes features not found in the other electronic readers (**Figure 14.9**).

Features of Palm Reader

◆ Mark favorite sections by tapping the Bookmark icon (■).

◆ Add notes to the text by tapping the Annotations icon (▣).

◆ Invert the screen for better readability (especially with backlighting on) by tapping the Invert Screen icon (◼).

◆ For those times when you get engrossed in a book, be sure to check the hour by tapping the Current Time icon (▦).

◆ Change the screen orientation and the tapping control of the screen by choosing Screen Orientation from the Options menu (**Figure 14.10**).

✔ Tip

■ Palm Reader now understands Doc files (earlier versions didn't), so you can use it to swap between multiple text formats on your handheld.

Reading and Editing Microsoft Word Files

If you're like a lot of people, you may not want to read books or preformatted files on your handheld. Instead, wouldn't it be great to take some of your word processor documents with you and edit them on the road?

DataViz's Documents To Go (http://www.dataviz.com/) and Cutting Edge Software's Quickoffice (http://www.cesinc.com/) enable you to do just that. Drag files in Microsoft Word and other formats to Documents To Go (**Figure 14.11**) or Quickoffice (**Figure 14.12**) to convert them with styles and most formatting (including tables) intact (**Figure 14.13**). Both programs also include modules for viewing Microsoft Excel spreadsheets on the handheld as well.

✔ Tips

- For a faster method of specifying files to be converted by Documents To Go, select the file in the Finder (Mac) or Explorer (Windows), then either Control-click (Mac) or right-click (Windows) to select Take File to Go from the popup menu that appears. Under Windows, you can optionally select Documents To Go from the Send to submenu of the contextual menu.

- Although much of the document's original formatting is translated to the handheld, keep in mind that the file is being converted, not just sent directly between the PC and handheld. So, some formatting (like style sheets) may not be retained when you open the file again on the PC after editing it on the handheld.

- You can use Quickoffice or Documents To Go as a standalone word processor too: create a new file on the Palm, then transfer it back to your PC at the next HotSync.

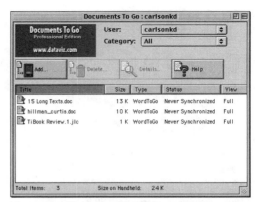

Figure 14.11 Simply drag Word files to the Documents To Go window to prepare them for installation at the next HotSync operation.

Figure 14.12 Quickoffice also converts Word files to a format that's editable under the Palm OS.

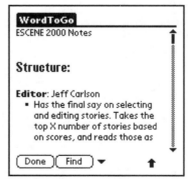

Figure 14.13 Documents To Go retains formatting from the word processor that created the original file.

Figure 14.14 Use iSilo's desktop tool to grab Web pages for viewing on your handheld.

Figure 14.15 iSilo formats text defined by the underlying HTML, and includes links to other converted pages.

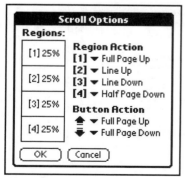

Figure 14.16 Control the page scroll rate by defining four screen regions.

Viewing HTML Documents

iSilo (http://www.isilo.com/) takes HTML pages and formats them for viewing on a handheld. You can use it to read an individual HTML file, or point to a Web site and specify how many levels of links to follow.

To convert a file for viewing with iSilo:

1. Using either the Windows or Macintosh iSilo application, select an HTML file you wish to convert (**Figure 14.14**). You can also provide a Web address that iSilo will connect to.

2. After the file has been converted, HotSync your organizer.

3. On the handheld, launch iSilo and choose the page(s) you installed. If you converted several pages of a Web site, you can tap the dotted-underlined words to bring up linked pages (**Figure 14.15**).

✔ Tip

■ Most text readers for the Palm OS separate the screen into two areas, usually top and bottom, to control whether the text advances up or down when you tap it. iSilo wisely splits the screen into four equal areas, letting you control the amount of scrolling based on where you tap (**Figure 14.16**).

Viewing PDF Documents

Adobe's Portable Document Format (PDF) began as a method of displaying print materials onscreen in a format that would retain the layout, fonts, and appearance of the original file, without requiring that the user own QuarkXPress, PageMaker, or other page-layout application. Over time, PDF has become a way to view nearly any document on any computer, so it's only natural that you can now view PDF files on a Palm OS handheld.

Two programs enable you to convert PDF files for viewing on the handheld: Adobe Acrobat Reader for Palm OS (http://www.adobe.com/products/acrobat/readerforpalm.html) and AportisDoc PDF Converter (http://www.aportis.com/). Each utility is available only for Windows as of this writing.

To convert a PDF file:

1. Simply drag a PDF file to the main window of either program; alternately, click the Add PDF to transfer list button in Adobe's application, or click the handheld icon button in the Aportis program (**Figures 14.17** and **14.18**). The PDF is converted to a format optimized for the handheld.

2. HotSync your handheld to transfer the files. Depending on the settings in AportisDoc PDF Converter, you may have to manually install the converted file.

3. Launch the reader application to view the PDF document (**Figure 14.19**).

✔ Tip

■ Adobe provides an Acrobat Reader application for the Palm OS. Aportis, however, uses its existing AportisDoc program to view the converted PDF.

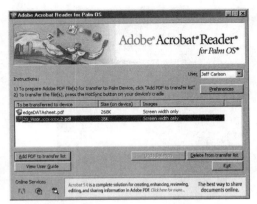

Figure 14.17 Adobe Acrobat Reader for Palm OS prepares PDF files for your handheld.

Figure 14.18 Taking a minimalist approach, AportisDoc PDF Converter simplifies the process.

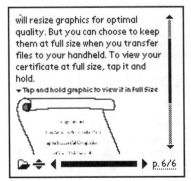

Figure 14.19 You won't forget you're viewing a device with a small screen, but the information (including images) from a PDF is available on the handheld.

Managing Your Time

Believe me, I'm not a slick-suited time management guru, a master of every minute and second. The truth is, I've never really been *great* at time management, which is what led me to buy a handheld in the first place.

What I am is a full-time freelancer/free agent/independent contractor (pick your favorite term) who has managed to get control of his schedule and tasks with the help of a remarkable pocket-sized gadget. When I started using a handheld, I was amazed to discover that it wasn't a tool people used only during business hours. Organizers soon became integrated into their owners' lives, instead of gathering dust on the corner of their desks.

We're all trying to manage our time, whether that means setting up an efficient workflow system at work, or keeping track of where to take the kids throughout the week. It's likely you carry your Palm device everywhere—use it to help take control of your time.

Track Your Time

I always enjoy stories or movies where the hero has to track something through an impenetrable jungle or forest. In these scenes, the star is the Expert Guide who inspects every branch, leaf, and mismatched clump of dirt to divine the path of his or her prey. It's that attention to detail that I find fascinating, of looking at the same thing everyone else is viewing, but seeing something different.

If there ever was an impenetrable wilderness to be explored, it's the schedule that many of us live with every day. Your desire to tame it may have led you to buy a Palm organizer in the first place. Like the Expert Guide who notices all details, it's important that you do some tracking before you can reach your goal of personal organization.

Many people have a natural aversion to tracking their time, myself included. If I'm recording every minute, I sometimes feel I'm focused more on tracking than on whatever task I need to accomplish. However, it's important that you know where your time is going before you can redefine where you want it to go. Keep track of where (or when) you spend your time for a week or a month.

For a visual approach that's built-in to your handheld, consider using Date Book to track your time (**Figure 15.1**). Instead of scheduling only upcoming events, mark things as you do them.

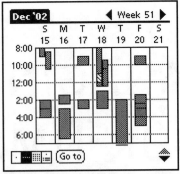

Figure 15.1 Your calendar will start to fill up, but by tracking everything you do plus your appointments, you can see how much time your tasks are taking.

Figure 15.2 To make it easier to differentiate between appointments and tracked items, use a special character (such as ~) to indicate your tracking.

To track your time using Date Book:

1. Launch the program by pressing the plastic Date Book button on the front of the case. This also displays today's events in the Day view.

2. Tap New, or tap the current time to create a new event. Write your activity on the event's title line.

3. If you know how long the activity will last, tap the Details button and enter an end time. If not, just stick with the default one hour time span.

4. When you've finished, go back into the record and adjust the end time, then start a new record for your next activity.

✔ Tips

■ To keep scheduled events and tracked events separate, mark the title with a unique character or word; you can set up a ShortCut (see Chapter 2) to quickly enter the notation (**Figure 15.2**).

■ This can be a good opportunity to also add notes about your activity for reference later. Tap the Note button in the Event Details screen, or select Attach Note (✓-A) from the Record menu.

■ If you don't want your Date Book screens cluttered with appointments *and* tracking information, mark the tracking events Private (see Chapter 4). They won't be visible, but they will be stored.

■ Don't purge the old records from your Date Book until you've finished your time-tracking period.

TRACK YOUR TIME

Use a Tracking Program

A few applications have been designed specifically to track time. One application I use is HourzPro (http://www.zoskware.com/), which lets me record my billable hours as well as non-billable time that I want to keep tabs on. Other similar applications include TEAK (http://www.eb7.com/) and Timesheet (http://hotpalm.n3.net/).

To track your time using HourzPro:

1. Launch HourzPro (**Figure 15.3**). Tap one of the view icons at the lower left to choose between the project view (⊞) and the day view (▢). Tap the New button to create a new record.

2. From the Project popup menu, choose Edit Projects to set up a new activity; if this is a business-related project, enter the client name and rate. Tap OK and then select the activity from the popup menu.

3. The timer begins when you create a new record, which will be shown on the HourzPro Entry screen (**Figure 15.4**). Tap Done to return to the main screen.

4. When finished with the activity, tap the stopwatch icon to the right of the description to stop the timer; the duration (and charge, if you entered a rate) is automatically calculated.

✔ Tip

■ If you're interrupted by something that you don't necessarily need to record, open your record and enter the amount of interrupted time in the Break field.

Figure 15.3 HourzPro offers many advanced options for tracking your time.

Figure 15.4 When you create a new entry, the timer begins tracking. Specify a project and task for later reference.

USE A TRACKING PROGRAM

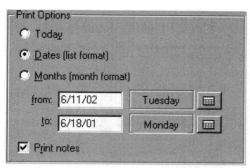

Figure 15.5 Specify Dates (list format) when printing your Date Book entries to see your events' details and save some paper.

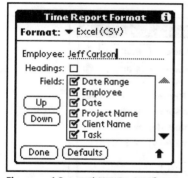

Figure 15.6 Set up the contents of your reports for when you export them.

```
┌─────────────────────────────┐
│ Reportz List                │
│ • ⊙ 9/24 Hourz-Report   $0  │
│ • ⊙ 9/24 filing         $0  │
│ • ⊙ 9/24 lunch          $0  │
│ • ⊙ 9/24 meetings       $0  │
│ • ⊙ 9/24 proj mgmt      $0  │
│                             │
│                             │
│ ( Time Report  ) (⊙)        │
│ ( Expense Report ) ($)      │
└─────────────────────────────┘
```

Figure 15.7 Generate comma-delimited time reports that can be opened in Excel on your PC.

Review Your Tracks

When you're finished recording your moves, you will have a wealth of raw data. Seeing where your time actually goes isn't always heartening, but at least you'll have a basis to build upon and improve. The next step is to analyze that data.

If you used the Date Book method mentioned earlier, go back and review where you spent your time. One easy method of doing this is to make a printout of the time period you spent tracking. If you're using HourzPro, a companion application, Reportz, makes it easy to create reports.

To generate a Date Book report:

1. Perform a HotSync to update your Palm Desktop records.

2. Choose Print from the File menu, or press Control/Command-P. The Print Options dialog box appears.

3. Under Print Options, choose Dates (list format) (**Figure 15.5**). Only days with events on them will print. Click OK.

To generate an HourzPro report:

1. From the HourzPro screen, tap the Reportz icon (🖹), or choose Go To Reports from the Options menu.

2. Tap the Time Report button to create a new report. You'll have to specify an employee (you) and default export format the first time you run Reportz (**Figure 15.6**). Tap Done when finished.

3. Name the report in the Title field, then select criteria from the Project, Period, Status, and Action popup menus.

4. Tap Create to generate the report. It will be added to the Reportz List (**Figure 15.7**). At your next HotSync, the reports will be transferred to your PC.

Fine Tune Your Time Management

Now that you have your data, look it over carefully. Are you spending too much time preparing for meetings? Too little? Do phone calls routinely interrupt your workflow? Examining this type of schedule overview tends to make previously minor annoyances or hidden successes stand out.

Know your own schedule

Most people have an internal clock that seems to pay no attention when they need to crunch on a deadline or be awake for poorly scheduled important meetings. Look at how you space your activities throughout the day, then restructure accordingly.

If you're a walking corpse at 3 p.m., don't plan meetings or appointments or important tasks; high doses of caffeine can sometimes overcome mid-afternoon sluggishness, but not always. Set up a repeating event ("Siesta" perhaps?) that spans 3:00–4:00 each business day (**Figure 15.8**).

Be alarming

Have you ever been so involved in a project that several hours can slip by without notice? Date Book's alarm features help keep me focused on when I need to shift gears.

I've set up my Date Book preferences so that every event is assigned a 10-minute alarm. Select Preferences from the Option menu (✓-R) and mark the Alarm Preset checkbox (**Figure 15.9**). Make sure you're being realistic about the alarms—adjust each event's alarm preset to take into account things like travel time and preparation (yes, you should shave before dinner with the boss).

Another option is to use reminder software like BugMe! (http://www.bugme.net/) (**Figure 15.10**).

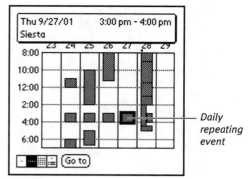

Daily repeating event

Figure 15.8 A scheduled break can help you get through the most unproductive time of the day.

Figure 15.9 I'd rather endure multiple alarms during the day than miss an appointment. Each new event is assigned an alarm when you activate the Alarm Preset option.

Figure 15.10 Think of BugMe! as a helpful Post-it note that's stuck to you.

Figure 15.11 Agenda lets you see which events and tasks are coming up by tapping the tabs at the top of the screen.

```
┌─────────────────────────────────┐
│ Today  Tomorrow  Week  ☑! ⌂    │
│  9:00 a Call Robert Shuster 20...  D │
│  9:30 a TidBITS ad ideas         D │
│ 10:00 a Coffee with Doug Tho...   D │
│ 12:00 p Fly to DC - #WAHBOA       D │
│  2:45 p Rue the Day               D │
│  5:00 p State Dinner              D │
│ Due  Finish screenshots        1 T │
│ Due  Make dinner reservati...  2 T │
│ Due  TidBITS issue draft       3 T │
│ Due  Prep class outline        4 T │
│                                    │
│  Feb 21, 2002   11:17 am           │
└─────────────────────────────────┘
```

Figure 15.12 Put off until tomorrow what you can view ahead today using the utility Today.

Prioritize events and tasks wisely

Is everything really a number-one priority on your To Do list? I find myself sometimes entering To Do items without paying attention to their priority settings—as long as they're on the list, that should be good enough, right?

Maybe that works for some people, but being smart about prioritizing items generally improves my ability to deal with them in a timely manner. If you have to manually scan through the list each time you finish a task, you may be wasting valuable time. If, on the other hand, you figured out each item's priority ahead of time, you can jump through the list quicker.

Seeing the bigger picture

The Palm OS is great at taking lots of little scraps of information and organizing them in one place. The problem is, your information is then all "hidden" behind the current application—you can't see what's coming up if you don't look at your schedule or To Do List. The saying "out of sight, out of mind" can be apt, but not beneficial, for Palm owners. (I've seen people with handhelds in larger carrying cases that are festooned with sticky notes.) Use a "big picture" utility such as TealGlance (http://www.tealpoint.com/), Agenda (http://www.dovcom.com/) or Today (http://www.synsolutions.com/) to get an overview of what's lurking beneath the surface (**Figures 15.11** and **15.12**).

✔ Tip

■ Give yourself some breathing room between appointments. A common scheduling mistake is to run meetings together, made all the easier because the Date Book defaults to hourly blocks of time. Use the alarm preset option to give you a breather before the next appointment.

Mark items for quick scanning

Don't start a memo with "Memo" or "Important Note," or list a To Do item as "business stuff." Assume that you're going to be quickly scanning through the items most of the time—you don't want to waste time with two or three taps just to decipher something you wrote two hours ago. Launch right into the meat of it, and explain later. You should be able to identify the memo, task, or event just by looking at its title in a list.

Use ShortCuts

The Palm OS's ShortCuts feature is one of its most underutilized aspects (see Chapter 2). ShortCuts are great for saving several Graffiti strokes when writing long words, and they're also ideal for frequently used items.

Look back at your time report and mark which events or keywords are most often repeated. Then go to the Prefs application, choose ShortCuts from the popup menu in the upper-right corner, and create ShortCut strokes for those items (**Figure 15.13**).

Figure 15.13 Figure out which tasks and events you write often, and create ShortCuts for them.

The Palm OS's Personal Touch

Another amazing thing about Palm devices is that they aren't just business devices. People schedule birthdays, anniversaries, reminders to watch favorite TV shows, etc. Your schedule is your life's schedule, which is why many more "non-business" people are buying handhelds.

However, some people think that if you enter a personal appointment (such as "dinner with Kim") into your impersonal gadget, then somehow that person has been "impersonalized." Not true—scheduling personal and family time is just as (or more) important than scheduling a meeting with the boss.

Build Your Time Management Skills

Now that you have a better idea of where your time has gone and how to get more of it in the present, you can begin taking steps to shape where it will go in the future.

Notes: your secret workhorses

They seem so inconsequential, making an appearance only when the little note icon shows up to the right of an item. However, notes can be one of the most useful features you'll find. I attach notes to everything: alternate addresses, driving directions, and miscellaneous data (such as spouse and children's names to Address Book items). Meeting notes, flight schedules, and even people notes get added to records in my handheld ("Andrea: wore cream-colored suit and cool glasses; quick responses, good ideas, but poked fun at my good-luck teddy bear"). In the Date Book, Address Book, and To Do applications, select Attach Note from the Record menu (✓-A).

Categorically speaking

One of the first things I did when I started using my organizer was to reassign the categories (see Chapter 2). "Business" and "Personal" are just too broad for practical use, and invite catch-all disorganization (it's similar to creating a folder called "Misc" on your desktop—everything ends up there).

Try to be as precise as you can: "Office Phone Calls," "Kids," etc. That way, you've started creating an organizational system before there's anything to organize (the pile of unfiled bills and receipts on my desk is a testament to the benefits of setting up categories prior to accumulating stuff).

The Power of Motion

One of the more important aspects of time management is being able to stick to the schedule you've created. Yet, there are times when an effectively plotted out day gets bogged down: phone calls, fatigue, a difficult project, whatever. These are the times that I need to get off my posterior and move around a little.

Take a break. If you're pressed for time, create a Date Book event that signals an alarm in ten minutes. Better yet, if you find yourself working for long stretches of time without resting (a practice that looks good from management's viewpoint, but can quickly lead to health problems and burnout), set up several repeating events that signal alarms every two hours or so. If you're using DateBk4 (see later in this chapter), create a floating event that you can dismiss until later if you absolutely can't get away at that moment.

Or, set up a To Do item that reminds you to take a break, get some coffee, or step outside for two minutes of fresh air. Position its priority so that after you complete the first one or two items on your list, you feel compelled to take a break in order to mark it off your list.

Motion has power, so it's in your best interest to keep moving, even if you spend most of your day in front of a computer. Remember that this type of motion is not counterproductive to "real work."

Overcome the endless To Do List

This is my worst problem. Stuff that doesn't get done each day gets rolled over to the next day. It's hard sometimes to feel like anything is ever completed.

The solution? Mark long- and short-term tasks with their own category. When you finish your pressing items, view your short-term list and reassign those tasks (**Figure 15.14**). If you don't want them to show up when you view All records, mark them hidden—just don't forget they're there! (And remember, categories don't have to be just "Business" or "Personal.")

✔ Tip

■ Stay realistic. Including "World Peace" on your To Do list is admirable, but not practical for day-to-day use (unless you really want a constant reminder—set up a low-priority, dateless To Do item that will never go away).

Be generous with time estimates

Estimating accurately how long a project will take is a skill built upon experience. Until you've done something at least once (and it usually takes several times), it's hard to nail a realistic estimate. A seasoned contracter once advised me to estimate a project's time commitment, then double the result. It sounds like overkill, but at some point— usually on deadline—you'll realize that the higher estimate was probably closer to reality.

Figure 15.14 Set up long-term and short-term categories so you're not just thinking about your immediate tasks.

Linking Records with DateBk4 and Actioneer

One of the most frequently voiced complaints about the built-in applications is that they aren't tied together well. Although you can perform phone lookups within other applications, you can't create a To Do item and have it show up on your schedule, for example. Two developers have come up with methods of bypassing this limitation.

DateBk4 (http://www.pimlicosoftware.com/) builds upon the strengths of Date Book by adding "floating" appointments, which get copied to successive days until marked Done.

To create a floating appointment in DateBk4:

1. Create a new event at the time and date you want to work on it, then tap Details.

2. In the Type category, tap the Float button (**Figure 15.15**). In DateBk4 you can also set up categories for events under the Category popup menu.

3. Tap OK. When you return to the Day view, you'll notice a circle icon at the far right of the event's name. After completing the task, tap the circle to checkmark it, or tap the Done button in the Event Details screen.

Actioneer (http://www.actioneer.com/) works ahead of the built-in applications by scanning what you write for keywords (such as times, days of the week, names, and others that you can set up).

To create new events and tasks using Actioneer:

1. Launch Actioneer and write your event or task. As you write, the icons on the right will become highlighted if a matching keyword is found (**Figure 15.16**).

2. If you want to refine Actioneer's matches before exiting, tap the icons to view options that can be added to your event.

3. When you're satisfied, tap OK. The record will appear in each application that Actioneer highlighted.

Figure 15.15 DateBk4 adds categories and the concept of "floating" events to the normal Date Book features.

Figure 15.16 Actioneer looks for keywords in what you write, then creates new records in the built-in applications.

LINKING RECORDS

Prepare ahead

Finally, some of the best advice I've received from others is to prepare for tomorrow today. I know, it sounds like a bad insurance commercial, but you'd be surprised at the results. Before you leave work or go to bed at night, take some time to go over the next day's appointments and tasks.

Set up tomorrow before you're in the thick of it; that much more time will be saved the next morning, when unexpected pressures and tasks are likely to begin appearing. For many people, knowing how tomorrow is going to work out makes them sleep easier the night before.

MANAGING YOUR DATA

I've gone on and on about how simple the Palm OS platform is, how its design is based on the idea that an *extension* of one's PC is better than an attempt at a miniaturized PC, and how this "less is more" approach is one key to the Palm OS's lead in the market.

"Yes, okay, fine, we *get it* already."

And yet, after owning a handheld for only a few weeks, many of us find it crammed with information other than what the built-in applications support. With thousands of programs available for downloading, and up to 8 MB of memory available in off-the-shelf devices, we can't help but store and manipulate all sorts of data. My Palm is stuffed with outlines, ideas, sketches, spreadsheets, stories to read, groceries to buy, and important numbers—and that pales compared to some other people's organizers I've run across in the past.

A Palm OS-based organizer is ideal for storing all sorts of data, anything that you need to access or edit without opening a laptop computer or driving to the office late at night. Despite the volume of data, the resources for organizing it all are able to do more with less.

Outlining and Brainstorming

I never liked outlining in school, preferring instead to just begin writing and see what I ended up with. After a few less-than-encouraging grades on some of my reports, I realized that perhaps some advance planning and structure might help me after all. Now, I do quite a bit of outlining, not only for writing, but also to organize thoughts, plans, and even which videos to rent.

I use Aportis's BrainForest (`http://www.aportis.com/`), which is what I'll use as an example in this chapter; other good outliners include Hi-Note (`http://www.cyclos.com/hi-note.htm`), ThoughtManager (`http://www.handshigh.com/html/thoughtmanager.html`), and Arranger (`http://www.olivebr.com/pilot.htm`). Of course, you can also achieve similar, though far limited, results with the built-in Memo Pad application.

To understand how BrainForest works, you have to think hierarchically in terms of trees and branches: an outline is the tree, the main entries are branches, and entries filed under the branches are leaves.

To create outlines with BrainForest:

1. Launch BrainForest, then tap the Create button, or choose Create Tree (✓-U) from the Tree menu (**Figure 16.1**). An empty tree is created.

2. To create a branch, tap the New button or choose New Branch from the Tree menu (✓-N). Write the branch's title in the popup text field that appears, then tap the checkmark to finish (**Figure 16.2**).

3. You can either create more branches, which exist at the same level of importance as the first, or add leaves (subsidiary information) to the branch. Select New Leaf from the Tree menu (✓-1).

Figure 16.1 BrainForest makes it easy to create and edit hierarchical outlines.

Figure 16.2 When creating a new branch or leaf, BrainForest uses a popup text field to enter information.

A solid line indicates where the item will move to when dropped.

Figure 16.3 Rearranging outline topics is as easy as tapping and dragging them to new locations.

Figure 16.4 Tabbed lines in Memo Pad are read as lower-level items when imported into BrainForest.

4. By default, trees are set up as actions (to-do items), with checkboxes running down the left side of the screen for each entry. To turn a tree, branch, or leaf into a standard item (identified by a black dot to the left), choose Toggle Action from the Edit menu (✓-T).

To edit outlines with BrainForest:

1. At the main screen, select the outline you want and tap the Open button, or choose Open Tree from the Tree menu (✓-L).

2. Tap and drag items to reposition them within the tree; a horizontal line appears to indicate where the item will end up when you lift your stylus (**Figure 16.3**).

To place an item under another item in the hierarchy (reducing its importance, as opposed to moving its position), drag and drop it onto the branch you wish to use as a parent item; the indicator line will disappear, and the parent will be highlighted before you drop it.

3. To rename a branch or leaf, double-tap its title to display the popup text field.

✔ Tips

■ If you're brainstorming and don't want to tangle with BrainForest's trees and branches, go ahead and write your ideas in the Memo Pad. Later, when you have more time, choose Import from the Tree menu (make sure the plug-in "BF Text Plug.prc" has been installed) to bring your notes into BrainForest.

■ If you do write a note using the Memo Pad, add tab characters (·⌐) at the front of each line based on the level in the hierarchy the item will reside (**Figure 16.4**).

Making Lists

The first time I walked into the grocery store with a hastily scrawled list in one hand and my organizer in the other, I knew that one would have to go. Now, in addition to saving some paper, I have a shopping list that remembers everything I normally buy so I don't have to start from scratch every time.

Lists, of course, go beyond noting the things I need to pick up at the store. You can create reusable checklists of procedures, clothing to pack when you travel, music you want to buy…the list of lists is practically unending. For generating lists of all kinds, try List-Maker (http://www.synsolutions.com/); JShopper (http://www.land-j.com/) is an advanced list tool that's tailored for shopping, with support for 15 different stores, item lookups, and even the ability to track coupons.

For Palm OS purists, the To Do List application can also expand its usefulness to include other types of lists.

To create lists using the To Do List:

1. Open the To Do List.

2. Tap the category popup menu in the upper-right corner of the screen and choose Edit Categories.

3. Each built-in application can support up to 15 categories, but there's no rule saying that they have to all be related (**Figure 16.5**). Tap the New button and name your category (such as "Grocery store").

4. When you want to access your list, simply launch the To Do List and select that category from the popup menu. You may want to mark the Show Completed Items checkbox in the To Do Preferences screen (✓-R), so you can uncheck items when you need them again (**Figure 16.6**).

Figure 16.5 The To Do list can be used for other purposes in a pinch. Set up a new category representing your topic.

Figure 16.6 Turning on the Show Completed Items option lets you go back and unmark the items you've completed to "reset" the list.

Figure 16.7 Priorities and due dates can be used to sort your lists.

✔ Tips

- Attach notes to items that require more explanation. In a grocery store list, you could include specific brand names in the note.

- If you already use several categories, things might get confusing if you choose to display them all at once; mark the non-task records Private to hide them during everyday use.

- To reorder items in your list, assign priorities or set varying due dates to the records (**Figure 16.7**).

A Spirited Use of Address Book

While visiting California recently, I ran into Doug Wilder, a wine expert for Dean & DeLuca. To easily keep track of the wines he tastes and sells, he stores the information in his Address Book under a Wine category. When a question comes up, he can check the Palm for details, and frequently beams the information to folks who also have Palm handhelds. (Email dougwilder@earthlink.com to subscribe to his electronic wine newsletter.)

Databases and Spreadsheets

It's always been the job of database and spreadsheet software to elevate computers above the "toy" stage into the realm of "serious business." The next time someone asks you if your Palm device is some sort of handheld gaming device, show them how you can crunch data with one of these programs (*then* you can get back to that game of YahtC—see Chapter 19).

JFile, MobileDB, HanDBase, and FileMaker Mobile

For actual database functionality, turn to JFile (http://www.land-j.com/), MobileDB (http://www.mobilegeneration.com/), or HanDBase (http://www.ddhsoftware.com/). If you use FileMaker on your PC, FileMaker Mobile (http://www.filemaker.com/) can read and edit, but not create, FileMaker databases. There are a number of existing databases available to download, ranging from subway schedules to medical references.

To create a database:

1. Tap the New DB (JFile) or the New (MobileDB and HanDBase) button.

2. Write the name of the database, then enter the field names in the lines provided (**Figure 16.8**). Click Done.

3. Within your new database, tap the New button (MobileDB and HanDBase) or Add button (JFile) to create a new record.

4. Enter the field data for that record (**Figure 16.9**). Tapping New on this screen creates a new blank record.

5. Tap Done (or OK) to go back to the list of records, where you can sort the records, perform searches, or choose other options (**Figure 16.10**).

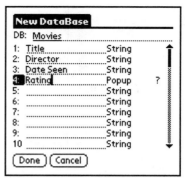

Figure 16.8 When creating a new database in JFile, enter the column headings in the New Database fields.

Figure 16.9 Once you're in a database (JFile shown here), you can enter your data next to the field titles you set up.

Figure 16.10 View, sort, and find the records from the database's main screen (HanDBase shown here).

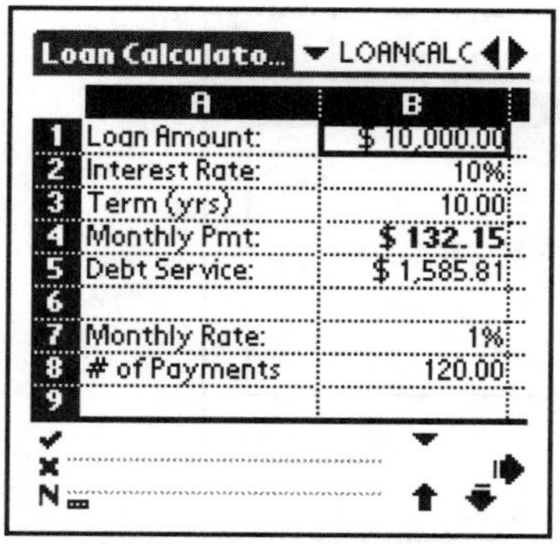

Figure 16.11 Quicksheet looks and acts like a desktop spreadsheet program.

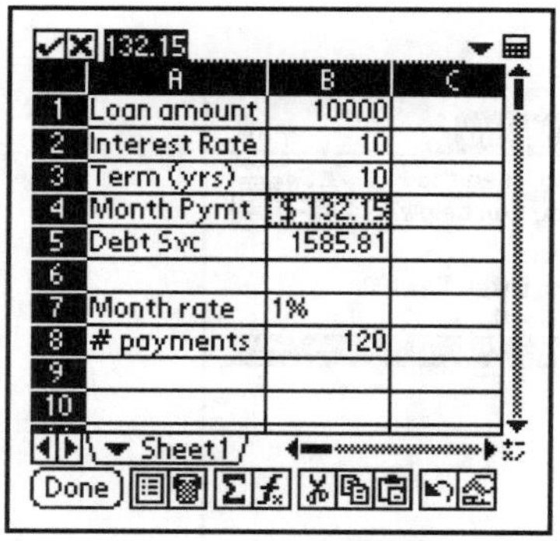

Figure 16.12 TinySheet turns out to be not so tiny after all.

Figure 16.13 The SheetView component of Documents To Go displays and edits Excel spreadsheets.

✔ Tip

- You can also get a variety of programs that let you interface your handheld database with one on your PC. Check the Web sites of each database application for links.

Quicksheet, TinySheet, and Documents To Go

If you spend much of your time locked in Microsoft Excel's data cells, you'll be happy to know that Quicksheet (http://www.cesinc.com/), TinySheet (http://www.iambic.com/), and Documents To Go (http://www.dataviz.com/) put a true spreadsheet onto your handheld's small screen, complete with built-in functions, linking of named spreadsheets within workbooks, and a surprisingly easy method of maneuvering lots of data within a small space (**Figures 16.11**, **16.12**, and **16.13**).

All three spreadsheets include conduits that synchronize the data on your device with the data on your hard disk.

✔ Tip

- If you're a regular spreadsheet user, you might seriously consider getting a HandEra 330 organizer. The higher resolution screen can display more cells, but more important, the Graffiti area can be hidden to make full use of the 3-inch tall screen. Tap the minimize arrow at the top of the Graffiti area.

Printing from Your Palm

Remember all the hoopla about paperless offices? A Palm device would seem to be the perfect antidote to mass paper consumption, but every now and again it would be handy to print something from your handheld. A few utilities will do just that: TealPrint (`http://www.tealpoint.com/`), PalmPrint (`http://www.stevenscreek.com/palm/`), and PrintBoy (`http://www.bachmannsoftware.com/printboy.htm`) enable you to connect to a variety of printers using either a special cable or, better yet, via infrared.

To print from your Palm device:

1. Launch your printing utility (I'm using PrintBoy as an example), and select the type of document you wish to print, or choose which application to print from (**Figure 16.14**).

2. If the printer is equipped with an infrared port, aim your handheld at the printer and tap the Print button (**Figure 16.15**).

✔ Tips

- If your printer doesn't have a built-in infrared port, consider buying the InfraReady adapter, an IR adapter that plugs into a printer's serial port (`http://www.bachmannsoftware.com/`).

- Sometimes it's just easier to print out a portion of your schedule and share it with someone. If you're not near your PC, use one of these printing programs to output your appointments over a span of time (**Figure 16.16**).

Figure 16.14 Don't wait to HotSync before printing something. Most document types can be printed directly from your handheld.

Figure 16.15 Printing from the Memo Pad is as simple as reading a memo.

Figure 16.16 If you want to share a week's schedule, don't beam every event to someone else. Simply print the week's appointments.

TRAVELING WITH YOUR PALM

17

One of the reasons the laptop computer really took off was the demand from business travelers who needed to take their data with them. Palm handhelds are no exception; I've heard of people who are now refusing to lug around a bulky laptop on trips when they can take a handheld instead.

But simply carrying your handheld doesn't make it any more unique of a tool—you probably used to carry a paper-based notebook, too. In addition to the bulk saved by storing information electronically, there are a number of advantages for travelers in terms of software and hardware: add-ons that will help you get to your location, figure out what to do while you're there, and then get you home again.

And who can resist the temptation of having a GPS (Global Positioning Satellite) signal receiver operating within their handheld? Finally, you get the chance to definitively say, "Here I am, world!"

The Well-Equipped World Traveler

If you do a lot of traveling, you're probably familiar with that odd, surreal sense when your body's clock is nowhere near the clocks in your new location. These utilities will help you gain some sense of equilibrium.

Travel Clock

Travel Clock (http://www.boswell.demon.co.uk/) keeps track of the current time, but also lets you specify an "away" location (perfect if you travel to the same location frequently). With two taps of the stylus, your handheld's clock can be adjusted to the current time (**Figure 17.1**).

Palm Zone Pro

Palm Zone Pro (http://www.geocities.com/SiliconValley/Campus/7631/software.html) lacks an alarm, but can automatically switch locations at pre-specified times (**Figure 17.2**).

TravelPal

For an extra boost of usefulness, install TravelPal, by the same developer (**Figure 17.3**). TravelPal includes the same time-tracking features as Palm Zone Pro, but adds a trip log and currency converter—perfect for those of us who sometimes have trouble counting our own currency, much less factoring in another country's exchange rate. Be sure to download the latest version of TravelPal's currency conversion database, which is updated regularly.

✔ Tip

- When you travel, record your parking space, frequent flyer number, ticketless travel numbers, etc. in your organizer for easy access later.

Figure 17.1 You may not have to rely on a wake up call to get up each morning while you're on the road.

Figure 17.2 Palm Zone Pro makes it easier to cross time zones without having to manually change settings.

Figure 17.3 TravelPal rolls a time tracking utility in with a trip log and currency converter.

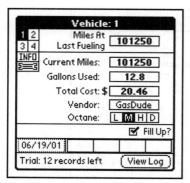

Figure 17.4 Keep track of your gas fill-ups as well as any maintenance done on your car with Kar Kare.

Figure 17.5 The miles may go by in a haze, but you'll have something to show for them besides yet another in-flight magazine.

Information that Travels with You

It's helpful to keep important travel-related information with you on your handheld. For drivers, Kar Kare (http://www.geocities. com/ResearchTriangle/6608/) tracks your mileage, fuel consumption, and maintenance dates and locations. You also can set it to remind you when the next service or check up is due (**Figure 17.4**).

If you're a heavy-duty frequent flyer, consider using a program such as AirMiles (http:// www.handshigh.com/), which keeps your airline frequent flyer numbers close at hand (**Figure 17.5**). You can keep track of your flights for reference later (when you need to trump the guy at the hotel bar stool next to you who's bragging about how many miles he's flown so far).

INFORMATION THAT TRAVELS WITH YOU

Vindigo: Navigating City Life

Although I enjoy traveling, I'm not a big fan of finding myself in an unfamiliar city with no idea where to go. Sure, I could pick up a telephone book or newspaper, but what I really want is the equivalent of a personal guide to the city.

So far, Vindigo (http://www.vindigo.com/) is the best product I've seen that feels most like being with a good friend who has lived in a city for years (without the bad puns and prying questions, of course!). It currently supports 20 cities worldwide, and updates its content when you HotSync your handheld the same way AvantGo does (see Chapter 10).

Other similar services include Lonely Planet's CitySync (http://www.conceptkitchen.com/) and the Zagat Restaurant Guide (http://www.landware.com/).

To find a destination in Vindigo:

1. Make sure your current location is set in the popup menu at the upper-right corner, then choose selection criteria in the left-hand column (**Figure 17.6**).

2. Tap the name of a destination that appears in the main column to see more detail about the place and its location.

3. Tap the Review tab to read a commentary, or tap the Map tab to get an overview of where the destination is in relation to your location (**Figure 17.7**).

4. When you've decided where to go, tap the Go tab to view walking directions from your location (**Figure 17.8**).

✔ Tip

■ Vindigo will work with a GPS receiver to pinpoint your current location.

Figure 17.6 Specify your location using the popup menu at upper right, then select a type of location (in this case, a Cajun restaurant).

Figure 17.7 With a destination selected, tap the Map tab to get a sense of where you are in relation to the place.

Figure 17.8 Tapping the Go tab provides walking directions from your current location.

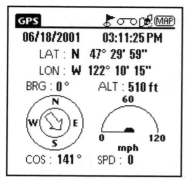

Figure 17.9 Find your place in the universe (okay, just Earth) with a GPS receiver.

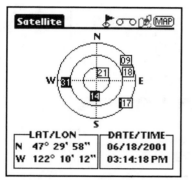

Figure 17.10 You can see how many satellites are overhead, and their signal strengths (black squares mean better reception).

Finding Your Way with GPS

Let's take a step back for a moment and consider the realm of Cool Technology. As you may have guessed, I think handhelds in general are extremely cool and even futuristic sometimes. That said, I think GPS narrowly trumps palmtops in sheer geeky coolness.

The GPS (Global Positioning Satellite) system is a collection of satellites that can be used to pinpoint one's location to within inches. And although this capability was once the toy of the military, now anyone with a small receiver can do the same thing.

Currently there are a few GPS devices available for Palm organizers, such as Magellan's GPS Companion (http://www.magellangps.com/) and the Rand McNally StreetFinder family of devices (http://www.randmcnally.com/). There are also Visor Springboard modules like Nexian's HandyGPS (http://www.nexian.com/) and GeoDiscovery's Geode (http://www.geodiscovery.com/).

Each device comes with its own software, but the general method of using them is quite similar. I'm using the HandyGPS Springboard module for this example.

GPS module basics

◆ When you insert the module, it must first locate the nearest satellites. When it does, a host of information is displayed, including latitude, longitude, altitude, and even speed if you're in motion (**Figure 17.9**).

◆ To see how many satellites are contributing to the Handy GPS module's calculations, select Satellite from the Preference menu or write ╱-S (**Figure 17.10**).

continues on next page

FINDING YOUR WAY WITH GPS

◆ To add context to your location data, download a map of your area from the vendor's Web site. Switch to the mapping software. When the GPS module has located you, a pulsing circle appears. You can zoom in and out by tapping the plus and minus buttons at the bottom of the screen (**Figure 17.11**).

◆ In UbiGo, the HandyGPS mapping software, you can use the pencil tool to scribble a note on the map and save it for later viewing (**Figure 17.12**). Please write something more informative than my example.

◆ The GPS device's mapping software should also include methods of recording a trip, plus storing locations in order to build trip plans. Over time, it's not unusual to end up with a map that's dotted with a mass of flagged locations.

✔ Tips

■ Palm-based GPS receivers typically aren't very powerful, so try to keep as few obstacles as possible between you and the satellites. You can probably get by with setting the handheld on the dashboard of your car, but don't expect any coverage indoors. For this reason, too, don't be surprised if it takes several minutes for the module to first latch onto the satellites.

■ GPS technology is sophisticated, but don't rely 100 percent on it to guide you—especially when driving. A GPS satellite can't tell you if a road is closed, for example, and sometimes the distances (say, between you and the edge of that cliff there) might be off.

■ If you're planning a trip where getting lost or disoriented could be potentially dangerous, consider other dedicated devices with better power supplies.

Figure 17.11 Once you've been found, you can zoom in and out of the map by tapping the plus and minus buttons.

Figure 17.12 A collection of lines and the odd street name can still be confusing. Use the pencil tool to customize your map and save it for later viewing.

Managing Your Money

I've often heard the expression "time is money," but rarely do I hear the phrase, "money is sure a lot like time." As sayings go it kind of stinks, I'll admit—yet in my experience, this nugget of wisdom has repeatedly proven itself true. As with time, you can burn through money without noticing it if you're not careful. Also like time (or rather, deadlines), bills have the uncanny ability to sneak up on you quickly.

Fortunately, I can use my handheld to keep track of my finances as well as to help me manage my time. Having that information at my disposal allows me to update my checkbook register when I'm away from my computer, minimizing the number of faded paper receipts that I'd normally have to organize.

Track Your Personal Finances

If your spending seems out of control, or you just want to get a better idea of where your money is going, track your usage for a week or a month—just as you tracked your time in Chapter 15.

The built-in Expense application is all set up to make it easy for you to track your money's trajectory from wallet to the outside world.

To track your cash flow with Expense:

1. To create a new record, tap New or begin writing either the expense amount or the first letter of the expense type in the Graffiti area.

2. With the record still highlighted, tap the Details button to enter the Vendor, City, and any other information you want to store (**Figure 18.1**).

3. At the end of the tracking period, perform a HotSync and then tap the Expense button in Palm Desktop for Windows. You'll be able to open the data in an Excel spreadsheet and get an overview of where your money went (**Figure 18.2**).

✔ Tip

■ I created a master list of the bills I pay each month, so that even if my income varies from month to month (one curse of freelancing), I know how much I need to pay. That list has made its way onto my handheld, first in the form of a Memo Pad entry, and lately as a spreadsheet.

Figure 18.1 The more information you add to expense items, the better you'll be able to track your money.

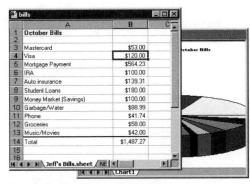

Figure 18.2 Gather your raw data into a program such as Excel to get an overview of your expenses.

Figure 18.3 Personal Money Tracker is an all-in-one financial center residing on your handheld.

Figure 18.4 Keep track your various accounts with Pocket Quicken (Balances have been changed to protect my accountant's integrity.)

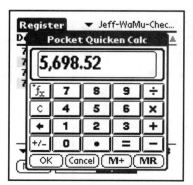

Figure 18.5 The built-in calculator keeps you within the Pocket Quicken application.

Manage Your Financial Accounts

My checkbook used to serve only as a convenient place to store money-related papers like ATM withdrawal receipts, upcoming bills, and more than a few overdraft notices. Then I bought a copy of Quicken (http://www.quicken.com/), which allowed me to see how and where I spent my cash.

A few financial applications have appeared for the Palm organizer. Pocket Quicken (http://www.landware.com/) syncs directly with Quicken on the PC. QMate (http://www.wco.com/~sdakin/qmate.html), one of the first financial apps, can take data from the handheld to be imported into Quicken. And there are others as well that don't need a desktop program, such as Personal Money Tracker (find it at http://www.palmgear.com/) (**Figure 18.3**).

Getting started in Pocket Quicken

One of the great things about LandWare's Pocket Quicken is that all you need to do is install the desktop conduit and perform a HotSync operation. Your Quicken account names and balances are transferred to the handheld (**Figure 18.4**). Optionally, you can have your categories transferred as well.

✔ Tips

■ You can add accounts on the handheld if you want, but they won't be created on the desktop after you HotSync.

■ Great feature alert: Pocket Quicken 2.0 includes a calculator that you can use without having to exit the application to launch the Palm OS calculator (**Figure 18.5**). Select Use Calculator from the Activities menu, or write ╱-M.

To enter a transaction in Pocket Quicken:

1. From the Account List screen, tap the Register button, or select Use Register from the Activities menu to view an account's register (**Figure 18.6**).

2. Tap the New button and choose the type of transaction from the popup menu that appears: Payment, Deposit, or Transfer. The transaction looks like Quicken's check format (**Figure 18.7**).

3. Write the information in the fields provided, or tap the field titles to access more information like categories.

4. Pocket Quicken supports split transactions. Tap Split to break out individual components (**Figure 18.8**).

5. Tap Done to apply the transaction, or Cancel to delete it.

✔ Tips

- Start writing the payee's name in the Graffiti area to create a new transaction.

- In the Category & Transfer List screen, tap the shortcut letters at the top to take you to that block of categories. Tapping each one repeatedly cycles through the letters; for example, tapping mno once takes you to the top of the "m" list, but tapping it again jumps down to the "n" categories.

- Pocket Quicken also supports features like memorized, cleared, and voided transactions. Plus, if a payee isn't in your list of memorized transactions, you can look up a name from the Address Book.

Figure 18.6 The Register lists individual transactions, with much better handwriting than my checkbook's register.

Figure 18.7 Pocket Quicken's transaction screen looks almost like the checks buried at the bottom of your purse or briefcase, without the paper.

Figure 18.8 Splitting transactions makes it easier to identify expenses when you run reports in Quicken.

Figure 18.9 QMate accounts need to share the same names of related accounts in Quicken.

Figure 18.10 The New Transaction window roughly resembles a check, with options for marking the record's status.

Table 18.1

Number Field Codes		
SHORTCUT	CODE	DESCRIPTION
A	ATM	Automatic Teller Machine
C	CCARD	Credit Card
D	DEP	Deposit
E	EFT	Electronic Funds Transfer
K	—	Advances check number by one
P	PRINT	Printed check
S	SEND	
T	TXFR	Transfer
W	WITHD	Withdrawal
X	XMIT	Transmission

To set up accounts in QMate:

1. From the main Accounts window, tap the New button to create a new account. Make sure its name exactly matches the name of your corresponding Quicken account (**Figure 18.9**).

2. Choose an account type from the Type popup menu.

3. Enter the account's current balance in the Balance field. Tap OK to save the account's information.

To enter a transaction:

1. Once your account is set up, tap the Transactions button, or double-tap the account name to open it. The transaction is structured like a check (**Figure 18.10**).

2. Tap the Date, Payee, or Cat (category) button to view a list of memorized transactions; or, write the information in the fields provided. Tap OK to apply the transaction, or Cancel to get rid of it.

✔ Tips

- To easily change the date in the New Transaction window, tap the date itself (not the Date button): tapping the year advances by a day, tapping the month falls back by a day.

- The Number field can display more than just numbers. Write the letters in **Table 18.1** to bring up the action codes.

To transfer data to Quicken:

1. Perform a HotSync under Windows.

2. Run the QSync application, which creates a Quicken .qif data file for your accounts.

3. In Quicken, choose the account you want to update and choose Import from the File menu.

Manage Your Investments

I remember being in school and not caring one whit about stocks, bonds, or anything else related to investing. I didn't have great stashes of money to throw at the stock market, so why bother? Now, in our recent era of IPOs and millionaires sprouting like weeds, stock tracking is moving to the masses. (If your stock portfolio took a big hit during the downturn in the economy, as mine did, think of these utilities as mere entertainment.)

Several solutions exist to track one's investments on a Palm device. Programs like Personal Stock Tracker (find it at http://www.palmgear.com/) enable you to enter your stocks and trades manually (**Figure 18.11**). For the more serious (or more fanatical) trader, a handheld connected to the Internet offers market information whenever you log on. Popular services such as E*Trade have created free Palm Query Applications (PQAs) that can tie into your accounts and make transactions (**Figure 18.12**). (See Chapter 10 for more information about PQAs.)

✔ Tip

■ If you do have a wireless Net connection and a Web browser on your Palm, you can access many online financial services just as you would on your computer. Not all browser software will work, however, as most financial Web sites use encrypted data and Web cookies to identify you while you're on their sites. Check the specs of the browser software.

Figure 18.11 Monitor your investments by entering your stocks and trades into Personal Stock Tracker.

Figure 18.12 Online users can get up-to-the-minute information on how their favorite stocks are performing, including buying and selling stock.

MANAGE YOUR INVESTMENTS

GAMES & ENTERTAINMENT

You're a working professional with a lot to accomplish in a limited time. Since purchasing your handheld, you've discovered new ways to squeeze your workload into the tight confines of your daily schedule, and finally carved out the quality time you've been dreaming about for months.

And yet, while on the bus or train, standing in line at the grocery store, or waiting at the airport—transitional time that would be ripe for reviewing the latest project outline—you just don't have it in you to *work*. These are the moments when a Palm device really shines, when you realize the full power of your investment. *These are the times to play games.*

I couldn't hope to cover all the games that are available for the Palm OS platform, but my conscience wouldn't allow me to write a book about these splendid devices without including a chapter about games and entertainment. The following programs are games I've become addicted to at one time or another, or are beguiling diversions that just deserve notice.

Stress Relievers

Vexed

There are games that try to squeeze the best 3D graphics performance out of their processors, but every once in a while a simple gem arrives and gets all of the attention. Vexed (http://spacetube.darktech.org/Projects/Vexed/) asks you to clear the screen of patterned tiles by making two or more touch and disappear. The 59 levels vary from easy to fiendishly obscure, and will occupy your thoughts as well as your time (**Figure 19.1**).

YahtChallenge

"Hmm," I thought, "a Yahtzee game... this should be entertaining for a few minutes." If I had only known then that YahtChallenge (http://home1.pacific.net.sg/~kokmun/) would occupy all of my spare time. Roll dice and come up with combinations to score the most points against a friend or the Palm.

PocketChess

This excellent chess program provides all the functions an average chess player needs, and takes up only 39K (**Figure 19.2**). And lest you think that the handheld's teeny processor can't provide enough challenge, just try to play on level eight. PocketChess (http://www.tinyware.com/) sometimes kills me—I mean, um, friends of mine—on level one!

Bejeweled!

Bejeweled! has a simple premise: move jewels into rows of three to get rid of them and bring on new gems (**Figure 19.3**). Like its spiritual ancestor Tetris, Bejeweled will cause you to put off work in favor of playing for just one more minute...

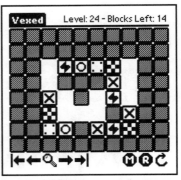

Figure 19.1 Vexed seems easy enough, though you might not think that when you've run your batteries down trying to get past its 59 levels.

Figure 19.2 PocketChess packs a well-designed chess engine into 39K.

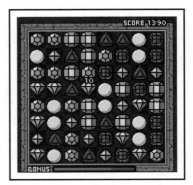

Figure 19.3 Bejeweled! is yet another classic battery-draining obsession.

STRESS RELIEVERS

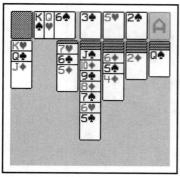

Figure 19.4 The most-often used Windows program is on the Palm OS!

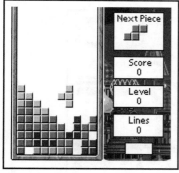

Figure 19.5 Spinning, shifting, rotating, interlocking...the obsession known as Tetris will keep you entertained on even the longest plane trips.

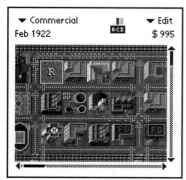

Figure 19.6 SimCity brings the megalomaniacal power of running a city to your handheld.

Klondike and FreeCell

No consumer electronic device should exist without a solitaire game installed. These two variations, the traditional Klondike and the more nefarious FreeCell (both at http://www.electronhut.com/pilot/), can occupy your hours without the need for table space to set up real cards (**Figure 19.4**).

Tetris

Cultural anthropologists are going to stumble upon Tetris one day, and either wonder at how backward our society was or marvel at how fast the human mind could move shapes into place in order to get rid of horizontal rows (http://www.pocketexpress.com/). I'd ponder this some more, but I really must clear a few more rows... just one or two... really, I can stop when I want to... (**Figure 19.5**).

SimCity Classic

You're the city mayor, responsible for promoting growth, prosperity, and above all the adulation of your citizens. SimCity Classic (http://www.ateliersoftware.com/palm/) is just like the original hallmark game on the Mac or PC (**Figure 19.6**), complete with fires, earthquakes, hurricanes, and the dreaded monster attacks.

DopeWars

Are you a budding entrepeneur, looking for the high life? Does the thrill of making deals pump through your veins? Then perhaps you need to try your hand at DopeWars (http://www.pdaguy.com/dopewars/), a game geared toward making as much money as possible within a given timeframe. If you're uncomfortable with the DopeWars theme, install Taipan (http://mdbowen.ne.mediaone.net/taipan/) instead and trade across the high seas of the Orient.

STRESS RELIEVERS

Notable Diversions

Zap!2000 and Zap!2016

Zoom through space blasting everything in sight in Zap!2000 (http://www.astraware.com/). The game play is fast, the graphics are crisp, and the color version, Zap!2016, takes advantage of the thousands of colors available on some devices' screens (**Figure 19.7**).

Tricorder II

More than a few people have noticed that the Visor is about the same size and shape as a Star Trek tricorder, an all-in-one device with the power to scan and analyze nearly anything. Jeff Jetton (http://www.jeffjetton.com/) took that one step further by developing the software for this fictional device (**Figure 19.8**). When you're finished scanning the household pets for baryon particle build-up, be sure to peruse the program's Read Me file, certainly one of the best I've read in years.

Tiger Woods PGA Tour Golf

A celebrity endorsement of a game on the Palm OS? These days, anything can happen. Electronic Arts ported this impressive golf game to the Palm OS (**Figure 19.9**), complete with grayscale graphics and a roster of golf pros to keep you at the top of your game (http://www.easports.ea.com/games/tigerpalm/main.html).

Figure 19.7 One of the best uses of color, Zap!2016 is beautiful and action-packed.

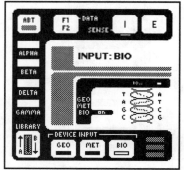

Figure 19.8 Tricorder II finally lets you scan for your television's tachyon emissions. Now you're ready for that away mission, Ensign...sorry, what was your name?

Figure 19.9 Hit the links from anywhere, even if it's raining outside.

Basic
Troubleshooting

My handheld is one of the most trustworthy electronic devices I've ever owned, but that doesn't mean it doesn't act up on occasion. Often the cause of problems and error messages is a conflict among the installed applications (some system extensions can be picky neighbors with other programs' code; see Chapter 8). Occasionally the problem is hardware-related, ranging from the components of the device itself, to upgrade cards, to batteries. Knowing how to deal with possible problems will go a long way toward reducing that first moment of panic when something isn't working.

If the problem requires you to send it back to the manufacturer, the situation is actually rather good. Although I've only needed to send back one device (knock on wood), when my original PalmPilot Personal developed a black smudge on the screen, Palm sent a padded shipping container marked with the correct postage. After doing a complete backup of my data, I sent it off, then was amazed when it returned three days later—including the shipping time. Your mileage may vary, as they say, but in general the companies understand the value of keeping their customers happy.

Back Up Your Data

When you perform a HotSync, the data on your handheld gets copied to your user directory on your PC or Macintosh—or rather, *most* of it gets copied. The data from third-party applications may get backed up at HotSync, but the applications themselves sometimes don't, depending on which version of the Palm OS you're running (versions prior to Palm OS 3.3 can be problematic in this respect). In the event of a hard reset, where all data on the device is lost (see next section), it's great to be able to restore everything to the state it was in before the reset. To ensure that you're getting a full backup, I recommend two essential utilities: BackupBuddy (http://www.bluenomad.com/) and, for Macintosh users only, Palm Buddy (http://perso.wanadoo.fr/fpillet/).

Both programs allow you to back up and restore your full data, as well as perform incremental backups (**Figure A.1**). If you have to do a complete restoration of your data, BackupBuddy users simply do a HotSync. Palm Buddy owners drag the data from their backup folder in the Finder to the active Palm Buddy window (**Figure A.2**).

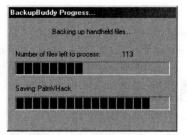

Figure A.1 BackupBuddy backs up all of your handheld files—even those stored in ROM—during HotSync.

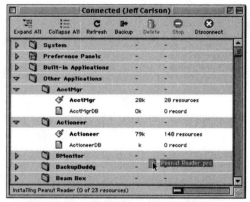

Figure A.2 Restore your programs and databases after a crash by dragging them from the Mac OS Finder to Palm Buddy's directory window.

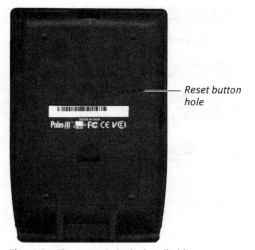

Reset button hole

Figure A.3 The reset pin in the handheld's stylus slides into the reset hole and presses the button inside.

Reset pin

Figure A.4 Most Palm handhelds include a reset pin in the tip of the stylus. A straightened paperclip also works in a pinch.

Resetting Your Handheld

Like turning your desktop computer off and on, a Palm organizer occasionally needs to be reset (though infrequently). Three methods of resetting the device are available.

A *soft reset* is like rebooting a computer, initializing its internal system files and libraries. All of your data will remain intact.

If something is giving you errors as your device starts up from a soft reset (such as a system update patch, for example), try doing a *warm reset*. This is analagous to booting Windows in Safe Mode or starting a Mac with extensions turned off.

A *hard reset* is the action of last resort, erasing all of your data and taking the handheld back to its original state. Be sure you have a recent backup of your information.

To perform a soft reset:

Insert the straight end of the stylus's reset pin into the reset hole on the back of the device (**Figures A.3** and **A.4**).

To perform a warm reset:

1. Hold down the plastic Scroll Up button on the front of the device case.

2. Insert the reset pin into the reset hole on the back of the device, then release the button. The screen should flash, then restart normally.

To perform a hard reset:

1. Hold down the power button.

2. With the power button still held down, insert the reset pin into the reset hole on the back of the device, then release the power button.

3. A confirmation message appears on the screen. Press the Scroll Up button to erase the memory, then restore your data.

Restoring applications after a hard reset

For the most part, performing a HotSync operation after a hard reset should reinstall your data files and any applications that were loaded on your handheld. However, a glitch in system versions prior to Palm OS 3.3 would sometimes cause applications you had deleted from the handheld to be reinstalled. This was because deleted programs still hang out in your User folder, but the handheld knew they should be ignored. Palm OS 3.3 improved the way it treats backed-up files, so now doing a HotSync operation resets the device to the state of the last HotSync.

To determine which version of Palm OS you are running, go to the Applications screen and choose Info from the App menu or write /-I. Tap the Version button at the bottom of the screen (**Figure A.5**).

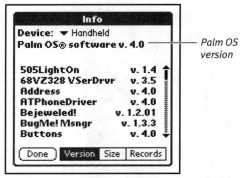

Palm OS version

Figure A.5 The Info screen displays the version numbers of your applications as well as the Palm OS.

Hardware Troubleshooting

Palm organizers are mass-produced electronic devices, and as such, there's bound to be problems. Although there's no miracle cure if you accidentally drop your handheld into a filled bathtub, some hardware problems are easily fixed.

Palm V won't turn off after an alarm, or it continually beeps

The Palm V design is revolutionary among handhelds, but the disadvantages of a few details managed to crop up. The scroll button sticks out from the case, so if an alarm goes off and the Palm V is in a carrying case, the pressure of the case walls could be holding the scroll button down. Since the device thinks you're inputting data, it won't turn off, making a continuous beeping noise and draining the battery. Palm OS 3.3 allegedly fixed the problem, though it still happens to me. PalmVHack (http://www.rgps.com/) disables the scroll button during alarms.

Another solution is to take a rubber washer, cut about a third of it, and mount it above the scroll button so that the Palm V's cover pushes on the washer instead of the button.

Rechargeable device won't turn on

Most likely, the battery has drained to the point where it's passed all of the low battery warnings. Put the device into its charging cradle to feed it a little power. Perform a soft reset, then let it charge for at least three hours.

HARDWARE TROUBLESHOOTING

HotSync Troubleshooting

If you have any troubles at all, they're likely to be related to HotSync. Although in practice HotSync is a simple process, it relies on several factors that control the communication with your computer.

Common HotSync fixes

◆ In Palm Desktop, check that your settings in the HotSync Setup screen are correct.

◆ Under Windows, exit HotSync Manager, then launch it again. On a Macintosh, make sure Local HotSync is enabled; if it is already on, disable it manually, wait a few seconds, then re-enable it.

◆ Verify that the HotSync cable or cradle is plugged into the correct port on your computer.

◆ Reduce the port speed in the Setup screen.

◆ Disable any software that might be sharing the communication ports. Fax software is often the culprit, because it's always monitoring for incoming faxes.

◆ Under the Mac OS, turn off AppleTalk by opening the Chooser and clicking the AppleTalk Inactive button.

◆ If you're using a USB hub, try plugging the HotSync cradle directly into the USB connection on the computer.

To set Macintosh memory allocation:

1. Try increasing the memory allocated to the Conduit Manager application. On your hard disk, open the Palm folder and click on the Conduit Manager.

2. Choose Memory from the Get Info submenu under the File menu.

3. Increase the number in the Preferred Size field, then close the Get Info window.

Windows COM port conflicts

If the previous suggestions don't produce a successful HotSync, your COM ports may be misconfigured or confused. COM ports are the physical ports used to hook up devices such as modems and mice to the back of your computer. Some machines also use COM ports for internal devices.

To work together, these ports communicate with the computer's processor over Interrupt Request (IRQ) channels. Often, one IRQ channel is shared by two COM ports, which means they can both be vying for attention (COM 1 and COM 3 usually share an IRQ, while COM 2 and COM 4 share another IRQ). If you have the option of doing so, move your HotSync cable to a different COM port. If not, and if you're skilled in complex computer configuration, try reassigning the port settings.

Keep in mind that tinkering with IRQ settings has the potential to cause conflicts where none existed before. Make changes one at a time; if they don't fix the problem, undo the change and reboot your computer before making any more changes.

To modify Windows COM settings:

1. Double-click the System icon from the Windows Control Panels.

2. Click the Device Manager tab, then click the plus sign next to Ports (COM & LPT).

3. Double-click the Communications Port you want to change.

4. Click the Resources tab. If the Use automatic settings checkbox is on, click to unmark it.

5. Choose an alternate configuration from the Settings based on popup menu.

6. When finished, click OK, then restart your computer.

Macintosh HotSync problems with certain models

Owners of computers based on the "Tanzania" motherboard design (Power Macintosh G3s, 5400, 6400, 4400, PowerBook 3400, and clones from Motorola, Umax, APS, and Power Computing) have had more than their share of HotSync problems. Fortunately, there are two possible solutions to try.

To reverse HotSync steps:

1. Open the HotSync control panel.

2. Turn HotSync monitoring off.

3. Put your device in its cradle and press the HotSync button to start synchronizing.

4. After the handheld has begun its portion of the HotSync process, turn HotSync monitoring back on.

Install Serial DMA

Some people have reported success with this fix, but it doesn't seem to be a cure-all. Download and install Apple's Serial DMA v2.1 extension (`ftp://ftp.info.apple.com/ Apple_Support_ Area/Apple_Software_ Updates/US/Macintosh/Networking- Communications/Other_N-C/SerialDMA/`). Note that this does not apply to the Power-Book 3400. Also note that on more recent Mac models, Serial DMA can actually be the culprit of errors. If you have it installed, try removing it and HotSync again.

Time out errors

If you have a slower (older) computer, or you're synchronizing a lot of data, you may receive a message that the handheld timed out while transferring the information. To get around this, try activating the "developer's backdoor" feature, which disables the set amount of time the handheld will wait to receive data.

To activate the Developer's Backdoor:

1. On the organizer, go to HotSync by selecting it from the Applications screen (don't press the HotSync button on the cradle).

2. Hold down the up and down scroll buttons on the front of the case.

3. With the buttons still pressed, tap the upper-right corner of the screen. You'll see the message DLServer Wait Forever is ON in the DEVELOPER'S BACKDOOR dialog box that appears. Tap OK and perform a HotSync again. The feature will be disabled after the HotSync, or if you power off your handheld.

GRAFFITI REFERENCE

Normal and Alternate Characters

LETTER	GRAFFITI		LETTER	GRAFFITI
A	∧		N	N ∿ ∼
B	ß B 3		O	O O
C	C ‹		P	P P ſ
D	D Q ℓ		Q	O U
E	Ɛ ≤ 6		R	R R ſ
F	Γ ſ		S	S ʃ b
G	G 6		T	⊓
H	h		U	U
I	l		V	V V
J	⌡ ⌐		W	ɯ ɯ
K	≺		X	X ∞
L	L ⌐		Y	ɣ ɣ ſ
M	ɯ ɯ		Z	Z

Graffiti Numbers and Special Strokes

LETTER	GRAFFITI		LETTER	GRAFFITI
1	l		8	8 8 / ɣ
2	2 ≿		9	9
3	3		0	O O
4	∟ C ‹		backspace	⟍
5	5 ɔ S		return	∕
6	6		shift	↓
7	⊓ ⊃		space	—

Graffiti Navigation Strokes

COMMAND	GRAFFITI	COMMAND	GRAFFITI
cursor right	—	next field	↑
cursor left	⟍	shortcut	ℓ
previous field	↑	command	∕

Graffiti Punctuation (with Alternates)

Symbol	Graffiti	Symbol	Graffiti
.	• •	+	• ∝
,	• ∕	=	• Z
'	• ၊	|	• ၊
?	• ? ⌐	‹	• <
!	• ၊	›	• >
-	• ‒	\	• \
(	• (	{	• Ɛ
)	•)	}	• 3
/	• ∕	[	• Ɛ
$	• S	]	• 3
@	• O	~	• N ~
#	• ᴎ h	`	• \
%	• ᪰	;	• ∕
^	• ∧	:	• ၊
&	• 8	"	• N
*	• ⤬	tab	• ⌐
—	• ‒		

Graffiti Symbols/Extended Characters

Symbol	Graffiti	Symbol	Graffiti
●	\ ·	×	\ ∕
TM	\ ᴍ	÷	\ ᪰
®	\ ᴙ	=	\ Z
©	\ C	¢	\ C
'	\ ⌐	¥	\ ४
,	\ ⌐	£	\ L
"	\ N	¿	\ L
"	\ ᴎ	i	\ ၊
§	\ S	ß	\ B
·	\ O	µ	\ ᴍ
+	\ ∝	f	\ S
–	\ ‒	Ø	\ O

Graffiti Accent Characters

Symbol	Graffiti	Symbol	Graffiti
à	∧ \	è	Ɛ \
á	∧ ∕	é	Ɛ ∕
â	∧ ∧	ê	Ɛ ∧
ä	∧ ᪰	ü	U ᪰
å	∧ O	ç	C
ñ	N N	æ	Ɛ

RESOURCES

Essential Information

Palm Organizers
Visual QuickStart Guide Web site
http://www.peachpit.com/vqs/palm/

Calvin's PalmPilot FAQ
http://www.palmgear.com/faq/

Palm, Inc.
http://www.palm.com/

HandEra
http://www.handera.com/

Sony CLIÉ
http://www.sonystyle.com/micros/clie/

Kyocera Smartphone
http://www.kyocera-wireless.com/kysmart/

Software Libraries

Palm Gear HQ
http://www.palmgear.com/

PDA.Tucows.com
http://pda.tucows.com/palm/

EuroCool
http://www.eurocool.com/

Handango
http://www.handango.com/

Palm Boulevard
http://www.palmblvd.com/

Electronic Texts

MemoWare
http://www.memoware.com/

Peanut Press
http://www.peanutpress.com/

Healthy PalmPilot (health care information)
http://www.healthypalmpilot.com/

Online Originals
http://www.onlineoriginals.com/

Fictionwise
http://www.fictionwise.com/

Mailing Lists

PalmPilot list at Ultraviolet.org
pilot-pda-subscribe@freeside.
ultraviolet.org
http://www.ultraviolet.org/pilot.html

PalmPilot Power Boards (click the
PowerBoards link at the bottom of the page)
http://www.palmpower.com/

Usenet Newsgroups

alt.comp.sys.handhelds.pilot

comp.sys.handhelds.pilot

Magazines/News

PalmPower Magazine
http://www.palmpower.com/

Handheld Computing Magazine
http://www.hhcmag.com/

The Piloteer
http://www.pmn.co.uk/

PalmStation
http://www.palmstation.com/

Palm Boulevard
http://www.palmblvd.com/

Palm Infocenter
http://www.palminfocenter.com/

Smaller.com
http://www.smaller.com/

VisorCentral
http://www.visorcentral.com/

VisorVillage
http://www.visorvillage.com/

INDEX

B

INDEX

D

INDEX

New from Peachpit Press!